CARL PHILIPP EMANUEL BACH

The Complete Works

Series VIII
Volume 4.1

Series VIII: Supplement

1. *Miscellanea Musica*
2. Arrangements
3. Librettos
4. Portrait Collection
5. Historical Catalogues
6. Sources and Scribes
7. Indices

CARL PHILIPP EMANUEL BACH

Portrait Collection I

Catalogue

Edited by Annette Richards

Appendices Edited by Paul Corneilson

The Packard Humanities Institute

LOS ALTOS, CALIFORNIA
2012

Carl Philipp Emanuel Bach: The Complete Works

The Packard Humanities Institute
in cooperation with the Bach-Archiv Leipzig, the Sächsische Akademie
der Wissenschaften zu Leipzig, and Harvard University

11A Mount Auburn Street
Cambridge, MA 02138
http://www.cpebach.org

ISBN 978-1-933280-69-1

Series design by Dean Bornstein

CONTENTS

General Preface · vii

Abbreviations · 1

Introduction · 5

Catalogue of C. P. E. Bach's Portrait Collection · 27

Appendix A: Silhouette Collection · 199

Appendix B: Portraits of C. P. E. Bach and His Family · 209

Classified Index · 223

Index of Subjects · 229

Index of Artists · 234

GENERAL PREFACE

Carl Philipp Emanuel Bach: The Complete Works is an editorial and publishing project of the Packard Humanities Institute, in cooperation with the Bach-Archiv Leipzig, the Sächsische Akademie der Wissenschaften zu Leipzig, and Harvard University. Its goal is to make available, in both printed and digital formats, a critical edition of the composer's works.

The edition is organized into eight series:

    I.   Keyboard Music
   II.   Chamber Music
  III.   Orchestral Music
  IV.   Oratorios and Passions
    V.   Choral Music
  VI.   Songs and Vocal Chamber Music
 VII.   Theoretical Writings
VIII.   Supplement

It contains all authentic works by C. P. E. Bach that are known to survive, as well as selected works of uncertain authenticity (*incerta*); demonstrably spurious works are omitted. Ordinarily, the edition considers the latest known authorized version of a work to be the principal one. Authentic alternate versions of works or movements are printed in full whenever Bach significantly changed the musical substance. Less extensive variants in pitch, rhythm, and duration, as well as substantive variants in articulation, ornamentation, dynamics, tempi, and other details of notation (such as slurring) are described in the critical report. Sketches are printed along with the works to which they are related.

Like most of his contemporaries, Bach arranged and reused existing music for new purposes. Movements originally written for solo keyboard, for example, served as the basis for some of his sonatinas for keyboard and orchestra. Bach arranged much of his chamber music for different scorings, and he wrote alternate solo parts for several of his concertos. In the Hamburg vocal music, he frequently borrowed movements from himself and other composers to produce new works. The present edition treats Bach's arrangements in the same manner as his wholly original works, publishing the arrangements in the series corresponding to their instrumentation and genre.

Each volume contains a critical report that includes a comprehensive description and evaluation of all sources used for the edition, as well as shorter descriptions and evaluations of other sources known to date from the eighteenth century but not used for the edition. The critical report also includes a commentary that describes variant readings in the principal sources, as well as editorial emendations.

Although C.P.E. Bach's notation is basically modern, some aspects of it do not conform to modern engraving standards. The notation of the present edition reflects modern convention while respecting some of the idiosyncratic elements of the original. Generic titles are usually modernized, and spellings found in the sources are described in the critical report. Titles that can be shown to derive directly from Bach are given as they appear in the principal sources. Clefs are modernized and standardized, as are instrument names, dynamic and tempo markings, and the notation of triplets and similar groupings. Accidentals are adapted to modern convention; any departures are explained in the volume in which they occur. *Colla parte* and other shorthand notations used in the eighteenth century have generally been realized. Beaming and stem direction are standardized according to modern convention, except where the original notation may have a bearing on performance; such cases are discussed in the introduction or critical report. Slurring, the placement of dynamic markings, and the notation of articulation are faithful to the principal sources.

The edition is conservative in its approach to emendation. Within the main musical text of the edition, emendations are distinguished according to the following general principles:

- Headings, movement numbers, tempo indications, dynamic markings, trills, and other literal directives that appear in the principal sources are given in roman type. Editorial emendations to such markings are given in italics.
- Pitches, accidentals, rests, fermatas, and ornament signs that appear in the principal sources are printed full size, as are cautionary accidentals. Editorial emendations are given in smaller type.

- Editorial slurs and ties are given as dashed lines.
- Emendations to other articulation marks, as well as to clefs, appoggiaturas, and accidentals in appoggiaturas, are not distinguished typographically in the body of the edition, but are described in the critical report.

Alfred Wotquenne's *Thematisches Verzeichnis der Werke von Carl Philipp Emanuel Bach* (1905) has long been the standard catalogue of Bach's works, and the present edition employs Wotquenne numbers, abbreviated "Wq," for primary references to Bach's works. Because many Wotquenne numbers refer to larger groups of independent works, the edition follows conventional practice in appending an additional number to Wotquenne's original one in order to identify a particular work within the group. (Thus, for example, "Wq 116/12" points to the twelfth independent work listed under Wq 116.) Works not in Wotquenne are referred to by their numbers in E. Eugene Helm's *Thematic Catalogue of the Works of Carl Philipp Emanuel Bach* (1989), abbreviated "H." Works not in Wotquenne or Helm are marked "Wq/H *deest*" or "Wq/H *desunt*." Whenever appropriate, volumes include concordances of all principal catalogue numbers.

Finally, we want to recognize and thank the institutions, librarians, and individuals whose support has been essential in undertaking a complete works

Imitative harmonization of the family name, B–A–C–H,
autograph entry by C. P. E. Bach in an album of Carl Friedrich Cramer (9 June 1774).
Courtesy of the Universitätsbibliothek Kiel

edition for the music of C. P. E. Bach: Helmut Hell and the Staatsbibliothek zu Berlin—Preußischer Kulturbesitz, Musikabteilung mit Mendelssohn-Archiv; Johan Eeckeloo and the Koninklijk Conservatorium, Brussels; Jon Newsom and the Library of Congress, Music Division, Washington, D.C.; Otto Biba and the Gesellschaft der Musikfreunde, Vienna; Georg Graf zu Castell-Castell and the board of directors of the Sing-Akademie zu Berlin; and Elias N. Kulukundis, Greenwich, Connecticut.

The Editorial Board

ABBREVIATIONS

General Abbreviations

ACPB	Anna Carolina Philippina Bach, CPEB's daughter
CPEB	Carl Philipp Emanuel Bach
H	Helm catalogue number
JCB	Johann Christian Bach
JCFB	Johann Christoph Friedrich Bach
JMB	Johanna Maria Bach, CPEB's wife
JSB	Johann Sebastian Bach
SBB	Staatsbibliothek zu Berlin (D-B) and its predecessor institutions
WFB	Wilhelm Friedemann Bach
Wq	Wotquenne catalogue number

Bibliographical

BA 1789	*Verzeichniß auserlesener theologischer, juristischer, medicinischer, historischer, moralischer, ökonomischer, und in die schönen Wissenschaften einschlagender mehrentheils neuer gebundener Bücher, in allerley Sprachen, nebst einigen Musikalien und Kupferstichen. . . .* Hamburg, 1789.
Bach-Dokumente IV	*Bach-Dokumente.* Vol. 4, *Bilddokumente zur Lebensgeschichte Johann Sebastian Bachs./Pictorial Documents of the Life of Johann Sebastian Bach.* Edited by Werner Neumann. Kassel: Bärenreiter, 1979.
Biehahn 1961	Biehahn, Erich. *Kunstwerke der Deutschen Staatsbibliothek.* Berlin: Henschelverlag, 1961.
BJ	*Bach-Jahrbuch*
Burney 1775	Burney, Charles. *The Present State of Music in Germany, the Netherlands and United Provinces,* 2nd ed. 2 vols. London, 1775.
Cat. Poelchau	"Porträt-Sammlung von Georg Poelchau." MS in D-B, Mus. ms. theor. Kat. 131.
CPEB-Briefe	*Carl Philipp Emanuel Bach. Briefe und Dokumente. Kritische Gesamtausgabe.* Edited by Ernst Suchalla. 2 vols. Göttingen: Vandenhoeck & Ruprecht, 1994.

CPEB:CW	*Carl Philipp Emanuel Bach: The Complete Works*
CPEB-Letters	*The Letters of C. P. E. Bach.* Translated and edited by Stephen L. Clark. Oxford: Oxford University Press, 1997.
CPEB-Musik und Literatur	*Carl Philipp Emanuel Bach. Musik und Literatur in Norddeutschland: Ausstellung zum 200. Todestag Bachs.* Heide in Holstein: Westholsteinische Verlagsanstalt Boyens, 1988.
"Er ist Original!"	*"Er ist Original!" Carl Philipp Emanuel Bach: Ausstellung in Berlin zum 200. Todestag des Komponisten, 14. Dezember 1988 bis 11. Februar 1989.* Wiesbaden: Dr. Ludwig Reichert, 1988.
Fröhlich	Fröhlich, Anke. *Zwischen Empfindsamkeit und Klassizismus. Der Zeichner und Landschaftsmaler Johann Sebastian Bach der Jüngere (1748–1778).* Leipzig: Evangelische Verlagsanstalt, 2007.
GerberL	Gerber, Ernst Ludwig. *Historisch-Biographisches Lexicon der Tonkünstler.* Leipzig: Breitkopf, 1790–92.
GerberNL	Gerber, Ernst Ludwig. *Neues Historisch-Biographisches Lexicon der Tonkünstler.* Leipzig: A. Kühnel, 1812–14.
Heartz 2003	Heartz, Daniel. *Music in European Capitals: The Galant Style, 1720–1780.* New York: W. W. Norton, 2003.
Helm	Helm, E. Eugene. *Thematic Catalogue of the Works of Carl Philipp Emanuel Bach.* New Haven: Yale University Press, 1989.
Hortschansky 1987	Hortschansky, Klaus, Siegfried Kessemeier, and Laurenz Lütteken. *Musiker der Renaissance und des Frühbarock: grafische Bildnisse aus dem Porträtarchiv Diepenbroick.* Münster: Landschaftsverband Westfalen-Lippe, 1987.
Krüger 1769	*Première partie des antiquités dans la collection de sa majesté le roi de Prusse à Sans-Souci. Contenant douze planches d'après les plus beaux bustes, demi-bustes, et thermes dessinées et gravées par Krüger à Potsdam.* Berlin: Birnstiel, 1769.
Leaver 2007	Leaver, Robin A. "Überlegungen zur 'Bildniß-Sammlung' im Nachlaß von C. P. E. Bach." *BJ* (2007): 105–38.
Leisinger 1991	Leisinger, Ulrich. "Die 'Bachsche Auction' von 1789." *BJ* (1991): 97–126.
Leisinger/ Wollny	Leisinger, Ulrich, and Peter Wollny. *Die Bach-Quellen der Bibliotheken in Brüssel. Katalog.* Leipziger Beiträge zur Bach-Forschung 2. Hildesheim: Georg Olms, 1997.

Lemmer 1973	Lemmer, Manfred. *Facsimile of Reusner 1587, with biographical notes.* Leipzig: Edition Leipzig, 1973.
MGG[II]	*Die Musik in Geschichte und Gegenwart*, 2nd ed. Edited by Ludwig Finscher. 29 vols. Kassel: Bärenreiter, 1994–2008.
Mortzfeld	Mortzfeld, Peter. *Die Porträtsammlung der Herzog August Bibliothek Wolfenbüttel.* 50 vols. Munich: K. G. Saur, 1986–2008.
Musiker im Porträt	Salmen, Walter, and Gabriele Busch-Salmen. *Musiker im Porträt.* 5 vols. Munich: C. H. Back, 1982–84.
NBR	*The New Bach Reader: A Life of Johann Sebastian Bach in Letters and Documents.* Edited by Hans T. David and Arthur Mendel, rev. and enlarged by Christoph Wolff. New York: W. W. Norton, 1998.
NG[II]	*The New Grove Dictionary of Music and Musicians*, 2nd ed. Edited by Stanley Sadie and John Tyrrell. 29 vols. London: Macmillan, 2001.
NV 1790	*Verzeichniß des musikalischen Nachlasses des verstorbenen Capellmeisters Carl Philipp Emanuel Bach.* Hamburg, 1790.
Ottenberg	Ottenberg, Hans-Günter. *C. P. E. Bach.* Translated by Philip J. Whitmore. Oxford: Oxford University Press, 1987.
Reusner 1587	Reusner, Nikolaus. *Icones sive imagines virorum literis illustrium quorum fide et doctrinà religionis & bonarum literarum studia....* Argentorati, 1587.
Reusner 1589	Reusner, Nikolaus. *Icones sive imagines viuæ, literis cl. virorum, Italiae, Graeciae, Germaniae, Galliae, Angliae, Vngariae ...* Basileae, 1589.
Reusner 1590	Reusner, Nikolaus. *Icones sive imagines virorum literis illustrium, quorum fide et doctrina religionis et bonarum literarum studia....* Argentorati, 1590.
Rostirolla	Rostirolla, Giancarlo, ed. *Il "mondo novo" musicale di Pier Leone Ghezzi.* Milan: Accademia nazionale di Santa Cecilia, 2001.
Schmid 1988	Schmid, Manfred Hermann. "'Das Geschäft mit dem Nachlaß von C.Ph.E. Bach.' Neue Dokumente zur Westphal-Sammlung des Conservatoire Royal de Musique und der Bibliothèque Royale de Belgique in Brüssel." In *Carl Philipp Emanuel Bach und die europäische Musikkultur des mittleren 18. Jahrhunderts. Bericht über das internationale Symposium der Joachim Jungius-Gesellschaft der Wissenschaften Hamburg, 29. September–2. Oktober 1988.* Edited by Hans Joachim Marx. Göttingen: Vandenhoeck & Ruprecht, 1990. Pp. 473–528.

Schneider 1985	Schneider, Hans. *Der Musikverleger Heinrich Philipp Bossler, 1744–1812.* Tutzing: H. Schneider, 1985.
Versuch I, II	Bach, Carl Philipp Emanuel. *Versuch über die wahre Art das Clavier zu spielen.* 2 vols. Berlin, 1753–62; rev. ed., Leipzig, 1787–97.
Wolff 2000	Wolff, Christoph. *Johann Sebastian Bach: The Learned Musician.* New York: W. W. Norton, 2000.
Wotquenne	Wotquenne, Alfred. *Thematisches Verzeichnis der Werke von Carl Philipp Emanuel Bach.* Leipzig: Breitkopf & Härtel, 1905.

Library Sigla

A-Wn	Vienna, Österreichische Nationalbibliothek, Musiksammlung
B-Bc	Brussels, Conservatoire Royal de Musique, Bibliothèque. Koninklijk Conservatorium, Bibliotheek
B-Br	Brussels, Bibliothèque Royale Albert 1.er
D-B	Berlin, Staatsbibliothek zu Berlin—Preußischer Kulturbesitz, Musikabteilung mit Mendelssohn-Archiv
D-EIb	Eisenach, Bachhaus und Bachmuseum
D-F	Frankfurt am Main, Universitätsbibliothek, Musik- und Theaterabteilung
D-LEb	Leipzig, Bach-Archiv
D-W	Wolfenbüttel, Herzog August Bibliothek, Musikabteilung
F-Pn	Paris, Bibliothèque nationale de France, Département de la Musique
GB-Lbm	London, British Museum
US-AAu	Ann Arbor, University of Michigan, Music Library
US-CA	Cambridge, Harvard University, Harvard College Library
US-CAh	Cambridge, Harvard University, Houghton Library
US-I	Ithaca, Cornell University Music Library
US-NYp	New York, Public Library at Lincoln Center, Music Division

INTRODUCTION

At the time of his death in 1788, the portrait collection of Carl Philipp Emanuel Bach, as listed in Bach's estate catalogue (*Nachlaßverzeichnis*, hereafter
NV 1790), contained 378 portraits and an additional 37 silhouettes.[1] The sub-
heading in NV 1790 summarizes the contents: "Bildniß-Sammlung von Com-
ponisten, Musikern, musikalischen Schriftstellern, lyrischen Dichtern und
einigen erhabenen Musik-Kennern." (Portrait collection of composers, musicians, writers on music, lyrical poets, and other eminent music connoisseurs.)
That Bach was an avid collector of musician portraits was widely known to his
contemporaries. Charles Burney, who visited Bach in Hamburg in 1772, gave
the first published report of the collection:

> The instant I entered, [Bach] conducted me up stairs, into a large and elegant mu-
> sic room, furnished with pictures, drawings and prints of more than a hundred and
> fifty eminent musicians: among them, there are many Englishmen, and original
> portraits, in oil, of his father and grandfather.[2]

An introduction to the portrait collection was apparently the first order of business for visitors to the Bach house, before any music was heard or discussed. In
1772 the collection numbered at least 150 items,[3] but by the time of Bach's death
in 1788 it had increased to more than four hundred.

Accounts of the collection circulated in North Germany in the 1780s,[4] and
it soon became the focus of, and inspiration for, what amounted to a collect-

---

1. The picture collection as a whole is listed in three sections at the end of NV 1790: (1) "Bildniß-Sammlung"; (2) "Eine kleine Sammlung Musikalischer Silhouetten"; and (3) "Verzeichniß
verschiedener vorhandenen Zeichnungen," 65 works of Carl Philipp Emanuel's son, Johann
Sebastian the younger. For a catalogue raisonné of the latter's work, see Fröhlich 2007. See appendix A for a list of the silhouettes listed in NV 1790. Appendix B includes all the known portraits
of C.P.E. Bach and his family, most of which are not listed in NV 1790.

2. Burney 1775, 2:269.

3. This is the number given in Burney 1775, but it may refer only to the items on display. Others
may have been kept, unframed, in folders. This was standard practice for print collections, and
became Bach's only option in the later 1780s, as space on his walls filled up. In NV 1790 215 out
of 378 portraits are listed as framed.

4. In his *Magazin der Musik* in the 1780s, Carl Friedrich Cramer published a series of letters
from Gerber in which he assembled a preliminary list of available composer portraits, and asked

ing craze among Bach's contemporaries and admirers. Perhaps the most de-voted collector was Ernst Ludwig Gerber, whose portrait collection, modeled on Bach's, became the basis for his monumental music-biography project, the *Tonkünstler Lexicon* (1790–92).[5] But others collected too, including Major von Wagener, who was stationed with the Knobelsdorff infantry regiment at Stend-hal in the early 1780s;[6] Johann Nicolaus Forkel, the biographer of J. S. Bach and correspondent with C. P. E. Bach; Christoph Transchel, a student of J. S. Bach later residing in Dresden; and Johann Jacob Heinrich Westphal, a devoted collector of Bachiana. These collections contributed to the foundations of the vast nineteenth-century musician-portrait collections of two other important collectors of Bach materials: Georg Poelchau and Aloys Fuchs.

Until recently, it had been assumed that C. P. E. Bach's collection had been irretrievably lost, despite the fact that some items from it (mostly the Bach family portraits) were known to be in the Staatsbibliothek zu Berlin (SBB).[7] Recent research into the very large holdings of musician portraits there, how-ever, reveals that a much greater portion of C. P. E. Bach's collection than had been thought survives intact as part of the portrait collection bought by the SBB in 1841 from the estate of Georg Poelchau. Indeed, not only have hitherto unknown drawings and pastels come to light, but it appears that a substantial portion of prints in the Poelchau collection are from the C. P. E. Bach collection itself. Building on the foundation provided by the holdings in Berlin, and using the list of items in NV 1790, it has been possible to a great extent to reconstruct the Bach collection: many of the prints he owned were widely circulated, and

---

correspondents to send in more. See *Magazin der Musik* 1.2 (1783): 962–69, esp. 965. *Musikalische Bibliothek* 1 (1784): 123–30, also reported on composer portrait collections: "According to Dr. Burney, Kapellmeister C. P. E. Bach in Hamburg possesses one of the largest collections." (Nach Herrn Doctors *Burnei* Versicherung, sol der Herr Kapellmeister C. P. E. *Bach* in Hamburg eine ser [*sic*] große Samlung besitzen.)

5. See Thomas Tolley, *Painting the Cannon's Roar: Music, the Visual Arts and the Rise of an Attentive Public in the Age of Haydn* (Aldershot, England: Ashgate, 2001), 165.

6. *Magazin der Musik* 1 (1783): 962–63. Major von Wagener was possibly related to the painter Gottfried Christoph Wagener (d. 1772), and to the family of the Hamburg senator Anton Wagener, who was involved in Bach's hiring as director of music for Hamburg in 1767. Major von Wagener was perhaps also related to the nineteenth-century collector of Bachiana, Guido Richard Wagener (1822–1896). See Schmid 1988, 515–16.

7. For a selection of portraits in D-B, see Biehahn 1961.

exemplars survive in libraries and museums across Europe and in the United States. The *unica* are more difficult to recover: some were acquired by Poelchau in the forty or so years after Bach's death (see below) and eventually found their way to Berlin; others were bought by a number of different collectors and their whereabouts remain unknown today.

The Formation of the Collection

The origins of C. P. E. Bach's collection date to well before Burney's visit in 1772. Although there is no mention of portraits in the specification of J. S. Bach's estate, it is clear that at least some of Bach's pictures were inherited from his father. The Bach family portraits, related to the musical material in the "Alt-Bachisches Archiv," included the portraits in oil of C. P. E. Bach's grandfather Johann Ambrosius Bach (no. 27), his father J. S. Bach (no. 28), and his stepmother Anna Magdalena Bach (no. 29, now lost). C. P. E. Bach's acquisition of the other family portraits would have built on this foundation.

Robin Leaver has suggested that the basis of C. P. E. Bach's collection may have been not only the family portraits, but a collection started by his father that included engraved portraits of non-family members.[8] This would account for the presence in the collection of a number of the more obscure figures, especially the seventeenth-century theologians and sixteenth-century Reformation and Counter-Reformation polemicists. The connection to J. S. Bach might also account for the large number of organists, kapellmeisters, violinists, and lutenists in the collection. While no firm evidence can be given to support the view that the collection originated with J. S. Bach, it clearly reflects C. P. E. Bach's role as a curator of his father's legacy. If there are many individuals represented there who were part of his father's cultural milieu, figures whom Bach would have heard spoken of, would have been recommended to read, or would have met, growing up in the Bach household, the collection can be understood in part as a window into the intellectual and musical interests of the Bach family in the first half of the eighteenth century.

---

8. See Robin A. Leaver, "Überlegungen zur 'Bildniss-Sammlung' im Nachlaß von C. P. E. Bach," *BJ* (2007): 105–38.

However, the majority of the collection was acquired by C. P. E. Bach himself, and its scope is extraordinarily broad: here are gathered together family members, colleagues of his father and of his own in Berlin and Hamburg, poets and philosophers both present and past, music theorists, scientists, mythical figures, kings, and emperors. The view it offers of Emanuel Bach's knowledge of both contemporary and historical music, and of the long cultural legacy that culminates with him, is unparalleled. The portrait collection is a rich source of information on Bach's expansive geographical circle and the role art, its reproduction, and the crucial practice of collecting played in nurturing Bach's social, intellectual, and artistic networks, and indeed the culture of music in the period. These pictures were not treated simply as valuable images. They were meant to be cherished for conveying a sense of the accomplishments of the broadly conceived musical past and making immediate the richness of the musical present, in one of the most famous musical households in Europe.

Considerable insight into the way the collection was built can be gathered from Bach's letters in the 1770s and 1780s to Johann Gottlob Immanuel Breitkopf, Forkel, and J. J. H. Westphal. Mostly concerned with professional affairs, these letters include discussions of portraits and requests for items for the collection that shed light on the culture of portrait collecting, and on the cachet of the portrait, among members of this circle. On 20 April 1774, in correspondence with Forkel, whom he was supplying with information for a biography of J. S. Bach, Bach replied to a request for a portrait of his father with information about a pastel in his possession, and with a passing reference to the collection as a whole:

> . . . With the delivery of these psalms, which should occur as soon as I receive them at the fair, I will have the pleasure of sending you a recently finished, clean, and quite realistic engraving of my dear father's portrait. The portrait of my father that I have in my musical portrait gallery containing more than 150 professional musicians is painted in pastel. I had it brought here from Berlin by water, since such paintings with dry colours cannot tolerate the shaking over the axle; otherwise I would very gladly have sent it to you to be copied.[9]

---

9. "Beÿ Ueberschickung dieser Psalmen, welche, so bald ich sie mit der Meße kriege, so gleich geschehen soll, werde ich Ihnen einen kürzlich verfertigten saubern u. ziemlich ähnlichen Kupferstich von meines lieben seeligen Vaters Portrait zu überschicken, das Vergnügen haben.

Copying was a standard method for expanding a collection.[10] The letter continues with an inquiry about two portraits Forkel had mentioned, one of C. P. E. Bach's brother Wilhelm Friedemann and one of Bach himself, the latter painting a copy:

> Who, then, painted the portrait of me that you own? Perhaps it is a copy by Herr Reiffenstein, who painted me in Kassel in 1754 with dry colours. Perhaps I will be fortunate enough to present to you soon a clean engraving of my portrait, if it would otherwise be of value to you. The one you have does not have wrinkles, but the one I hope to send you will have all the more. Who painted my oldest brother?[11]

That Bach was concerned with portraits, and with family likenesses especially, comes across vividly from his letters. So too does the problem of making copies from fragile pastels; this is a topic that recurs some years later—this time again in conjunction with a portrait of Bach himself. In the margin of a letter to his Leipzig publisher, Engelhardt Benjamin Schwickert, on 27 January 1786, Bach wrote:

> Drop the expensive plans with the portrait. My only appropriate portrait is with dry colours, framed, under glass, and may not be sent. My family will not permit it. Someone will make a good copy here in oil for 4 ducats. Since I have been engraved badly often enough, who is looking particularly for something new?[12]

Meines Vaters Portrait, welches ich in meiner musicalischen Bildergallerie, worin mehr als 150 Musiker von Profeßion befindlich sind, habe, ist in pastell gemahlt. Ich habe es von Berlin hieher zu Waßer bringen laßen, weil dergleichen Gemählde mit trocknen Farben das Erschüttern auf der Axe nicht vertragen können: außerdem würde ich es Ihnen sehr gerne zum Copiren überschickt haben." *CPEB-Briefe*, 1:392; *CPEB-Letters*, 54. The pastel portrait mentioned here was not listed in NV 1790. On its possible identity as the so-called Meiningen pastel of J. S. Bach, see entry on Johann Ludwig Bach (no. 35).

10. It is possible that some of the lost paintings listed in NV 1790 may survive in copies by other artists (see J. C. F. Bach, no. 32, and Kirnberger, no. 189).

11. "Wer hat deñ mein Portrait, welches Sie besitzen, gemahlt? Vielleicht ist es eine Copie von H. Reifenstein, welcher mich anno 1754 in Caßel mit trocknen Farben abmahlte. Vielleicht bin ich so glücklich, weñ Ihnen anders damit gedient ist, bald mit einem saubren Kupferstich, von meinem Bildniß, aufzuwarten. Dasjenige, was Sie haben, hat keine Runzeln, aber, was ich hoffe, Ihnen zu schicken, desto mehr. Wer hat meinen ältesten Bruder gemahlt?" *CPEB-Briefe*, 1:392; *CPEB-Letters*, 54.

12. "Das Kosten machende Vorhaben mit dem Portrait laßen Sie liegen. Mein einziges getroffenes Bildniß ist mit trocknen Farben im Rahm, unter Glas u. läßt sich nicht verschicken.

Breitkopf in Leipzig, the city at the heart of the printing industry, was an important collaborator in the expansion of Bach's collection. In his exchanges with Breitkopf, one can see Bach taking the chance to pursue his hobby even as he carefully attended to his business affairs. "Do get for me Rhau's portrait, the book printer in Wittenberg at Luther's time. I will gladly pay for it," Bach wrote in the margin of a letter to Breitkopf on 9 October 1784; on 15 April 1785 he was still pursuing the print: "Is Rhau's portrait really not at all available? It is a woodcut engraving."[13] This kind of request had been going on for many years. A letter sent to Breitkopf in April 1775, ten years before the request for Rhau's portrait, includes the following comment:

> I purchased Herr [Johann Adam] Hiller's portrait here as soon as it was available and this honest worthy German has already been parading in my picture gallery for a long time. The portrait is in quarto. Herr [Christoph Daniel] Ebeling thinks the one in octavo is more realistic. If it is not much trouble, I would also like the latter. Give my best regards to this admirable man. Herr Schröter's portrait would be very welcome to me. I will pay everything with pleasure.[14]

Meine Familie läßt es nicht. Eine gute Copie in Oehl macht hier Jemand für 4 Dukaten. Da ich oft genug schlecht gestochen bin, wer verlangt sonderlich was neues." *CPEB-Briefe*, 2:1139–40; *CPEB-Letters*, 245. Bach must have been referring to the pastel portrait by Johann Philipp Bach (1752–1846), painted in 1775. At least two copies of this pastel survive; see appendix B. Other copies of items were made for the collections of C. P. E. Bach's friends: on 13 May 1786, he sent to Forkel a copy of his portrait of Padre Martini (itself a drawing): "The mail is about to leave, most esteemed friend; therefore in short! You are receiving herewith Pater Martini. The artist did his work rather well. Herr Capellmeister Naumann, who studied with him, told me it is a good representation of Martini when he was younger. I have enclosed a lyric poet, the honest Rist. I am making you a little present of both of them." (Die Post eilt, theuerster Freund; also kurz u gut! Hierbeÿ erhalten Sie Pater Martini. Der Zeichner hat seine Sachen ziemlich gut gemacht. Es soll Martini, wie er jünger war, gut gleichen; so sagte mir H. C. Mstr. Naumañ, welcher beÿ ihm studirt hat. Ich habe einen lÿrischen Dichter, den ehrlichen Rist beÿgelegt. Mit beÿden mache ich Ihnen ein kleines Präsent.) *CPEB-Briefe*, 2:1151; *CPEB-Letters*, 247.

13. "Schaffen Sie mir doch Rhaws des gelehrten Buchdruckers in Wittenberg zu Luthers Zeiten Portrait. Ich wills gerne bezahlen." *CPEB-Briefe*, 2:1044; *CPEB-Letters*, 216. "Ist deñ Rhaus Portrait gar nicht zu haben? Es ist ein Holzschnitt." *CPEB-Briefe*, 2:1074; *CPEB-Letters*, 227. Despite Bach's efforts to present a complete picture of the immediate circle around Martin Luther in the portrait collection, NV 1790 does not list Rhau's portrait.

14. "H. Hillers Portrait kaufte ich hier so gleich, als es zu haben war, und dieser würdige brave Teutsche paradirt schon lange in meiner Bilder-Gallerie. Das Portrait ist in 4to. H. Ebeling meÿnt, dasjenige in octav seÿ ähnlicher. Weñ es nicht viele Umstände macht, so wünschte ich dieses leztere auch." *CPEB-Briefe*, 1:497; *CPEB-Letters*, 79.

The Hiller portrait in "quarto" is listed in NV 1790 (no. 166), but the "octavo" image appears not to have been available as Bach had hoped (or if he did acquire it, he quickly passed it on). The Schröter portrait is mentioned again, in a letter on 11 July 1775, and yet again on 26 December 1775. By 17 January the following year, the determined collector was still trying to acquire the image, and suggested an alternative method: "My son, who is very negligent in writing to us, can possibly look into the portrait of Herr Schröter you kindly promised for me, since you do not have much time to spare."[15] All these efforts appear to have been unsuccessful, for the portrait is not listed in NV 1790.

This letter points to another collaborator in the development of the collection: Bach's son, the artist Johann Sebastian Bach the younger, who was at that time studying in Leipzig at the Kunstakademie with Adam Friedrich Oeser.[16] The close family involvement in the visual arts should be kept in mind when assessing Bach's portrait collection. The fine arts were a topic of real interest in the Bach household, and the collection offers plenty of evidence that C.P.E. Bach was a connoisseur of the visual arts, as of music. That J.S. Bach the younger chose to be a painter and was supported in this endeavor by his proud father suggests the importance of the elder Bach's interests and his collection in the professional path chosen by his son. J.S. Bach the younger appears to have assisted with the collection in several ways. He made drawings of painted portraits for it, including those of Caterina Regina Mingotti (no. 234) and Pierre-Gabriel Buffardin (no. 60); the now-lost drawings of Rudolf Agricola (no. 6), Padre Martini (no. 222), and Palestrina (no. 258) were also likely made by him from pre-existing paintings or engravings. The younger Bach also made portraits from life, such as the drawing of Johann Gotthilf Ziegler (no. 374, lost)[17] and the oil painting of Christian Friedrich Abel (no. 2, lost). Additionally, he may have acquired for his father some of the Italian drawings listed in NV 1790, between 1777 and 1778 on his study trip to Italy (where he died in

---

15. "Mein Sohn, der im Schreiben an uns sehr nachläßig ist, kan allerfals das mir von Ihnen gütigst versprochene Portrait von H. Schrötern auskundschaften, da Sie nicht viele Zeit übrigen haben." *CPEB-Briefe*, 1:556; *CPEB-Letters*, 82.

16. See Wolfgang Stechow, "Johann Sebastian Bach the Younger," in *Essays in Honor of Erwin Panofsky*, ed. Millard Meiss (New York, 1961); see also Fröhlich.

17. Maria Hübner, "Johann Sebastian Bach d.J. Ein biographischer Essay," in Fröhlich, 24.

1778). A poignant reminder of the personal currency of the portrait is provided by Bach's letter to Breitkopf, 19 December 1778, after his son's death:

> Most cherished compatriot, you will receive through Herr Professor Oeser a silhouette of my dear late son. I know you loved him too. The likeness is very good. A young artist here used this style to great advantage. Darker and better than those of Lavater. Inexpensive. Keep this portrait in memory of me.[18]

One important function of portraits was, indeed, as a reminder of friendship, a substitute for the personal presence of the sitter.[19] Bach wrote to his friend, the Braunschweig professor of literature and writer J. J. Eschenburg, with a request that he, "one of my best friends," should have his portrait drawn for the collection:

> . . . I already have Zacharaias' portrait, but how happy I would be if I could add your dear portrait, drawn, to my collection? You are not only an amateur and connoisseur of our art, but also an author, of which I have several, and NB one of my best friends.[20]

Specially commissioned portrait drawings appear to have been a theme for Bach in the 1780s. Distant friends such as Hans Adolf Friedrich von Eschstruth (no. 105), former pupils such as Nils Schiørring (no. 308), acquaintances and visiting musicians passing through Hamburg in the 1780s including the blind

---

18. "Liebwehrtester Herr Landsmann, Sie werden durch den Herrn Profeßor Oeser einen Schattenriß von meinem lieben seeligen Sohn erhalten. Ich weiß, Sie haben ihn auch geliebt. Er ist sehr gut getroffen. Ein junger Künstler hier hat diese Art sehr hoch gebracht. Schwärzer u. beßer, wie die Lavaterschen. Wohlfeil. Verwahren Sie dies Bild mir zum Andenken." *CPEB-Briefe*, 2:719; *CPEB-Letters*, 131.

19. For more on the portrait and friendship circles, see Roland Kanz, *Dichter und Denker im Porträt: Spurengänge zur deutschen Porträtkultur des 18. Jahrhunderts* (Munich: Deutscher Kunstverlag, 1993), esp. 121–71.

20. "Zachariä's Portrait habe ich nun schon: aber wie glücklich wäre ich, wenn ich Ihr liebes Portrait, gezeichnet, meiner Sammlung beyfügen könnte? Sie sind nicht nur Liebhaber und Kenner unserer Kunst, sondern auch Schriftsteller, dergleichen ich mehrere habe, und NB. einer meiner besten Freunde." *CPEB-Briefe*, 2:1049; *CPEB-Letters*, 218. Typically, Bach could not resist including additional requests in this letter for portraits of the two Braunschweig court musicians Johann Gottfried Schwanenberger and Friedrich Gottlob Fleischer. His request to Eschenburg concludes with the hint that "Herr Schwanenberger and Herr Fleischer will be very welcome to me." (Hr. Schwanenberger und Hr. Fleischer werden mir sehr wilkommen sein.) Ibid. Whether or not Eschenburg fulfilled the request is unknown, but none of the three drawings is listed in NV 1790.

flutist Friedrich Ludwig Dülon (no. 97), the blind piano virtuosa Maria Teresia
Paradies (no. 262), the violinists Regina Strinasacchi (no. 340) and Antonio
Lolli (no. 210), the singers Mme Mara (no. 216) and Mme Duschek (no. 98), all
appear to have been asked to provide portraits for the collection. On 25 Febru-
ary 1785 Bach wrote to Alexander Reinagle, whom he had met in Hamburg
with his brother Hugh two years earlier, to ask about his music and to make a
request for portrait drawings:

> At the same time I ask you to let me have your portrait and that of your brother,
> only drawn, to include them in my cabinet of portraits of musicians. That will
> serve to help me remember your friendship, for the return of which I am and will
> be always, Sir, your very humble servant . . ."[21]

In 1783 the 14-year-old Dülon played for Bach at his house in Hamburg, and
Dülon later recounted in his autobiography how he and his father had re-
sponded to a request from Bach for a portrait. The account is worth quoting
at length, for the light it sheds on Bach's practise of commissioning portrait
drawings:[22]

> Before I leave Lübeck again, I must mention yet another interesting acquaintance-
> ship with an artist, which gave rise to the following circumstance. The late Carl
> Philipp Emanuel Bach owned an exquisite collection of paintings of famous musi-
> cians. On that day that was so important for me, on which the above-mentioned
> story with the theme took place at his house,[23] he entreated my father to have me
> painted at some point for the said collection. How flattering that must have been

---

21. "En même tems je Vous prie de me faire avoir Vôtre portrait et celui de Ms. Vôtre frère,
seulement en dessin, pour les placer dans mon cabinet de portraits des musiciens. Cela me ser-
vira d'aide dans le souvenir de Vôtre amitié, dans le retour de la quelle je suis et serai toujours,
Monsieur, Vôtre très humble Serviteur . . ." *CPEB-Briefe*, 2:1069; *CPEB-Letters*, 225. Neither
Alexander nor Hugh Reinagle's portrait was added to the collection.

22. In the account the portrait is referred to as a painting (Gemälde), although it is listed in
NV 1790 as a drawing. Dülon may have misremembered (or, at fourteen years old, not have been
fully aware of the medium in which his portrait was being made); it is possible, however, that
the portrait was made in pastels, like that of Maria Theresia Paradies which NV 1790 lists as a
drawing, but which was described by its subsequent owner J. J. H. Westphal as a pastel.

23. As recounted by Dülon, and then in the Hamburg newspapers, Bach had given the young
flutist a theme in A major on which to improvise, in order to test his compositional skills. Dülon
executed the test to Bach's satisfaction, and his own pride. See Christoph Martin Wieland, ed.,
Dülons des blinden Flötenspielers Leben und Meynungen von ihm selbst bearbeitet, 2 vols. (Zurich,
1807–8), 1:164–69. See also Leta Miller, "C. P. E. Bach and Friedrich Ludwig Dülon: Composition

for me, one can easily understand. When we then heard coincidentally in Lübeck, that in that very place a skilled painter resided, this was very welcome news to us, and we wasted not a moment in making use of his artistry. When the painting was finished, the general verdict agreed upon by all who saw it, was that it lacked nothing but the faculty of speech. When we were then, a little later, in Hamburg again, my father presented it to the great Bach, who took great pleasure in it. The portrait collection was sold after his death, and it flattered me not a little, when the estate catalogue was read, to hear my name in it. The above-mentioned painter was not only first-rate in his art, but he also possessed a highly cultivated spirit, and the gift of endearing himself to those around him. . . . He was called Karstens. . . .[24]

In the last years of Bach's life perhaps the most important correspondent as regards the portrait collection was J. J. H. Westphal, who was not only occupied with gathering together as complete a collection as he could of the works of C. P. E. Bach, but was also busy amassing a portrait collection of his own in-spired by Bach's. Bach asked Westphal for help with his collection on 5 March 1787, in the year before his death, when all his other affairs were in order and his business dealings completed: "I have a large collection of engraved portraits of musicians and musical authors. Should you have the opportunity to obtain a

---

and Improvisation in Late 18th-Century Germany," *Early Music* 23 (1995): 65–80, and John A. Rice, "The Blind Dülon and His Magic Flute," *Music & Letters* 71 (1990): 25–51.

24. "Ehe ich Lübeck wieder verlasse, muß ich noch einer interessanten Bekanntschaft mit einem Künstler erwähnen, zu welcher folgender Umstand die Veranlassung gab. Der selige Karl Philipp Emanuel Bach besaß eine auserlesene Sammlung von Gemälden berühmter Tonkünstler. An jenem für mich so wichtigen Tage nun, an welchem die bereits erzählte Geschichte mit dem Thema in seinem Hause vorfiel, ersuchte er meinen Vater, mich doch bey Gelegenheit für die bewußte Sammlung malen zu lassen. Wie schmeichelhaft mir dies seyn mußte, kann man sich leicht vorstellen. Als wir nun in Lübeck zufälliger Weise erfuhren, daß sich ein geschickter Maler daselbst aufhalte, war uns dies sehr erwünscht, und wir säumten keinen Augenblick Gebrauch von seiner Kunst zu machen. Als das Gemälde fertig war, fiel das einstimmige Urtheil aller, die es sahen, dahin aus, daß demselben nichts weiter mangle als die Sprache. Als wir nun einige Zeit darauf wieder in Hamburg waren, überreichte es mein Vater dem großen Bach, welcher eine herzliche Freude darüber hatte. Die Bildersammlung wurde nach seinem Tode verkauft, und es schmeichelte mir nicht wenig, als man mir das Verzeichnis derselben vorlas, auch meinen Namen darin zu hören. Der erwähnte Maler war nicht nur vorzüglich in seiner Kunst, sondern besaß auch viele Geistesbildung, und die Gabe, sich durch seinen Umgang beliebt und angenehm zu machen. . . . Er nannte sich Karstens [Asmus Jakob Carstens (1754–1798)] . . ." *Dülons des blinden Flötenspielers Leben*, 1:319–21, 326ff.

few recruits for me, please do so; I will gladly pay for them."[25] On 4 August 1787 Bach wrote to Westphal in more detail about the portraits, revealing the extent of the collection (now expanded beyond the available display space on his walls) and conveying the complicated business of portrait exchange:

> Now something about the portraits. I can get Kellner's portrait for you. You have made me very embarrassed by your far too great kindness. I thank you most respectfully for Mme de Saint-Huberty and Herr Professor Engel. I wanted to keep the latter without a frame since, for lack of space in my hall, I now put my remaining portraits unframed in a portefeuille, and will deal with whatever new ones I receive in the same way. Well, I packed the Engel with the frame, but incompetent packer that I am, I was so unlucky as to break the glass, *en fin* I had to keep it and I am hereby sending the Engel without the frame back to you. As some compensation for you, I have enclosed seven portraits that you do not yet have. Forgive me, therefore, and make do with them. I am still waiting impatiently for a few recruits who were promised to me, then my catalogue of portraits shall certainly be printed.[26]

The catalogue that Bach mentioned in this letter had already been in preparation for some time; Carl Friedrich Cramer reported in the *Magazin der Musik* in 1784 that Bach had promised that it would soon be ready for publication. It did not appear before Bach's death, but was eventually printed in NV 1790. The list of the collection occupies 36 pages (pp. 92–128), and many of the entries are remarkably detailed. Each entry gives the name of the sitter, followed by a brief description, which usually includes the medium (whether the portrait is a woodcut, copperplate engraving, drawing, pastel or painting in oils); the paper

---

25. "Ich habe eine starke Saṁlung von Bildnißen der Musiker u. musikalischen Schriftsteller in Kupfer; sollten Sie Gelegenheit haben, mir einige Rekruten zu verschaffen: so bitte ich darum, ich bezahle sie gerne." *CPEB-Briefe*, 2:1198; *CPEB-Letters*, 259.

26. "Nun etwas von den Portraits. Kellners kriege ich. Durch Ihre allzugroße Gutheit haben Sie mich sehr verlegen gemacht. Für M. d. St. Huberti u. H. P. Engeln danke ich ganz ergebenst. Diesen leztern ohne Rahm wollte ich behalten, weil ich jetzt, aus Mangel des Raums in meinem Saale, alle übrige Portraits ohne Rahm in ein Portefeuille thue u. mit dem, was ich etwa noch kriege, eben so verfahren werde. Genug ich pakte den Engel mit dem Rahm ein, allein ich ungeschickter Einpaker war so unglücklich, das Glas zu zerbrechen, en Fin ich mußte ihn behalten, u. schicke Ihnen hierbeÿ den Engel ohne Rahm wieder zurück. Zu einiger Schadloshaltung für Sie habe ich 7 Portraits, die Sie noch nicht haben, beÿgelegt. Vergeben Sie mir also u. nehmen damit vorlieb. Ich laure nun noch auf ein Paar mir versprochne Recruten, alsdeñ soll mein Bildercatalogue gewiß gedruckt werden." *CPEB-Briefe*, 2:1221–22; *CPEB-Letters*, 267 (modified).

size; details as to whether or not the picture was framed, and if framed, whether in gold or black and under glass.

The Posthumous Fate of the Collection

Although materials from Bach's estate were auctioned in 1789,[27] a decision appears to have been made by his heirs to try to keep the portrait collection together. In 1790 Gerber emphasized the importance of the collection, and of keeping it intact: "Finally, Herr Bach, earlier than anyone else, owned a trove of 330 portraits exclusively of virtuosi, among which were to be found a particularly large number of paintings and drawings. It is to be hoped, that this valuable collection comes, intact, into good hands."[28] In 1797, however, following the death of Bach's widow, items began to be sold off piecemeal by Bach's daughter, Anna Carolina Philippina. Her principal advisor in this endeavor was J. J. H. Westphal. He was one of the first to be notified of plans for the sale, which she excused on account of advice from friends and lack of space on the walls of her new apartment.[29] Westphal helped to price the prints in the collection, marking up a copy of NV 1790 for Bach's daughter; the drawings

27. See Leisinger 1991.

28. "Endlich besaß Herr Bach, früher schon als jemand, einen Schatz von 330 unvermischten Virtuosenbildnissen, worunter sich besonders viele Gemälde und Zeichnungen befanden. Es ist zu wünschen, daß diese schätzbare Sammlung unzertheilt in gute Hände kommt." *GerberL*, 1:83. Gerber's count of 330 items refers to the portraits of what he considered practicing musicians (virtuosi), and excludes those of writers, mythical and historical figures, and the other less obviously musical portrait subjects.

29. In a letter to Westphal on 3 May 1797 ACPB wrote: "On the advice of various friends I have come to the point of selling off the musical portrait collection piecemeal, as soon as I have had it priced by an expert, for whom I am currently on the lookout." (Auf Anrathen verschiedener Freunde bin ich anjetzt gekommen, die musikalische Bildniß-Sammlung im einzelnen zu verkaufen, so bald ich sie werde, durch einen Sachverständigen, nach dem ich mich jetzt umthue, taxiren lassen.) On 24 May 1797 she wrote: "Partly I think that it will be difficult to find a Liebhaber who is interested in the whole collection, partly I was requested to do so [to sell the collection piecemeal], and partly it was made necessary to pursue this course on account of the lack of room on changing my apartment." (Theils glaube ich, daß sich zu der ganzen Sammlung schwerlich ein Liebhaber finden wird, theils werde ich so dazu aufgefordert, und theils nöthigt mich der Mangel an Raum bey Veränderung meiner Wohnung, diesen Weg einzuschlagen.) See Schmid 1988, 514–15.

and paintings were priced with the help of the Hamburg artist and engraver Friedrich Wilhelm Skerl, as well as the collector Wagener.[30] There appears to have been no attempt to sell the collection as a whole to a single individual; indeed, A.C. P. Bach's letters reveal a concern that many items would not be of interest to the print-collecting enthusiast, "for in this it largely comes down to hobby-collecting" (weil es hiebey hauptsächlich auf Liebhaberey ankömmt), and that many would not have the means to buy the paintings, drawings, and other more expensive items.[31]

To judge from annotations made by Westphal in his own copy of NV 1790, he himself appears to have acquired around 160 of the items listed in the catalogue.[32] Most of these were prints, but there is additional evidence, in fragmentary drafts of a catalogue of Westphal's collection that survive in B-Bc,[33] that Westphal also took some of the more expensive "treasures." On the draft pages of his catalogue, under the heading "Aus der Bachischen befinden sich in meiner Sammlung," are listed four items from NV 1790: the drawing of Bononcini (no. 54), the miniature of Fischer (no. 119), the drawing of Santa Stella Lotti (no. 211), and the portrait of Paradies (no. 262), listed in NV 1790 as a drawing, but emphatically described by Westphal as "NB Not drawn, but painted in pastels by Schubart." (NB nicht gezeichnet, sondern in Pastell gemahlt von Schubart.)[34] Furthermore, Westphal managed to acquire some of the busts

---

30. The copy of NV 1790 in B-Bc, 34,734 H.P., contains a handwritten note stating that Hofrath von Ehrenreich of Hamburg had provided descriptions of the works of J.S. Bach the younger; see Leisinger/Wollny, 126 and 458.

31. Certain that it would be easier to sell the prints than the much more expensive drawings and paintings, she wrote on 17 October 1797: "The paintings and drawings, of which there are a considerable number, and which are naturally much more expensive than the copperplate engravings, will not be sought after, since the enthusiasts are seldom so well off that they can spend very much on their hobby, and generally limit themselves to engravings." (Die Gemälde und Zeichnungen, deren Anzahl sehr beträchtlich ist, und die natürlicher Weise viel theurer, als die Kupferstiche sind, werden nicht gesucht werden, da die Liebhaber selten so bemittelt sind, daß sie für ihre Liebhaberey viel anwenden können, und sich bey ihrem Sammeln gemeiniglich nur auf Kupferstiche beschränken.) See Schmid 1988, 516.

32. See Schmid 1988, 481–83.

33. Both the complete catalogue and the collection itself are now lost.

34. The folder containing these pages, B-Bc, 34,734, also contains many other loose sheets. Most of these seem to be part of Westphal's project to collect portraits, or to list, in the manner

and reliefs: he lists "Telemann, . . . In Gips von Gibbons", "Noelly, in Gips . . .", "Noelly . . . in Wachs, von Sirl", and "Bach, C.P.E. in Gips von Schubart." The latter, the plaster bust of C.P.E. Bach, was a gift from A.C.P. Bach, thanking Westphal for his help in the sale of the collection. The waxen Noëlli had been part of negotiations with Bach before his death—Bach had planned to send it to Westphal, and the difficulty of packing it had been the subject of several letters. Eventually, Bach's widow sent the object on 24 September 1790.[35]

The fate of Westphal's collection is unknown. After his death in 1825, his library was eventually sold in 1838 to Fétis in Brussels,[36] but the portraits appear not to have been part of the sale; there is no trace in Brussels today, at either B-Bc or B-Br, of the several hundred portraits Westphal owned (in 1819 his collection stood at 518 items, by his own count).[37]

Among the less well-known and more wealthy collectors who acquired items from the Bach collection was Ernst Florens Friedrich Chladni (1756–1827). Chladni had already acquired several items from the estate, when A.C.P. Bach wrote to Westphal in October 1797 that an engraving of E.W. Wolf (no. 369) that Westphal had requested (letter of 15 June 1798) had already been in Chladni's possession for some time.[38] According to Gerber, Chladni had been particularly interested in the Italian drawings, and in 1815 owned drawings of Folega (by Tiepolo, no. 121), Pugnani (which Gerber thought was probably by Tiepolo, no. 278) and Palestrina (no. 258). Unlike the average collector, Chladni had the resources to buy some of the more expensive items, and it is possible that some of the other now-lost portraits, including paintings, were part of his collection. Information on his collection is scarce: in his autobiography of 1824 he described how he had saved his "very numerous and well-ordered collection

of Gerber, extant portraits and to provide additional information to Gerber for the second edition of his *Tonkünstler Lexicon*. Of particular interest is No. 25 (reprinted in Leisinger/Wollny), which seems to have been the list sent with a letter of 21 July 1788 from Bach, supplying Westphal with 23 of Bach's duplicate copies, and asking for others.

35. Although it appears that Bach had in his possession two reliefs by Noëlli, only one is listed in NV 1790: a plaster relief on slate; perhaps this is the first Noëlli listed by Westphal as residing in his own collection. Both of these items are now lost. See Schmid 1988, 518.

36. See Leisinger/Wollny.

37. Letter to the Schwerin "Zahl-Kommisair" Henk, 30 June 1819; see Leisinger/Wollny, 74.

38. Schmid 1988, 518.

of portraits of musicians" (sehr zahlreiche und gehörig geordnete Sammlung von Tonkünstlerbildnisse) from fire; it is not known what happened to his collection after his death in 1827.

Anna Carolina Philippina Bach also mentioned that Gerber bought items from the Bach collection to expand his own,[39] and it is likely that Forkel also would have tried to acquire items to fill out his own collection. Forkel's estate catalogue (1818) lists a collection of portraits that includes several drawings (many of them copies of earlier portraits by a certain "Loggan"), 46 silhouettes, and well over 450 prints.

After the death of A.C.P. Bach in 1804, the rest of the Bach estate was sold at auction on 4 March 1805. It was at this sale that a number of the more expensive portraits, including those of Paolo Bedeschi (no. 42) and Mingotti, were bought by Georg Poelchau. Very actively acquiring items from the Bach collection, Poelchau also bought items from the Forkel estate, and from other sales later in the 1820s and early 1830s.[40] A number of the portraits which Poelchau annotated as having come from the Bach collection ("aus der Bachschen Sammlung") appear to have entered his own collection quite late. (See, e.g., Poelchau's annotations in the lower left and right corners of the drawing of Mara, no. 216, plate 169.) Poelchau's collection was sold to SBB in 1841; Poelchau's detailed handwritten catalogue of the collection is to be found in D-B, Mus. ms. theor. Kat. 131.

Reconstructing the Portrait Collection

The portraits assembled here reconstruct as far as possible the collection documented in NV 1790. The basis for this reconstruction is the Poelchau collection. Although many of the paintings are lost, several of the drawings and

---

39. In a letter of 11 January 1799 ACPB reported that she was sending a package of portrait prints, in answer to a prior request from Westphal, but that the portrait of Damião a Góis was not among them, since it had for a while already been in the collection of "Herr Gerber in Sondershausen." Schmid 1988, 519.

40. See Klaus Engler, *Georg Poelchau und seine Musikaliensammlung: Ein Beitrag zur Überlieferung Bachscher Musik in der ersten Hälfte des 19. Jahrhunderts* (Tübingen: s.n., 1984), and Paul Kast, *Die Bach-Handschriften der Berliner Staatsbibliothek* (Trossingen: Hohner, 1958).

paintings listed in NV 1790 are to be found in Poelchau's collection, and his annotations on many of them identify their provenance without doubt. Some items from the Poelchau collection lack these attributions, but can be identified by the artist and size of the image. In several cases, this provenance has led to important discoveries, including the identification of two drawings by J. S. Bach the younger, of Buffardin and Mingotti.[41] The Kniep drawing of Jürgensen (no. 180), and likewise the drawing of J. F. Reichardt (no. 289), were hitherto unknown. The provenance of the Kniep drawing of St. Cecilia (no. 62) has been identified for the first time here.

The majority of the collection consists of prints. Where possible, the images reproduced here for these have been taken from the Poelchau collection, although in most cases it cannot absolutely be ascertained whether a print in Poelchau's collection had come from Bach's collection. Indeed, prints were widely disseminated in the eighteenth century, and in a sense the object itself (the piece of paper) is of far less significance than the image printed on it (even whether or not the print was a first or later impression was also not of great significance to most collectors—these are not fine art prints). Nonetheless, it is very likely that many of the prints in Poelchau's collection, and now in D-B, were in fact bought from the Bach collection. These would include portraits of figures who were truly obscure by the beginning of the nineteenth century (especially those for whose presence in Bach's collection Gerber could find no explanation), as well as figures who had no strong connection to music (such as the sixteenth-century German legal scholar Nicolaus Cisner, no. 77). Into this category would fall some of the theologians and Reformation or Counter-Reformation figures, who may have had particular significance for the Bach family (and especially J. S. Bach), but who had little interest for other collectors of musical portraits in the nineteenth century (such as Joseph Müller or Aloys Fuchs). However, it is important to stress that many of the late-eighteenth-century prints listed in NV 1790 circulated fairly widely; it was precisely because they were relatively inexpensive that they were so attractive to the print collector. On the other hand, some of the older items were very rare (as Gerber notes), and it would have required great expertise, effort, and financial outlay

---

41. Fröhlich, 163–65.

to assemble a portrait collection of this size. Although the likelihood is strong that at least some of Poelchau's prints had been in Bach's collection, the actual provenance of individual sheets should not be overstated.

Concordant exemplars of prints listed in NV 1790 but not present in D-B have been traced to collections and archives across Europe and in the United States. The main collections consulted in this process have been the comprehensive collection of A-Wn (www.bildarchivaustria.at); the portrait collection of D-W (see Mortzfeld); the collection of US-NYp (digitalgallery.nypl.org/ nypldigital/index.cfm); the Department of Prints and Drawings of the British Museum (www.britishmuseum.org/pd/pdhome.html); and the National Portrait Gallery, London (www.npg.org.uk/collections.php). Other museums, libraries, and archives consulted online or visited in person include B-Bc and B-Br; the Kupferstichkabinett, Staatliche Museen zu Berlin; the Kupferstich-Kabinett, Staatliche Kunstsammlungen Dresden; the Art Institute of Chicago; the libraries of Cornell University and Harvard University; as well as many smaller museums and archives across Europe and the United States.

In gathering exemplars from other collections, every effort has been made to match the print with the portrait that was in C. P. E. Bach's possession. In cases where the names of original artist and engraver are given in NV 1790 and visible on the portrait, identification has been straightforward (although not all items have come to light). In cases where NV 1790 does not identify artists, the extensive appendix in *GerberL* has provided important information: since NV 1790 normally gives the approximate paper size, and Gerber always adds artists' names if possible, in many cases it has been possible to identify the print in question using Gerber's additional information. While many portrait prints were issued as single items or as series, others were published as frontispieces to books or music. Gerber usually gives the source for these portraits. In cases where no artists' names are given in NV 1790 or in Gerber, and where several different portraits of the same sitter appear to have been available, the entry in NV 1790 has been taken as a clue to the identity of the print: we have taken the portrait whose inscription conforms most closely to the rubric given in NV 1790. In several cases NV 1790 gives too little information for any definitive identification of the image to be made. NV 1790 does not cite a source for the woodcuts, but the most likely source (according to Gerber) is Nikolaus

Reusner, *Icones sive Imagines* (1587, 1589, 1590), several volumes of woodcuts of illustrious theologians and other cultural figures. Corroborating evidence for this is given in the NV 1790 entries, whose information generally reflects the inscriptions on the Reusner images.

Sizes given in NV 1790 are either indications of the paper size on which the image was engraved, or the dimensions of paintings and pastels. These can be used as a fairly reliable point of reference for the extant paintings, although NV 1790 is not without errors. With respect to the prints, the sizes do not always correspond well to the objects as they are today. In the majority of cases, the prints have been cropped to various degrees. Many are cropped to the plate line, and some beyond the plate line right to the image itself (or even into the image); in some cases the paper has been cut in such a way that the name of the subject, or a dedicatory verse, has been lost. It is not clear when this cropping took place, although traces of gray paper and glue in the corners of most of the Poelchau collection prints indicate that his prints were glued into albums, and were likely reduced in size as far as possible. In the case of NV 1790, measurements probably refer to the complete sheet of paper, and not the portrait image alone; the commentary in the present volume gives the sheet size where possible, and otherwise just the size of the image.

Notes on Using this Catalogue

The present volume presents the portraits and the commentary in the more-or-less alphabetical order in which they are listed in NV 1790; all items listed in NV 1790 are accounted for in the commentary (and numbered editorially according to their place in NV 1790). Items presented as plates in part II are also identified by plate numbers and presented in NV 1790 order. A classified index groups the portraits into four categories:

A. Items known to have been in the possession of Bach, including the extant paintings and drawings, as well as one print;

B. Engraved portraits concordant with items listed in NV 1790, many of them from the collection of Georg Poelchau, and perhaps originally in the possession of Bach;

C. Items possibly concordant with those listed in NV 1790, including portraits for which NV 1790 gives only partial information but for which a likely match is available, based on provenance, on portrait inscription, on rarity of portraits of a particular sitter, on the absence of artists' names, and on availability to Bach;

D. Lost items and those for which NV 1790 gives too little information for identification of an exact concordant exemplar to be made.

All items in the A, B, and C categories are included as plates in part II. An index of artists (alphabetical by surname) gives their birth and death dates (if known) and lists all portraits in the collection with which they were involved.

The commentary gives the NV 1790 entry for each portrait. Information supplied there refers to the subject, to the artists (if known), the size of the object, and the medium: "in Oel gemahlt" (oil painting); "mit trocknen Farben" (with dry colors, i.e., pastels); "gezeichnet" (drawing); "gestochen" (engraved); "Holzschnitt" (woodcut); "schwarze Kunst" (mezzotint). The NV 1790 entry also gives information as to whether the portrait was framed: "in goldenen Rahmen" (in a gold frame), "in schwarzen Rahmen" (in a black frame), or "in schwarzen Rahmen mit goldenen Stäbchen" (in a black frame with gilded inner edge). In the commentary, full names of artists follow, as well as the current size of the object (with image and sheet size where relevant), rounded to the nearest .5 cm. Transcriptions of all inscriptions on the prints have also been provided, with common abbreviations tacitly realized. These inscriptions offer an important glimpse into the kind of biographical-historical information portraits such as those provided to C. P. E. Bach and his contemporaries. Any annotations made by C. P. E. Bach are noted, but other markings or numberings in pencil or pen (usually by a previous owner or librarian) are not mentioned. Provenance is given for all unica (paintings, drawings, pastels), as far as it is known; provenance is generally not included for the prints except as indicated by the reference to numbering in Cat. Poelchau in the "References" line. The current location of prints and engravings is given using library sigla, with the shelf mark or identification number of the individual item as given by the holding institution.[42]

---

42. While several items reproduced here from collections other than the SBB are also listed in the Poelchau catalogue, this has not been noted here: references to Cat. Poelchau indicate the provenance of a particular item from the Poelchau collection. References to Mortzfeld indicate

The editorial board of CPEB:CW conceived this volume as a critical edition of NV 1790, including plates of the portraits owned by C. P. E. Bach, but without biographical information on the subjects.[43] Biographical information on many of the portrait subjects can be found in standard reference works. NG^{II} and MGG^{II} have been consulted in the preparation of this volume; many subjects who do not appear in those dictionaries can be found in eighteenth-century dictionaries that would have been available to Bach, and, in almost all cases, they are also found in *GerberL* or *GerberNL*. References to those works are cited along with any other relevant secondary literature on the portraits. Gerber's *Lexicon* (1790–92) is an important point of reference: not only does it represent the state of music historical-biographical knowledge around the time of Bach's death (1788), but it is very closely linked to C. P. E. Bach's portrait collection itself. As Gerber explains, his *Lexicon* grew out of the musician-portrait collection he had assembled based on the Bach model, and it is clear that NV 1790 was a vital primary source for the preparation of Gerber's *Lexicon*. Information on individuals, then, and explanations for their particular importance or relevance given by Gerber, are likely indications of the type of knowledge possessed by Bach and his circle.[44]

---

the location of that particular item in the Wolfenbüttel collection, and its discussion in Mortzfeld's critical commentary.

43. I am currently completing a separate study of CPEB's portrait collection that presents the critical and biographical information needed to relate the portraits and their subjects to Bach's musical, social, and intellectual world.

44. This catalogue represents my research on CPEB's portrait collection through March 2011. As the volume was going to press, I came upon engravings by Andreas Ludwig Krüger of busts of Aelius Dionysius, Homer, Horace, Socrates, and Virgil (see Krüger 1769; online edition available at http://resolver.staatsbibliothek-berlin.de/SBB000058A300010000, accessed 12 December 2011). Additionally, at least one of the "lost" portrait drawings is believed to be in the possession of Andreas Beurmann, but at the time of going to press we have been unable to confirm this. These and any other portraits that come to light will be made available as part of the "Addenda & Corrigenda" of CPEB:CW.

Acknowledgments

My initial discovery of items from C. P. E. Bach's portrait collection in the Staatsbibliothek zu Berlin was made during a research period generously funded by an Andrew W. Mellon Foundation New Directions Fellowship; I was able to work partly on this project in the course of the following year as an Alexander von Humboldt Foundation Fellow in Berlin. To both foundations I owe the sincerest thanks. The preparation of this volume would not, however, have been possible without the support of The Packard Humanities Institute. Many individuals and institutions helped to supply images for this volume, and I am indebted in particular to Martina Rebmann at the Staatsbibliothek zu Berlin—Preußischer Kulturbesitz, Musikabteilung mit Mendelssohn-Archiv; other archives, museums and libraries which have assisted include the Kupferstichkabinett, Staatliche Museen zu Berlin; the Bach Museum Leipzig; the Bibliothèque Royale de Belgique, Cabinet des Estampes, Brussels; the Herzog August Bibliothek, Wolfenbüttel; the Österreichische Nationalbibliothek, Bildarchiv; the National Portrait Gallery, London; the British Museum, Department of Prints and Drawings; the Universitätsbibliothek Frankfurt am Main, Sammlung Manskopf; the Art Institute of Chicago; Harvard University, Houghton Library, Isham Memorial Library, and Loeb Music Library; Cornell University, Division of Rare and Manuscript Collections; and The New York Public Library.

Invaluable research help was provided by Mathieu Langlois and Evan Cortens at Cornell; Matthew Hall and Ruth Libbey at the CPEB:CW editorial office, and Marko Motnik in Vienna, gave expert assistance at the editorial stages. Lisa DeSiro assisted in preparing the indices. My thanks go also to the editorial board of CPEB:CW for welcoming this project into their magisterial project, and to Paul Corneilson for guiding this volume through to completion with acuity and patience. Kerstin Wiese's enthusiasm for this project came at a critical moment, and I am especially grateful to her and her colleagues for the beautiful exhibition of the portraits presented at the Bach Museum, Leipzig (1 September–1 December 2011), as well as for her professional advice and help. Research in London was crucially supported by Nicola Thorold and Patrick Dillon at the Kennington Centre for 18th-Century Studies, and in Brussels and Berlin by the incomparable hospitality and intellectual stimulation of Jean Ferrard, Stefanie Hennecke, and Christian Wilke. For helping in innumerable ways musicological and practical—that is, for putting me up in Ithaca, New York, and for putting up with me there and everywhere else, I thank David Yearsley.

Annette Richards

CATALOGUE

Leopold August Abel
(1718–1794)

NV 1790, pp. 92–93: [no.1] "*Abel, (Leopold August)* Violinist in Ludwigslust. Von ihm selbst gezeichnet. Gr. 4. In schwarzen Rahmen mit goldenem Stäbchen unter Glas." [PLATE 1]

Self-portrait drawing in gray pencil, black and colored chalk, India ink and wash with white highlights on gray paper; 27 x 22.5 cm

Inscription below image, in the hand of the artist, in brown ink: "Leopold. August. Abel. Musicien. Dessiné par mon propre Main. Ludewigslust: Anno 1779, den 24 März."

Location: D-B, Mus. P. Abel, Leop. Aug. III, 1

Provenance: CPEB's estate—Georg Poelchau—SBB (1841)

References: Cat. Poelchau no. 3; *GerberL*, 1:3–4; Biehahn 1961, 9

Carl Friedrich Abel
(1723–1787)

NV 1790, p. 93: [no. 2] "*Abel, (Carl Fried.)* Violdigambist in London. In Oel gemahlt von *Joh. Sebast. Bach*, 1774. 20 Zoll hoch, 16 Zoll breit. In goldenen Rahmen."

Oil painting by Johann Sebastian Bach the younger; c. 51 x 40.5 cm

Lost

* * *

NV 1790, p. 93: [no. 3] "Derselbe gezeichnet von *E. H. Abel*, 1786. Gr. 4. In schwarzen Rahmen mit goldenem Stäbchen, unter Glas." [PLATE 2]

Drawing by Ernst Heinrich Abel, in black, white, and colored chalk with India ink and wash on gray paper; 25 x 21 cm

Inscription below image: "Dessiné par E. H. Abel: 1786:."

On verso at lower left, in Poelchau's hand: "aus Em. Bachs Sammlung. Poelchau."; on verso at lower right edge: "Carl Friedrich Abel. Violdigambist in London. Gez. von E. H. Abel. 1786."

Location: D-B, Mus. P. Abel, Carl Friedrich I, 6

Provenance: CPEB's estate—Georg Poelchau—SBB (1841)

References: Cat. Poelchau no. 2; *GerberL*, 1:4–5; *GerberNL*, 1:4–7; *CPEB-Briefe*, 1:188; *CPEB-Letters*, 19

Mariangelo Accorso
(1489–1546)

NV 1790, p. 93: [no. 4] "*Accursius, (Marinus Angelus)* Musikus und Poet. Holzschnitt. 8." [PLATE 3]

Woodcut from Reusner 1589; 10 x 8 cm on sheet 16.5 x 10.5 cm

Inscription above image: "MARINVS ANGELVS AC- | CVRSIVS POETA."; below image: "Angelus Aonidum decus & laus magna Marinus, | Et Latium & Tuscum quàm bene canto melos! | IOAN."

Location: A-Wn, PORT 00002468_01

References: *GerberL*, 1:8

NV 1790 does not cite the source for the woodcut, but Gerber indicates that it is to be found in Reusner 1589. This and other publications by Reusner are the likely source for the majority of the woodcuts of illustrious theologians and other cultural figures in the CPEB portrait collection. Corroborating evidence for this is given in the NV 1790 entries, whose information generally reflects the texts accompanying the Reusner images.

Johan Joachim Agrell
(1701–1765)

NV 1790, p. 93: [no. 5] "*Agrell, (Joh.)* Nürnbergischer Kapell-meister. In schwarzer Kunst von *Preisler. Fol.* In schwarzen Rahmen, unter Glas." [PLATE 4]

Mezzotint by Valentin Daniel Preisler after Johann Justin Preisler, 1754; 33 x 22 cm on sheet 37 x 24.5 cm

Inscription below image:

IOANNES AGRELL | SVECVS EX GOTHIA ORIENTALI LOTHIGIAE NON PROCVL
A NORCOPIA ORTVS HONESTISQVE ET INGENVIS PARENTIBVS NATVS MVSI-
CAM ARTEM HVMANIORESQVE LITTERAS IN GYMNASIO LINCOPIENSI ACA-
DEMIAQVE VPSALIENSI FREQVENTAVIT ET EXCOLVIT IBIQVE RECEPTVS
EST A SERENISSIMO PRINCIPE HASSIAE-CASSELLANO MAXIMILIANO INTER
MVSICOS CVBICVLO SVO DESTINATOS ILLINCQVE A SENATV NORIMBERGENSI
VOCATVS DEMANDATO MVNERE, QVOD CHORI MVSICI PRAEFECTVS ET DIREC-
TOR GERIT, BENE LAVDABILITERQVE FVNGITVR.

Production details at bottom left: "J.J. Preisler pinx."; at bottom right: "Val. Dan. Preisler sc. et exc Nor. 1754"

Location: D-B, Mus. P. Agrell, I, 1

References: Cat. Poelchau no. 6; *GerberL*, 1:16; *GerberNL*, 1:24

Rudolf Agricola
(1444–1485)

NV 1790, p. 93: [no. 6] "*Agricola, (Rudolphus) Theol. Philos.* und Musikus. Gezeichnet von *Joh. Seb. Bach.* 8. In schwarzen Rahmen, unter Glas."

Drawing by Johann Sebastian Bach the younger

Lost

References: *GerberL*, 1:18; *GerberNL*, 1:33–34

Heinrich Cornelius Agrippa
(1486–1535)

NV 1790, p. 93: [no. 7] "*Agrippa, (Henr. Cornel.)* Schriftsteller. 4."
[PLATE 5]

Engraving after Robert Boissard, 1669; 13.5 x 9 cm on sheet
15 x 10.5 cm

Inscription in arch above image: "HENRICUS CORNELIUS AGRIPPA Med. & IC. EQU."

On plaque below: "Nascitur Colon. | Agrip. | Obiit Anno 1538. || Stemmate natus Eques, Medicus Magus atque peritus | Juris et Imperij consul Agrippa fuj."
Location: US-NYp, Muller Collection (digital ID 110736)
References: *GerberL*, 1:18

NV 1790 gives no identifying details for this portrait beyond its size. A woodcut of Agrippa was published in Reusner 1587 and 1590, but the absence of the indication "Holzschnitt" and the fact that NV 1790 lists the image as quarto rather than octavo size suggest that Reusner was not the source for this portrait. Gerber indicates that the source for the quarto-sized portrait of Agrippa (included here) was Boissard's *Bibliotheca Chalcographica*.

Alardus Amstelredamus
(1491–1544)

NV 1790, p. 93: [no. 8] "*Alardus*, Schriftsteller. Holzschnitt. 8."
[PLATE 6]
Woodcut from Reusner 1587; 10 x 8 cm on sheet 15 x 9 cm
Inscription above image: "ALARDVS AMSTELREDAMVS | Philosophus.";
below image: "Si Logicâ laus est præcellere in arte, Rodolphum | Par laus Agricolam debita, meque manet."
References: Lemmer 1973, 452

According to Gerber, images of Alardus were available in quarto and octavo sizes; only the octavo is listed by Gerber as a woodcut, published in Reusner.

Albertus Magnus
(c. 1195–1280)

NV 1790, p. 93: [no. 9] "*Albertus, Magnus*, Schriftsteller. Holzschnitt. 8." [PLATE 7]
Woodcut from Reusner 1590; 10 x 8 cm on sheet 15 x 9 cm
Inscription above image: "4 | ALBERTUS MAGNUS EPI- | scopus Ratisponensis."; below image: "Magnus eram Sophiæ doctor, Præsulque sacrorum: | Abdita naturæ vis mihi nota liquet. || M. CCCXXCII."

Location: D-W, Portr. I 163
References: *GerberL*, 1:23–24; *GerberNL*, 1: 52; Mortzfeld, A 203

Leon Battista Alberti
(1404–1472)

NV 1790, p. 93: [no. 10] "*Albertus, (Leo Baptista) Musicæ &c.*
summe peritus. Holzschnitt. 8." [PLATE 8]
Woodcut from Reusner 1589; 10 x 8 cm on sheet 15 x 9 cm
Inscription above image: "LEO BAPTISTA ALBERTVS |
PHILOLOGVS."; below image: "Par mihi nec Zeusis, nec erat Vitruuius ingens: |
Doctior hic libris fiet, & ille meis."
Location: US-I, Petrarch N7575.R44 1589
References: *GerberL*, 1:23

Alcaeus
(c. 620–after 580 BCE)

NV 1790, p. 93: [no. 11] "*Alcæus.* Lyrischer Dichter, *Musices scientissimus.* 12."
Engraving
References: *GerberL*, 1:27–28; *GerberNL*, 1:57–58

NV 1790 provides too little information for this image to be conclusively identified.

Andrea Alciati
(1492–1550)

NV 1790, p. 93: [no. 12] "*Alciatus, (Andreas)* Schriftsteller.
Holzschnitt. 8." [PLATE 9]
Woodcut from Reusner 1589; 10 x 8 cm on sheet 15 x 9 cm
Inscription above image: "ANDREAS ALCIATVS | IVRISCONSVLTVS."; below

image: "Suada, Thaleia, Themis fauit mihi semper amica: | Inclytus eloquio carmine, iure feror."

Location: US-I, Petrarch N7575.R44 1589

References: *GerberL*, 1:28; *GerberNL*, 1:58

Jean le Rond d'Alembert
(1717–1783)

NV 1790, p. 93: [no. 13] "*Alembert, (Jean le Rond d')* Schrifsteller [*sic*] in Frankreich. 4. In schwarzen Rahmen, unter Glas." [PLATE 10]

Engraving by Claude Henri Watelet after Charles Nicolas Cochin the younger; 18.5 x 14 cm on sheet 22 x 17.5 cm

Inscription below image: "J. D'ALEMBERT."

Production details at bottom left: "C.H. Watelet sc. 1754."; at bottom right: "Cochin filius delineavit."

Location: A-Wn, PORT 00121405_01

References: *GerberL*, 1:29–30; *GerberNL*, 1:63–64

NV 1790 does not give an artist's name in connection with this portrait. Gerber lists two available quarto-size engravings: one by Cochin/Watelet, the other a mezzotint by Haid. Had the item in CPEB's collection been a Haid mezzotint, that information would have been given in the catalogue, as it is for Saint Cecilia (no. 61) and others. It is likely that the engraving in question is the one shown here; the extremely small size of the artists' names etched on the lower margin of the print perhaps accounts for their absence in the NV 1790 description.

Alexander the Great
(356–323 BCE)

NV 1790, p. 93: [no. 14] "*Alexander Magnus, ex nummo argenteo*, hat die Cyther gespielt. Von *Heynsius*. 8." [PLATE 11]

Engraving by Johann Ernst Heinsius; 12 x 6.5 cm

Inscription: "ALEXANDER MAGNUS | ex nummo argenteo."

Greek text: "εἶδος Ἀλεξάνδρου τὸ δ' ἔην | κόσμοιο τρόπαιον. | ἐκ γενεῆς, θνητῶν, τοῦ διὸς | ἐκ κεράτων. || Heynsius."

Location: A-Wn, PORT 00041516_06

Maddalena Allegranti
(1754–after 1801)

NV 1790, p. 94: [no. 15] "*Allegranti*, Sängerinn. Von *Stölzel*. G. 8. In schwarzen Rahmen, unter Glas." [PLATE 12]

Engraving by Christian Friedrich Stölzel after D. Casse; 15.5 x 11 cm on sheet 17 x 12 cm

Inscription below image: "SIGNORA ALLEGRANTI"

Production details at bottom left: "D. Casse pinx:"; at bottom right: "Stoelzel sc."

Location: A-Wn, PORT 00002723_01

References: *GerberL*, 1:33; *GerberNL*, 1:72

Johann Heinrich Alsted
(1588–1638)

NV 1790, p. 94: [no. 16] "*Alstedius, (Joh. Heinr.)* Schriftsteller. Gr. 8." [PLATE 13]

Engraving; 10 x 12 cm on sheet 15 x 20 cm

Inscription in oval frame: "IOHANNES-HENRICUS ALSTEDIUS, PHILO-SOPHIÆ SACRÆ AC PROFANÆ DOCTOR. ÆTATIS LII."; below: "Sedulitas anagramma tibi quia tradidit, ergo | Exposcunt operas oppida cuncta tuas."

Location: US-NYp, Muller Collection (digital ID 1100779)

References: *GerberL*, 1:34; *GerberNL*, 1:76–77

The image included here, which gives no artists' names, circulated widely. Gerber lists only one available engraving of Alsted, giving the size as quarto, but again listing no names. It is likely that both NV 1790 and Gerber refer to the engraving shown here.

Saint Ambrose
(340–397)

NV 1790, p. 94: [no. 17] "*S. Ambrosius*, Mayländischer Bischoff, hat viele geistliche Lieder gemacht. Schwarze Kunst von *Bürglen. Fol.*"
Mezzotint by Christoph Leonhard Bürglin, c. 1760
Lost
References: *GerberL*, 1:36

Johann André
(1741–1799)

NV 1790, p. 94: [no. 18] "*André, (Joh.)* Musik-Director in Berlin. Von *Berger.* 8." [PLATE 14]
Engraving by Daniel Berger after Johann Christoph Frisch, 1780; 15.5 x 11 cm on sheet 20.5 x 14 cm
Inscription below image: "IOHANN ANDRÉ."
Production details at bottom left: "J.C. Frisch del."; at bottom right: "D. Berger Sculp. 1780."
Location: A-Wn, PORT 00003030_01
References: *GerberL*, 1:38–42; *GerberNL*, 1:98–99

Jean-Henry d'Anglebert
(1629–1691)

NV 1790, p. 94: [no. 19] "*Anglebert, (J. H.)* Königl. französischer Kammer-Musikus und Organist. Von *Vermeulen.* 4." [PLATE 15]
Engraving by Cornelis Vermeulen after Paul Mignard; 23.5 x 20.5 cm
Inscription in oval frame: "JEAN HENRY D'ANGLEBERT ORDINAIRE DE LA MUSIQUE DE LA CHAMBRE DU ROY POUR LE CLAVECIN"
Production details at bottom left: "P. Mignard pinxit"; at bottom right: "C. Vermeulen sculp."

Location: D-B, Mus. P. Anglebert, Jean Henri d' I, 1
References: Cat. Poelchau no. 21; *GerberL*, 1:46

Nicholas Lanier
(1588–1666)

NV 1790, p. 94: [no. 20] "*Anier (Nic. l')* Musik-Direktor und Mahler in England. Von *Vostermans. Fol.* In schwarzen Rahmen, unter Glas." [PLATE 16]

Engraving by Lucas Vorsterman after Jan Lievens; 24 x 19.5 cm on sheet 35 x 26.5 cm

Inscription below image: "Nicoläo L'anier. In aula Serenissimi Caroli Magnæ Britanniæ Regis Musicæ Artis | Directori, admodum Insigni Pictori, Cæterarumque Artium Liberalium maximè | Antiquitatum Italiæ Admiratori et Amatori Summo, Mœcenati suo Vnicè | Colendo."

Production details at bottom left: "Ioannes Lijvijus pinxit."; at bottom center: "Franciscus vanden Wijngaerde excudit."; at bottom right: "Lucas Vostermans sculpsit."

Location: US-NYp, Muller Collection (digital ID 1269446)

References: *GerberL*, 1:785; Jeremy Wood, "Connoisseurship of the Arts," in *Nicholas Lanier (1588–1666): A Portrait Revealed* (London: The Weiss Gallery, n.d.); Hortschansky 1987, 83

This portrait was one of several commissioned by Lanier from distinguished artists including Anthony van Dyck, Jacob Jordaens, Guido Reni, and Jan Lievens. The now-lost Lievens painting on which the Vorsterman engraving was based likely dates from the early to mid-1630s during Lievens' sojourn in London. The engraving was made in Antwerp and subsequently published in London.

Domenico Annibali
(c. 1705–c. 1779)

NV 1790, p. 94: [no. 21] "*Annibali, (Domenico)* Altist am Dresdner Hofe. *Carricatur* von *Oesterreich. Fol.* In schwarzen Rahmen, unter Glas." [PLATE 17]

Engraving by Matthias Oesterreich after Pier Leone Ghezzi; 30 x 20.5 cm

Plate 19 from *Raccolta di XXIV Caricature Disegnate colla penne dell Celebre Cavalliere Piet. Leon. Ghezzi Conservati nell Gabinetto di Sua Maestà il Re di Polonia Elett: di Sassonia. Matth: Oesterreich Sculpsit* (Dresden, 1750)

Inscription below image: "Eq P: L: Ghezzi: Delin: Oesterreich: Sculps: | Nell Gabinetto di S: M: il Ré di Pol: Ellett: di Sassonia: || MO sculpsit 1750:"; plate number in lower left corner: "XIX."

Location: US-CAh, Typ 720.50.423 F

References: *GerberL*, 1:50; *CPEB-Briefe*, 2:1151, 1153; *CPEB-Letters*, 247

The index to the *Raccolta* identifies plate XIX as "Domenico Annibali." This same print (without the number XIX) appears in the second edition of the *Raccolta* (1766) as plate 4; in that volume the index identifies the sitter as "Il Signior — Annibali, in Vesta di Cammera, Virtuoso di Sua Maestà il Ré di Polonia. Elettore di Sassonia." A different Ghezzi/Oesterreich caricature of Annibali was made in 1751; this image bears the inscription "Virtuoso di Camera | Di Sua Maestà di Polonia Elettore di Sassonia | Il Disegno si conserva nell Reggio Gabinetto" and appears to come from a now-lost album of prints. That Bach owned the earlier 1750 portrait is clear from his letter to Forkel, 13 May 1786, in which he writes: "Of the caricatures by Oesterreich I have only the Bresciani, Jommelli (under which is written Maestro in Vaticano) and Annibali sub No. XIX." (Von Carricaturen Oesterreichs habe ich nur die Bresciani, Jomelli (wo drunter steht Maestro in Vaticano) u. Annibali sub No. XIX.)

Apollo

NV 1790, p. 94: [no. 22] "*Apollo, Inventor Musicæ.* Von J. M. Preisler. Gr. Fol." [PLATE 18]

Engraving by Johann Martin Preisler; c. 21 x 11 cm

Plate 15 from *Philippo L. Baroni de Stoch, Statuas hasce antiquas . . .* (Nuremberg, 1732)

Inscription below image: "APOLLO | Inventor Musicæ Festudinem Pede premens. Florentiæ Museo | Magn. Duc. Etr."

Production details at bottom left: "Cum. Priv. Sacr. Cæs. Mai."; at bottom right: "Joh. Mart. Preisler sc."

Location: B-Br, Cabinet des Estampes, S. I 34637

Guido of Arezzo (Guido Aretino)
(c. 991–after 1033)

NV 1790, p. 94: [no. 23] *"Aretino, (Guido)* Musik-Director im *Ferarischen,* war ein *Benedictiner* Mönch, und Erfinder der *Solmisation.* Holzschnitt. *Fol.* In schwarzen Rahmen, unter Glas."
Woodcut
References: *GerberL,* 1:561–65

NV 1790 provides too little information for this image to be conclusively identified.

Aristotle
(384–322 BCE)

NV 1790, p. 94: [no. 24] *"Aristoteles.* Von *J. B. L.* Gr. 8."
[PLATE 19]
Engraving; 14.5 x 8 cm on sheet 30.5 x 18 cm
Inscription in oval frame: "PERIPATETICÆ DISCIPLINÆ PRINCIPIS VERA ARISTOTELIS STAGIRITÆ EFFIGIES."; below:
"Vt Leo bruta, Sop^{h}os sic vincit acumine cunct≠os | Summus ARISTOTELES, ARTIS enim ipse LEO EST."
Production details at bottom left: "I.B.L. | M & P.C."
Location: A-Wn, PORT 00003768_02
References: *GerberL,* 1:58

Saint Augustine of Hippo
(354–430)

NV 1790, p. 94: [no. 25] *"S. Augustinus, (Aurelius) Bischoff. Schriftsteller. Schwarze Kunst von Bürglen. Fol."*
Mezzotint by Christoph Leonhard Bürglin, c. 1760
Lost
References: *GerberL,* 1:68

Bacchus

NV 1790, p. 94: [no. 26] *"Bacchus*, der Weingott und Stifter musikalischer Schulen. 8."

NV 1790 provides too little information for this image to be conclusively identified.

Johann Ambrosius Bach
(1645–1695)

NV 1790, p. 95: [no. 27] *"Bach, (Ambrosius)* Hofmusikus in Eisenach, des folgenden *J.S.* Vater. In Oel gemahlt. 3 Fuß, 2 Zoll hoch, 2 Fuß, 9 Zoll breit. In goldenen Rahmen." [PLATE 20]

Oil painting, after 1671; 92 x 78 cm

Location: D-B, Mus. P. Bach, Ambrosius V, 1

Provenance: CPEB's estate—Georg Poelchau—SBB (1841)

References: *GerberL*, 1:76; Conrad Freyse, "Das Porträt Ambrosius Bach," *BJ* (1959): 149–55; Biehahn 1961, 10; *Bach-Dokumente* IV, 365, 409; Wolff 2000, 15–21; Leaver 2007, 111–12

Johann Sebastian Bach
(1685–1750)

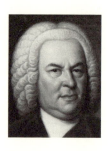

NV 1790, p. 95: [no. 28] *"Bach, (Johann Sebastian)* Kapellmeister und Musik-Director in Leipzig. In Oel gemahlt von *Hausmann.* 2 Fuß, 8 Zoll hoch, 2 Fuß, 2 Zoll breit. In goldenen Rahmen." [PLATE 21]

Oil painting by Elias Gottlob Haußmann, 1748; 76.3 x 62.8 cm

Inscription on verso: "Hl. Johañ Sebastian Bach C. M. | Dir. mus. Lips. | Hausmañ pinx: Lips: 1748."

Location: William H. Scheide, Princeton, New Jersey

Provenance: CPEB's estate—Johann Christian Kittel— Walter E.E. Jenke—William Scheide

References: *GerberL*, 1:86–92; *GerberNL*, 4:735; *CPEB-Briefe*, 3–9; *Bach-Dokumente* IV, 353–56, 397–400; cf. *Musiker im Porträt*, 3:34–35; Wolff 2000, 391; Leaver 2007, 111

The portrait is most likely a copy, by Haussmann, of his original portrait of 1746. It is presumed to be identical with the portrait listed in the 1809 estate catalogue of Johann Christian Kittel. According to Gerber, Kittel acquired the portrait in 1798, perhaps from the estate of the Duchess Friderike of Weissenfels. In 1950 the painting was in the possession of Walter E. E. Jenke, whose family acquired it in Berlin after 1800. Since 1953 it has been in the collection of William H. Scheide of Princeton, New Jersey.

Anna Magdalena Bach
(1700–1760)

NV 1790, p. 95: [no. 29] "*Bach, (Anna Magd.)* Sopranistin, *J.S.* zweyte Frau. In Oel gemahlt von *Cristofori.* 2 Fuß, 1 Zoll hoch, 23 Zoll breit. In goldenen Rahmen."
Oil painting by Antonio Cristofori; c. 63.5 x 58.5 cm
Lost
References: *GerberL*, 1:76; Leaver 2007, 112; Michael Maul, "'von Cristofori'—Zum Maler des verschollenen Porträts Anna Magdalena Bach?" *BJ* (2011): 251–54

The painter, only recently identified as Antonio Cristofori, was a court chamber musician (violoncellist) in Eisenach from 1730 and also known as a master painter. The painting may have been made in Eisenach (J. S. Bach and his wife passed through the town twice in 1732 on their way to Cassel) or in Leipzig, if Cristofori traveled there.

Wilhelm Friedemann Bach
(1710–1784)

NV 1790, p. 95: [no. 30] "*Bach, (Wilh. Friedemann)* Musik-Director in Halle, *J.S.* ältester Sohn. Mit trocknen Farben von *Eichler.* 4. In goldnen Rahmen, unter Glas."
Pastel by [Joseph] Eichler
Lost
References: *CPEB-Briefe*, 1:392; *CPEB-Letters*, 54; for other known portraits of WFB, see Biehahn 1961, 10–11; *Bach-Dokumente* IV, 383–84, 427

Carl Philipp Emanuel Bach
(1714–1788)

NV 1790, p. 95: [no. 31] "*Bach, (C. P. E.)* in Hamburg, *J.S.* zweyter Sohn. In Gips von *Schubart.*"

Plaster bust or relief by Schubart

Lost

References: Schmid 1988, 518

The bust was acquired by J.J.H. Westphal. See appendix B for surviving portraits of CPEB.

Johann Christoph Friedrich Bach
(1732–1795)

NV 1790, p. 95: [no. 32] "*Bach, (Joh. Christoph Friedr.)* Bückeburgischer Concertmeister, *J.S.* dritter Sohn. In Oel gemahlt. 1 Fuß 8 Zoll hoch, 13 Zoll breit. In goldenen Rahmen." [PLATE 22]

Oil painting by Georg David Mathieu; 44 x 35.5 cm

Inscription on verso, in Poelchau's hand: "Christian Bach in London | Matthieu pinx. 1774"; below: "Aus Forkels Sammlung"

Location: D-B, Mus. P. Bach, Joh. Chr. II, 4

References: *Bach-Dokumente* IV, 392, 436

This oil painting, by the Ludwigslust court painter Mathieu, was formerly in the collection of Forkel. Both Forkel and its subsequent owner, Georg Poelchau, thought it portrayed Johann Christian Bach. The painting, however, is not of JCB, but rather of JCFB; possibly it was in CPEB's collection before going to Forkel, or was a copy of CPEB's. The dimensions of this painting, listed in Forkel's estate catalogue as folio-sized, do not exactly correspond with those listed in NV 1790 (c. 51 x 33 cm), nor does NV 1790 mention a painter's name.

Johann Christian Bach
(1735–1782)

NV 1790, p. 95: [no. 33] *"Bach, (Joh. Christian) in London, J.S. jüngster Sohn. In Miniatur von F. H. Abel. In goldenen Rahmen, unter Glas."*
Miniature by Ernst Heinrich Abel
Lost

Hans Bach
(c. 1555–1615)

NV 1790, p. 95: [no. 34] *"Bach, (Hans) ein Gothaischer Musikus. Gezeichnet 1617. 8. In schwarzen Rahmen, unter Glas."* [PLATE 23]
Engraving, 1617; 13.5 x 10.5 cm
Inscription in oval frame: "HANS BACH; MORIO CELEBRIS ET FACETUS: FIDICEN RIDICULUS: HOMO LABORIOSUS SIMPLEX ET PIUS."; within frame, at right: "Obijt Sexagenarius | penult. Nov. 1615."
Production details at bottom right: "M. W. S. | fecit. | Nirtingae. | Anno | 1617."
Location: D-B, Mus. P. Bach, Hans I, 1
References: *GerberL*, 1:83; W. Irtenkauf and H. Maier, "Gehört der Spielmann Hans Bach zur Musikerfamilie Bach?" *Die Musikforschung* 9 (1956): 450–52; Leaver 2007, 112

NV 1790's description of the portrait of Hans Bach as "drawn in 1617" indicates the correspondence between the portrait in CPEB's possession and this print. The Hans Bach shown here was a violinist [Spielmann] and jester at Stuttgart under Duke Ludwig of Württemberg. In 1593 he went with the Duke's widow, Duchess Ursula to the Nürtingen court, where this engraving of him was made, posthumously, in 1617. An etching from 1605 also survives. He may have been a distant relation of Veit Bach (d. 1619), founder of the Wechmar line of the Bach family, to which JSB and CPEB traced their ancestry, but he was not a direct forebear, nor was he a "musician from Gotha" (NV 1790's designation, repeated in Gerber). Presumably CPEB confused this Hans Bach with the contemporary son of Veit of the same name (1580–1626), who had trained in Gotha.

Johann Ludwig Bach
(1677–1731)

NV 1790, pp. 95–6: [no. 35] "*Bach, (Joh. Ludw.*) Meinungischer Kapellmeister. Mit trocknen Farben von *Ludw. Bach*, seinem Sohne. Kl. 4. In goldenen Rahmen, unter Glas." [PLATE 24]
Pastel by Gottlieb Friedrich Bach; 15.5 x 12.5 cm

Inscription on verso, at top, in black ink: "Gemaelde von Gott-
lieb Friedrich, J. Ludwigs Sohn. †1785."; below, also in black ink: "Joh: Ludwig Bach | Capellmeister in Sax: Meiningen | gebohren 1677 gestorben 1730. | Dessen Vater war Jacob Bach | Cantor in der Kirche geb. 1655."; various owners' stamps and numberings are also on the verso

Location: D-B, Mus. P. Bach, Joh. Ludwig I, 1

Provenance: CPEB's estate—Georg Poelchau—SBB (1841)

References: Cat. Poelchau no. 40; *CPEB-Briefe*, 616, 392; Biehahn 1961, 11; *Bach-Dokumente* IV, 381, 397, 424; Leaver 2007, 112–13

Gottlieb Friedrich Bach, Johann Ludwig's son, was an exact contemporary of CPEB, and he made portraits of his father and also of his distant cousins CPEB and WFB (later, his own son also made a portrait in pastels of CPEB; see appendix). According to family tradition in the Meiningen branch of the Bach family, this portrait was sent to CPEB in exchange for the pastel portrait of JSB mentioned by CPEB in a letter to Forkel on 20 April 1774: "My father's portrait, which I have in my musical portrait gallery, in which more than 150 musicians are to be found, is painted in pastels. I have had it brought here from Berlin by water, because this kind of painting with dry colours cannot stand being shaken on the road; otherwise I would gladly have sent it to you for copying." (Meines Vaters Portrait, welches ich in meiner musicalischen Bildergallerie, worin mehr als 150 Musiker von Profeßion befindlich sind, habe, ist in pastell gemahlt. Ich habe es von Berlin hieher zu Waßer bringen laßen, weil dergleichen Gemählde mit trocknen Farben das Erschüttern auf der Axe nicht vertragen können: außerdem würde ich es Ihnen sehr gerne zum Copiren überschickt haben.)

Johann Beer

(1655–1700)

NV 1790, p. 96: [no. 36] "*Baer, (Joh.)* Weissenfelsischer Concert-meister. In schwarzer Kunst von *Schenck.* Gr. 4. In schwarzen Rahmen, unter Glas." [PLATE 25]

Mezzotint by Pieter Schenck, 1700; 25.5 x 19 cm

Inscription below image: "IMMATURO FUN- | ERE RAPTUS. || Johannes Bähr, Austriacus Superior, Serenissimi Principis Saxo-Weissenfelsensis | Magister Concertorum et in Camera Musicus. Ann: natus XLIV."

Production details below left: "Pet. Schenk fec: et. exc: Amstelo. Cum Privil: 1700."

Location: D-B, Mus. P. Bähr I, 1

References: Cat. Poelchau no. 45; *GerberL,* 1:96–97; *GerberNL,* 1:236

See also Johannes Schenck (no. 307) and Sybrandt van Noordt (no. 252)

Charles Ernest, Baron de Bagge

(1722–1791)

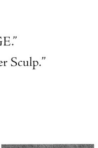

NV 1790, p. 96: [no. 37] "*Bagge, (Baron de)* in Paris. Von *Miger.* 12. In schwarzen Rahmen, unter Glas." [PLATE 26]

Engraving by Simon Charles Miger after Charles Nicolas Cochin the younger, 1781; 7.5 cm circle on sheet 14 x 20.5 cm

Inscription in circular frame: "C. ERNEST BARON DE BAGGE."

Production details below image: "C. N. Cochin del. 1781. S. C. Miger Sculp."

Location: US-NYp, Muller Collection (digital ID 1100969)

References: *GerberL,* 1:98; *GerberNL,* 1:237–38

Ernst Gottlieb Baron

(1696–1760)

NV 1790, p. 96: [no. 38] "*Baron, (E. G.)* Lautenist in Berlin. 8. In schwarzen Rahmen, unter Glas." [PLATE 27]

Engraving by Johann Wilhelm Stör, 1727; 13.5 x 9.5 cm on sheet 17.5 x 12 cm

Inscription below image: "Ernst Gottlieb Baron | Candidatus Juris—"
Production details at bottom right: "J. W. Stör sculp. Norib. 1727."
Location: D-B, Mus. P. Baron, E. G. I, 1
References: Cat. Poelchau no. 51; *GerberL*, 1:107–8; *GerberNL*, 1:266; *CPEB-Briefe*, 2:1209; *CPEB-Letters*, 262; *Bach-Dokumente* IV, 388, 431; Leaver 2007, 126

In a letter of 8 May 1787 to J. J. H. Westphal, CPEB referred to Baron's portrait: "Since you have Baron's book, you should also have his portrait. You have not listed it. If you should happen not to have it, it is also available to you, like the enclosed not-very-well-executed portrait of me." (Da Sie Barons Buch haben, so müßen Sie auch sein Portrait haben. Sie habens nicht angeführt. Wenn Sie es nicht haben sollten, so steht es Ihnen ebenso, wie mein beÿkommendes nicht gut getroffenes Portrait zu Diensten.)

Caspar Bartholin
(1655–1738)

NV 1790, p. 96: [no. 39] *"Bartholinus, (Caspar)* Schriftsteller. 12. In schwarzen Rahmen, unter Glas." [PLATE 28]
Engraving from Bartholin's *De Tibiis veterum, et earum antiquo usu Libri Tres*, 2nd ed. (Amsterdam, 1679); 10.5 x 6 cm
Inscription below image: "CASPARUS BARTHOLINUS | THOM. FIL. CASP. NEP. | A°. C. M D CLXXVI. ÆT. XXII."
Location: A-Wn, PORT 00072217_01
References: *GerberL*, 1:111; *GerberNL*, 1:276–77

Ann Bastard [mistaken for La Bastardella]
(1743–1783)

NV 1790, p. 96: [no. 40] *"Bastardella, (Lucret. Angujari,* genant) eine Sopranistinn. Von *Corbutt.* Gr. 8. In schwarzen Rahmen, unter Glas." [PLATE 29]
Mezzotint by Richard Purcell (Charles Corbutt) after Sir Joshua Reynolds; 15 x 11.5 cm
Inscription below image: "Mrs Bastard."

Production details at lower left: "J. Reynolds pinx^{t}"; at lower right: "C. Corbutt fecit"; center: "Printed for Robt. Sayer, N°. 53 in Fleet Street."

Location: GB-Lbm, Department of Prints & Drawings (registration no. 1902,1011.3690)

References: *GerberL*, 1:19, 1:113; Edward Hamilton, *A Catalogue Raisonné of the Engraved Works of Sir Joshua Reynolds* (London: Colnaghi, 1884), 80

NV 1790 lists a portrait of Lucrezia Aguiari engraved by Corbutt; no such image is known in Corbutt's output, but his engraving of Mrs. Bastard does bear some resemblance to the Italian singer. It seems likely that NV 1790 refers to this print, which may have been sold to CPEB as a portrait of La Bastardella.

John Beard
(c. 1717–1791)

NV 1790, p. 96: [no. 41] *"Beard*, Sänger in London. Schwarze Kunst von *Faber. Fol.* In schwarzen Rahmen, unter Glas." [PLATE 30]

Mezzotint by John Faber the younger after John Michael Williams, 1749; 31 x 26 cm on sheet 36.5 x 27 cm

Inscription below image: "M:^{r} Beard."

Production details at lower left: "John Michael Williams Pinx."; at lower right: "J. Faber fecit 1749."; center: "Price 2^{S}. Sold by J. Faber, at the Golden Head in Bloomsbury Square."

Location: D-B, Mus. P. Beard, John II, 1

References: *GerberL*, 1:121; *GerberNL*, 2: 297–98

Paolo Bedeschi
(1727–1784?)

NV 1790, p. 96: [no. 42] *"Bedeschi, (Paolo)* Königl. Preußischer Sänger. Gezeichnet von *Franck. Gr. Fol.* In goldenen Rahmen, unter Glas." [PLATE 31]

Drawing by [Johann Heinrich Christian?] Franke, in black chalk with white highlights on blue-gray paper (now severely foxed); 43 x 34 cm

On verso, at bottom edge in Poelchau's hand: "Paolo Bedeschi: genannt Paolino, Sopranist in der königl. Kapelle zu Berlin (geb. in Bologna 1727 †1784) Gezeichnet von Franck. Aus der Bachschen Sammlung. G. Poelchau 1805"

Location: D-B, Mus. P. Bedeschi, P III, 1

Provenance: CPEB's estate—Georg Poelchau—SBB (1841)

References: Cat. Poelchau no. 54a; *GerberL*, 1:125–26; Charles Walthall, "Portraits of Johann Joachim Quantz," *Early Music* 14 (1986): 500–518

NV 1790 lists "Franck" as the artist, possibly the same artist who made the drawings of Quantz and Pisendel in CPEB's collection (although the style of those drawings is markedly different).

Pietro Bembo
(1470–1547)

NV 1790, p. 96: [no. 43] *"Bembus, (Petrus) Cardinalus,* Lyrischer Dichter. Holzschnitt. 8." [PLATE 32]

Woodcut from Reusner 1589; 14 x 9 cm

Inscription above image: "PETRVS BEMBVS PATRICIVS | Venetvs Cardinalis."; below image: "Bembus amor Phœbi, Tuscæ Latiæque Camœnæ | Gloria, Cardinei luxque, decusque chori. || Petrvs"

Location: D-B, Mus. P. Bembo, Petro I, 2

Franz Benda
(1709–1786)

NV 1790, p. 96: [no. 44] *"Benda (Franz)* Concertmeister in Berlin. Schwarze Kunst von *Schuster. Fol.* In schwarzen Rahmen, unter Glas." [PLATE 33]

Mezzotint by Johann Matthias Schuster after Joachim Martin Falbe, 1756; 33 x 21.5 cm on sheet 38.5 x 27 cm

Inscription below image: "François Benda | Premier Violon de Chambre | de Sa Majesté le Roi de Prusse."

Production details at bottom left: "Peint par M\u1d31 Falbe."; at bottom right: "Gravé par J. M. Schüster, Berlin 1756."

Location: D-B, Mus. P. Benda, Franz II, 1

References: Cat. Poelchau no. 63; *Bach-Dokumente* IV, 381, 425

* * *

NV 1790, p. 96: [no. 45] "Derselbe ganz alt. Von *Sckerl*. 4."
[PLATE 34]

Engraving by Friedrich Wilhelm Skerl, 1783; 19 x 13.5 cm

Inscription below image: "François Benda | Maitre de Concert de Sa Majeste le Roi de Prusse."

Production details at bottom right: "grave a l'eau forte par Sckerl 1783"

Location: D-B, Mus. P. Benda, Franz, I, 1

References: Cat. Poelchau no. 61; *GerberL*, 1:131–33; *CPEB-Briefe*, 2:1009; *CPEB-Letters*, 242; *Musiker im Porträt*, 3:66–67

Georg Benda
(1722–1795)

NV 1790, p. 96: [no. 46] "*Benda, (George)* Gothaischer Kapellmeister. Von *Geiser*. 8. In schwarzen Rahmen, unter Glas."
[PLATE 35]

Engraving by Christian Gottlieb Geyser after Jacob Wilhelm Mechau; 14.5 x 8.5 cm on sheet 18 x 12 cm

Inscription below image: "G. BENDA."

Production details at bottom left: "Mechau dèl"; at bottom right: "Geyser sc"

Location: D-B, Mus. P. Benda, G. I, 1

References: Cat. Poelchau no. 64; *GerberL*, 1:134–35; *Musiker im Porträt*, 3:94–95

Maria Felicitas Benda
(1756–after 1788)

NV 1790, p. 97: [no. 47] "*Benda, (Madame)* Sängerinn in Ludwigslust. Gezeichnet von *Hardrich*. Kl. 4. In schwarzen Rahmen mit goldenem Stäbchen, unter Glas." [PLATE 36]

Drawing by Hardrich, 1781, in black chalk on white paper; 26 x 20.5 cm

Inscription on back of the sheet to which the drawing is attached, in pencil, in an unknown hand: "Maria Felicitas Benda | gebohren Ritz in der Rolle der Parthen | aus dem Alcest nach dem Leben gezeichnet | Von Herderich im Monat August 1781"; below: "Zu Würtzburg gebohren den 15 Martii, 1755"

Location: D-B, Mus. P. Benda, M. F. I, 1

Provenance: CPEB's estate—Georg Poelchau—SBB (1841)

References: Cat. Poelchau no. 66; *GerberL*, 1:137

Little is known about the artist Hardrich, who appears to have been based in Hamburg and was active in the 1780s. Also by Hardrich are the portraits of Antonio Lolli (no. 210) and Thomas Christian Walther (no. 363).

Antonio Maria Bernacchi
(1685–1756)

NV 1790, p. 97: [no. 48] "*Bernacchi, (Antonio)* Sangmeister aus *Bologna*, war in Bayerischen und Oestereichischen Diensten. In *Carricatur* von *Oesterreich. Fol.* In schwarzen Rahmen, unter Glas."

Engraving by Matthias Oesterreich

Lost

References: *GerberL*, 1:144–45; cf. Rostirolla, 153, 354–56

Jean-Baptiste Besard
(c. 1567–after 1616)

NV 1790, p. 97: [no. 49] "*Besardus, (Joh. Bapt.) Dt. Juris,* Lautenist und Schriftsteller. *Fol.* In schwarzen Rahmen, unter Glas."
[PLATE 37]

Engraving by Lucas Kilian, 1617; 19.5 x 12.5 cm

Inscription in oval frame: "NOBILIS ET CLARISSIMVS IOANNES BAPTISTA BESARDVS CIVIS BISVNTINVS AC LL. DOCTOR."; in ledge below sitter: "ET PALLADE ET | PHOEBO"; below, in cartouche: "ECHO. | Anne Besardus hic est? ᴱᶜᴴ· Sic est. Quid opuscula? Suades | Illa teram? An censes digna latere? ᴱᶜᴴ· Tere."; in surrounding scrollwork: "Anno. 1617."

Production details at bottom center: "Lucas Kilian Aug. ad uivum delineauit et sculp:"

Location: D-B, Mus. P. Besardus, Joh. Bapt. I, 1

References: *GerberL*, 1:154; *GerberNL*, 1:381; Hortschansky 1987, 90

NV 1790 does not specify artist or medium for Besard's portrait. The Kilian engraving (plate 37) is the only known portrait of Besard. CPEB's exemplar may have been cropped to the inner oval frame, thus cutting out Kilian's name.

Heinrich Ignaz Franz von Biber
(1644–1704)

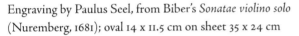

NV 1790, p. 97: [no. 50] *"Biber, (H. J. Fr.)* Salzburgischer *Vice-Kapellmeister, ein guter Violinist.* 4. In schwarzen Rahmen, unter Glas." [PLATE 38]

Engraving by Paulus Seel, from Biber's *Sonatae violino solo* (Nuremberg, 1681); oval 14 x 11.5 cm on sheet 35 x 24 cm

Inscription in oval frame: "HENRICUS I. F. BIBER, CELS:^{mi} AC REU^{mi} PRIN-CIPIS ET ARCHIEPI SALISBURG: CAPELLÆ VICE-MAGISTER, ÆTAT: SUÆ XXXVI. ANNORUM."; below image: "Viva Viri species parvo spectatur in orbe; | Paucos arte pares magnus at orbis habet. | Ingenio, fidibusque; fidem non præstat inanem, | Quando Chorum simul, & regia corda regit. | Ita honoris ergò accinuerunt | Philomusici Noribergensis."

Production details at lower edge of oval: "Paulus Seel Sculpsit"

Location: US-NYp, Muller Collection (digital ID 1105992)

References: *GerberL*, 1:160; cf. *Musiker im Porträt*, 2:138–39; Leaver 2007, 125

Francesco Bianchini
(1662–1729)

NV 1790, p. 97: [no. 51] *"Blanchinus, (Franc.)* Schriftsteller, *Canon. Rom. & Papæ Domest. Prælatus.* Von *Schönemann.* 8." [PLATE 39]

Engraving by Friedrich Schönemann, 1741; frontispiece to *Fort-gesetzte Sammlung von Alten und Neuen Theologischen Sachen . . . Zweyter Beytrag Auf das Jahr 1739* (Leipzig: Romanus Friedrich Braun); 10 x 9.5 cm on sheet 16 x 9.5 cm

Inscription below image: "Franc: Blanchinus | Canonicus Rom et Papæ domesticus | Prælatus"

Production details at bottom right: "F. Schönemann sc. Lips. 1741"

Location: D-W, Portr. I 1102

References: *GerberL*, 1:169–70; *GerberNL*, 1:423; Mortzfeld, A 1566

Quirinus Gerbrandszoon van Blankenburg
(1654–1739)

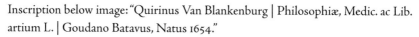

NV 1790, p. 97: [no. 52] *"Blankenburg, (Quirinus van) Musikus und Schriftsteller. Von Creite. Gr. 4."* [PLATE 40]

Engraving by Ernst Ludwig Creite after Jacob Jan Nachenius; 22 x 17 cm on sheet 23.5 x 20 cm

Inscription below image: "Quirinus Van Blankenburg | Philosophiæ, Medic. ac Lib. artium L. | Goudano Batavus, Natus 1654."

Verse on pedestal:

> Dit's 't beeld van Orpheus zoon die met vergode vingeren
> Der stemm' en orgelen banier met regt mag slingeren,
> Wijl hij, door wijsgeerte en door wiskonsts vasten stand,
> Den ouden nevel schift en 't licht voor eewig plant.
> J. de. Meester.

Production details at bottom left: "J. J. Nachenius del."; at bottom right: "Creite sc."

Location: US-NYp, Muller Collection (digital ID 1106041)

References: *GerberL*, 1:170

Giovanni Bona
(1609–1674)

NV 1790, p. 97: [no. 53] *"Bona, (Joh.) Cardinal, Schriftsteller. 4. In schwarzen Rahmen, unter Glas."*

References: *GerberL*, 1:183

NV 1790 provides too little information for this image to be conclusively identified.

Giovanni Bononcini

(1670–1747)

NV 1790, p. 97: [no. 54] *"Bononcini, (Joh.) Aus Modena.* Gezeichnet in Italien. Gr. 4.
In schwarzen Rahmen, unter Glas."
Drawing
Lost
References: *GerberL,* 1:223–24

The drawing was bought from the CPEB collection by J. J. H. Westphal.

Domenico Colas and his brother

(fl. 1749–1765)

NV 1790, p. 97: [no. 55] *"Bresciani, (Dom.)* mit seinem
Bruder, *Calasciocinisten. Carricatur* von *Oesterreich. Fol.*
In schwarzen Rahmen, unter Glas." [PLATE 41]
Engraving by Matthias Oesterreich after Pier Leone
Ghezzi; 33 x 23 cm
Plate 24 from *Raccolta de vari disegni dell Cavalliero Pietro Leone Ghezzi Romano è
di Giovanni Battista Internari Romano e di alcuni altri maestri incise in rame da Matteo
Oesterreich Hambourghese* (Potsdam, 1766).
Inscription below image: "Domenico con suo Fratello Bresciani. Il primo, che é di
faccià suona mirabilmente il Calascioncino | á due Corde: l'altro che é di Schiena,
l'accompagnava con la Chitarra. | Furono nel Mese di Aprile 1765; nell Palazze à Sanssouci, dove Sua Maestà il Ré di | Prussia li intese ambedue à Sonare."
Production details below frame, at left: "Cav. P. L. Ghezzi del. Romae"; below frame,
at right: "Matth. Oesterreich sculps: Dresdae 1752"; within frame, lower right, in reverse: "Matthæus Oesterreich Jncise Dresda a di 5 Marzo 1750 a di 27. Febraro: 1752:
La Mattina a 7 Ore e un Quarto à Mezzo."
Location: US-CAh, Typ 720.66.423 F
References: Rostirolla, 220, 408–9

The drawing of the two brothers on which this engraving is based was acquired
by the Saxon Count Brühl, and an earlier version of the print appeared as plate
15 in *Recueil de Quelques Desseins de Plusieurs Habiles Maitres tirès du Cabinet*

De S. E. ms.r le Prem: Ministre Comte de Brühl. gravés par Matthieu Oesterreich (Dresden, 1752). The 1765 version shown here bears a new caption, stating that the brothers performed that year for Frederick II at Sanssouci; CPEB might have heard them there.

Wolfgang Carl Briegel
(1626–1712)

NV 1790, p. 98: [no. 56] *"Briegel, (Wolfgang Carl)* Darmstädtscher Kapellmeister. Von *Nessenthaber.* 4. In schwarzen Rahmen, unter Glas." [PLATE 42]

Engraving by Elias Nessenthaler after Johann Heinrich Leuchter; 19 x 13 cm on sheet 21 x 16.5 cm

Inscription in oval frame: "WOLFFGANG CARL BRIEGEL FÜRSTℓ HESℓ CAPELLMEIS-TER IN DARMSTADT NATℓ Aₒ. 1626. ÆTATIS 65. Aₒ. 1691."

Verse below:

> Diß ist der werthe Mann der Hertz und Seelen rühret
> Durch Kunst=belobten Fleiß im Engel=süssen Thon;
> Herr Briegel lebet stets der Edle *Pallas* Sohn:
> Sein' Arbeit zeiget hier, daß ihm der Breiß gebühret.
>> Zu schuldwilliger Ehrenbezeugung setzet dieses Geringfügige bey
>> Joh. Benedictus Müller, Darmstadinus S. S. Th. in Acad. Giss. Stud.

Production details at left: "Joh. Henrich Leuchter pin:"; at right: "E. Nessenthaler sc."
Location: D-B, Mus. P. Briegel, W. K. I, 1
References: Cat. Poelchau no. 92; *GerberL,* 1:205; *GerberNL,* 1:512–14

Barthold Heinrich Brockes
(1680–1747)

NV 1790, p. 98: [no. 57] *"Brockes, (B. H.)* Lyrischer Dichter. Gemahlt von *Denner,* gestochen von *Wolfgang.* 4." [PLATE 43]

Engraving by Johann Georg Wolfgang after Balthasar Denner; 19.5 x 16 cm

Inscription in oval frame: "B. H. BROCKES. R. HAMB. SENATOR."

Production details at bottom right: "Gravé par Wolffgang, Graveur du Roy, à Berlin.";
in lower left of frame: "Denner pinx."

Location: D-B, Mus. P. Brockes, B. H. I, 1

References: Cat. Poelchau no. 94

Sir Thomas Browne
(1605–1682)

NV 1790, p. 98: [no. 58] *Brown, (Thomas) Dt. Med.* in Norwich,
Schriftsteller. 4." [PLATE 44]

Engraving by Robert White; 19 x 13.5 cm

Inscription below image: "THOMAS BROWN, | In syn Leven
Ridder en Doctor | in de Medicyne tót Norwich."

Location: A-Wn, PORT 00072483_01

References: *GerberNL*, 1:526–27

Gerber suggests that CPEB made a mistake in acquiring a portrait of Thomas
Browne, meaning instead to have a portrait of John Brown (1715–1766), author
of *A Dissertation on the Rise, Union, and Power, the Progressions, Separations,
and Corruptions, of Poetry and Music* (London, 1763), translated into German
by J.J. Eschenburg (Leipzig, 1769). CPEB's interest in Browne may, however,
have had to do with Browne's writing on physiognomy, especially in the *Religio
Medici* (1642), whose German translation (1748) was praised by Johann Caspar
Lavater.

Georg Heinrich Bümler
(1669–1745)

NV 1790, p. 98: [no. 59] *Bümler, (G. H.)* Anspachischer Kapellmeister. Von *Sysang*. 8. In schwarzen Rahmen, unter Glas."
[PLATE 45]

Engraving by Johann Christoph Sysang after [Johann Christian]
Sperling; 15 x 9 cm on sheet 22.5 x 16 cm

Inscription below image: "Georg: Henr. Bümler | Seren. Marchionis Brandenburg:

Onoldini | capellæ musicæ præfectus, Societ: scien: music: in | Germania florentis socius."

Production details at bottom left: "Sperling pinx"; at bottom right: "Sysang sc."

Location: D-B, Mus. P. Bümler, I, 1b

References: *GerberL*, 1:218–19; *Bach-Dokumente* IV, 391, 435; Leaver 2007, 128

Pierre-Gabriel Buffardin
(1690–1768)

NV 1790, p. 98: [no. 60] *"Buffardin, (Pet. Gab.)* Flötenist in Dresden. Gezeichnet von *Joh. Seb. Bach.* Fol. In schwarzen Rahmen, unter Glas." [PLATE 46]

Drawing by Johann Sebastian Bach the younger, in black chalk with white highlights on white paper; 43 x 30.5 cm

Location: D-B, Mus. P. Buffardin III, 1

Provenance: CPEB's estate—Georg Poelchau—SBB (1841)

References: *GerberL*, 1:217–18; *GerberNL*, 1:542; *CPEB-Briefe*, 1:617, 2:1151; cf. *CPEB-Letters*, 247; *Bach-Dokumente* IV, 388, 431; Fröhlich, 164–65

This drawing by CPEB's son was probably based on an earlier painting or pastel, like the drawing of Mingotti (no. 234). Until recently it was catalogued as by an unknown artist, but it has also been published with an attribution to Friedrich Wilhelm Skerl. A drawing of Buffardin by Skerl is listed in *GerberL* (belonging to Wagener), but that was a smaller picture (quarto size) and cannot have been the item shown here. CPEB mentioned his drawing in a letter to Forkel of 13 May 1786, in which he discusses the possibility of commissioning a copy for Forkel's collection: "Since you want to know, <u>for future purposes</u>, what such a [Martini] drawing costs: I must tell you that I gave 4 marks to Lübisch for it. Buffardin and Mingotti are much larger and more intricate. He will not copy them for less than a ducat. Expensive things!" (Da Sie jedoch wißen wollen, <u>wegen der Folge</u>, was dergleichen Zeichnung [Martini] kostet: so muß ich Ihnen sagen, daß ich 4 Mark Lübisch dafür gegeben habe. Buffardin u. die Mignotti [*sic*] sind viel größer u. mühsamer. Dergleichen will er unter einen Dukaten nicht machen. Theure Wahre!)

Saint Cecilia

NV 1790, p. 98: [no. 61] "*Cæcilia, (Sancta)* Schwarze Kunst von *Haid Fol.*"
Mezzotint by [Johann Jakob?] Haid
Lost

✳ ✳ ✳

NV 1790, p. 98: [no. 62] "Dieselbe, schön gezeichnet von *Kniep.*
Fol. In goldenen Rahmen, unter Glas." [PLATE 47]
Drawing by Christoph Heinrich Kniep, in Indian ink with wash;
33 x 28.5 cm
Annotation below image, in CPEB's hand, in black ink:
"S. Caecilia"
Location: Kupferstichkabinett, Staatliche Museen zu Berlin,
Inv.-Nr.: SZ Kniep 1
Provenance: CPEB's estate—Georg Poelchau—SBB (1841)
References: Georg Striehl, *Der Zeichner Christoph Heinrich Kniep (1755–1825)*
(Hildesheim: Olms, 1998), 33, 327

This drawing was likely made between 1778 and 1780, while Kniep was in Hamburg and before his departure for Italy. Striehl suggests that the drawing might date as late as 1782, but this seems unlikely, given its presence in CPEB's collection; while Striehl notes the relationship between Kniep and other Hamburg artists, he appears not to have known the connection to CPEB.

Callimachus (Filippo Buonaccorsi)
(1437–1496)

NV 1790, p. 98: [no. 63] "*Callimachus, (Phil.)* Schriftsteller.
Holzschnitt. 8." [PLATE 48]
Woodcut from Reusner 1589; 10 x 8 cm on sheet 15 x 9 cm
Inscription above image: "PHILIPPVS CALLIMACHVS |
POETA."; below image: "Sauit vt in vates Paulus, procul vrbe remotus | Exulo par
Græco Sarmata Callimacho. || PHILIP."
Location: US-I, Petrarch N7575.R44 1589
References: *GerberL*, 1:273

While NV 1790 does not specify artist or provenance of this woodcut, Gerber lists the Reusner image as the only available woodcut portrait of Callimachus. The inscription is a quote by the Italian poet Filippo Buonaccorsi, but Gerber apparently mistook the woodcut as a portrait of the Greek Callimachus.

Sethus Calvisius
(1556–1615)

NV 1790, p. 98: [no. 64] *"Calvisius, (Sethus)* Musik-Director in Leipzig. 4. In schwarzen Rahmen, unter Glas." [PLATE 49]
Engraving by Melchior Haffner; 19 x 16 cm
Inscription in oval frame: "SETHUS CALVISIUS ASTRON. CHRONOLOG. MUSIC POETA PERCELEBRIS NATUS. MDLV."
Production details at bottom left: "Melchior Haffner."; at bottom right: "Sculpsit. Aug."
Location: D-B, Mus. P. Calvisius I, 4
References: Cat. Poelchau no. 104; *GerberL,* 1:238; Leaver 2007, 121

Caspar Calvör
(1650–1725)

NV 1790, p. 98: [no. 65] *"Calvör, (Caspar)* Schriftsteller. Von Mentzel. Fol." [PLATE 50]
Engraving by Johann Georg Mentzel; 26.5 x 18 cm
Inscription below image: "CASPAR CALVÖR | Ecclesiar. commvnion. elector. | ac dvcal. in hercyn. svperint."
Production details at bottom left: "J.G. Mentzel sc."
Location: A-Wn, PORT 00153200–1
References: *GerberL,* 1:239; Leaver 2007, 130–31

Philippus Camerarius
(1537–1624)

NV 1790, p. 98: [no. 66] *"Camerarius, (Phil.)* Schriftsteller. Von *Kilian.* Gr. 8." [PLATE 51]

Engraving by Lucas Kilian; 13 x 9 cm on sheet 17.5 x 11.5 cm

Inscription below image: "D. PHILIPPVS CAMERARIVS ICTVS. | Tubingensis | *Diversorum Imperii Statuum et Reipublicæ* | *Norim-bergensis Consiliarius, et Academiae* | *Altdorfiniàe Procancellarius ab A. 1575.* | *Nat. A. 1537. Denat. d. 22. Jun. A. 1624.*"; motto in book held by sitter: "Horarum Subcisiva- | rum | Centuriæ. | III."

Production details at bottom right: "Kilian sc."

Location: US-NYp, Muller Collection (digital ID 1121082)

References: *GerberL*, 1:240; *GerberNL*, 1:615

Samuel Friedrich Capricornus
(1628–1665)

NV 1790, p. 98: [no. 67] *"Capricorn, (Sam.)* Würtembergischer Kapellmeister. Von *Kilian.* 8. In schwarzen Rahmen, unter Glas." [PLATE 52]

Engraving by Philip Kilian, 1659; 18 x 13 cm

Inscription in oval frame: "SAMUEL CAPRICORNUS | SEREN^{mi} DUCIS WÜRTEMB. CAPELLÆ MAGISTER. A.° ætat. 30."; below, in scroll: a musical setting, "Canon perpetuus à 6.v.", of the text "Sanctus Dominus Deus Sabbaöth"; below, in cartouche: "Quantum habuit Sculptor, dedit heîc; Quod restat, abundè | MUSICA FAMA TIBI, mî CAPRICORNE, dabit. || Jacobus Abel | Med. Doctor"

Production details at bottom left: "NL pinx"; at bottom right: "Philip Kilian S."; below: "1659."

Location: D-B, Capricornus, S. I, 1

References: Cat. Poelchau no. 109; *GerberL*, 1:245; *GerberNL*, 1:632–35; *Musiker im Porträt*, 2:92–93

Jeanne Cecile Cardinal

NV 1790, p. 99: [no. 68] *"Cardinal, (J. Cec.) Epouse d'Henry Mottet. Von François.*
Gr. 8. In schwarzen Rahmen, unter Glas."
Engraving by [Jean Charles] François
Lost
References: *GerberL*, 1:247

Giovanni Carestini
(1700–1760)

NV 1790, p. 99: [no. 69] *"Carestini, (Joh.)* Königl. Preußischer
Altist. Schwarze Kunst von *Faber. Fol.* In schwarzen Rahmen,
unter Glas." [PLATE 53]
Mezzotint by John Faber the younger after George Knapton,
1735; 37.5 x 27.5 cm
Inscription below image: "Joannes Carestini."
Production details at bottom left: "George Knapton Pinx^t."; at bottom right: "J. Faber
Fecit 1735."; below: "Sold by J. Faber at the Golden Head, in Bloomsbury Square."
Location: D-B, Mus. P. Carestini, Giov. II, 1
References: Cat. Poelchau no. 110; *GerberL*, 1:247–48; *GerberNL*, 1:641–42

Charlemagne
(742–814)

NV 1790, p. 99: [no. 70] *"Carolus Magnus, Imper. Rom.* Von *Fritsch.* 12. Derselbe, wie
er unter den Chorknaben singt. 12. Diese beyden Stücke sind zusammen in einen
goldenen Rahmen, unter Glas gefaßt."
Pair of engravings by [Johann Christian Gottfried?] Fritzsch
Lost
References: *GerberL*, 1:250

Charles V

(1500–1558)

NV 1790, p. 99: [no. 71] *"Carolus, V. Imp. Rom. 8."*
References: *GerberL*, 1:250

NV 1790 provides too little information for this image to be conclusively identified.

Charles VI

(1685–1740)

NV 1790, p. 99: [no. 72] *"Carolus, VI. Imp. Rom. Von Stör. 8."*
Engraving by [Johann Wilhelm?] Stör
Lost
References: *GerberL*, 1:250

René Descartes

(1596–1650)

NV 1790, p. 99: [no. 73] *"Cartes, (Renatus des) Von Meurs. 4"*
[PLATE 54]
Engraving by Jacob van Meurs after Frans Hals; 19.5 x 14.5 cm
Inscription below image: "RENATUS DESCARTES, NO-
BILIS GALLUS, PERRONI DOMINUS, SUMMUS, MATHEMA &
PHILOSOP[H] | natus Hagæ Turonum pridie cal. Apr. 1596. denatus Holmiæ cal.
Feb. 1650. | *Talis erat vultu* NATVRÆ FILIVS: *unus* | *Qui Menti in Mateis viscera*
pandit iter. | *Assignansque suis quævis miracula causis* | *Miraclum reliquum solus in orbe*
fuit."
Production details at bottom left: "F. Hals pinxit."; at bottom right: "J. v. Meurs sculp."
Location: A-Wn, PORT 00134828_01
References: *GerberL*, 1:254; *GerberNL*, 1:654–55

Elisabeth Sophie Chéron

(1648–1711)

NV 1790, p. 99: [no. 74] *"Cherron, (Elis. Soph.) celebre dans la Musique, Poes. & Peint.* 4. In schwarzen Rahmen, unter Glas."
[PLATE 55]

Engraving; 15 x 10.5 cm on sheet 22 x 30 cm

Inscription below image, in cartouche: "Elisabeth Sophie | CHERON femme de Jacques | le Hay. illustre dans la poiesie la pinture | et la musique. decedé a paris l'an 1711. agê de 63 ans."

Verse below:

> La Peinture et la Poesie
> et la musique ches Sophie
> se plaisoient a se reünir:
> toutes trois relevoient tellement son merite
> qu'on ne pouvoit pas deviner
> la quelle etoit sa favorite.

Location: D-F, Sammlung Manskopf, S36_G00610

References: *GerberL*, 1:275

Christophorus (Cristoforo Marcello)

(1480–1527)

NV 1790, p. 99: [no. 75] *"Christophorus, (M.)* Holzschnitt. 8"
[PLATE 56]

Woodcut from Reusner 1589; 10 x 8 cm on sheet 15 x 9 cm

Inscription above image: "M. CHRISTOPHORVS FLOREN- | TINVS L. P."; below image: "Si dedit ingenium Pallas, si Phœbus honorem: | Palladis & Phœbi nomine nomen habes. | VAL. THILO L. || BAPTISTA."

Location: US-I, Petrarch N7575.R44 1589

References: *GerberL*, 1:280

Marcus Tullius Cicero

(106–43 BCE)

NV 1790, p. 99: [no. 76] *"Cicero, (M. T.)* Von *Krüger* nach
einer alten Büste. *Fol."* [PLATE 57]

Engraving by Andreas Ludwig Krüger after Pompeo Battoni;
plate 8 in Krüger 1769; 21 x 19.5 cm on sheet 25.5 x 21 cm

Inscription on pedestal: ":M:T:C:"; below image: "Ciceron | Buste en Bronze |
Dans la Collection de sa Majesté le Roy de Prusse, à Sans Souci."

Production details at bottom left: "Po. Battoni fec. Rome."; at bottom right: "An. Lud.
Krüger Sculp."

Location: A-Wn, PORT 00146105_01

Nicolaus Cisner

(1529–1583)

NV 1790, p. 99: [no. 77] *"Cisnerus, (Nicol.)* Schriftsteller.
Holzschnitt. 8."* [PLATE 58]

Woodcut from Reusner 1587; 10 x 8 cm on sheet 15 x 9 cm

Inscription above image: "NICOLAVS CISNERVS | Iurisconsultus.";
below image: "Ius docui, dixique: scit Heidelberga Palatî | Imperij Schola scit Spira,
forumque sacri. | M. D. XXCIII."

References: Lemmer 1973, 457

Jean-Marie Leclair

(1697–1764)

NV 1790, p. 99: [no. 78] *"Clair, (J. M. le)* Französischer Violinist.
Von *François. Fol.* In schwarzen Rahmen, unter Glas."
[PLATE 59]

Engraving by Jean Charles François after Alexis Loir, 1741;
30.5 x 22 cm on sheet 34.5 x 30 cm

Inscription below image: "J. Marie LeClair | L'ainé de Lyon"

Production details directly below portrait, at left: "Gravé par François né en 1717"; at bottom left: "A. Loir pinx."; at bottom right: "François sc."; at bottom center: "Fratri frater Offerebat."

Location: A-Wn, PORT 00155787_01

References. *GerberL*, 1:283; *Musiker im Porträt*, 3:50–51

Claude Le Jeune
(1528/30–1600)

NV 1790, p. 99: [no. 79] "*Claude, le jeune*, Französischer Componist. 8. In schwarzen Rahmen, unter Glas."

Engraving

References: *GerberNL*, 2:774–76 (s.v. "Jeune")

NV 1790 provides too little information for this image to be conclusively identified.

Johannes Cochlaeus
(1479–1552)

NV 1790, p. 99: [no. 80] "*Cochlæus, (Joh.)* Schriftsteller. Holzschnitt. 8." [PLATE 60]

Woodcut from Reusner 1587; 10 x 8 cm on sheet 15 x 9 cm

Inscription above image: "IOANNES COCHLAEVS |
Theologus Pontificius."; below image: "Patria Noris erat: sed mens diuersa fidesque: |
Pontificum calamo tutor, & ore fidem.| M. D. LII."

References: *GerberL*, 1:291; Lemmer 1973, 457–58; Leaver 2007, 127

Marie Therese Cogho
(1736–1824)

NV 1790, p. 99–100: [no. 81] "*Cogho, (Mad. Ther. neé Petrini)* Mecklenburg Strelitzische Sopranistinn. In Oel gemahlt von ihrem Mann. 1 Fuß 9 Zoll hoch, 15 Zoll breit. In goldenen Rahmen."

Oil painting by Johann Samuel Cogho; c. 53 x 38 cm

Lost

References: *GerberL*, 1:292

Carlo Concialini
(1744–1812)

NV 1790, p. 100: [no. 82] *"Concialini, (Carlo)* Königl. Preußischer Sopranist. Gezeichnet von *Stranz. Gr. Fol.* In goldenen Rahmen, unter Glas." [PLATE 61]

Drawing by [Emanuel Gottlieb] Stranz, in black chalk with white highlights on cream paper; 41 x 32 cm

Inscription in the hand of Aloys Fuchs, in red ink on the ochre card onto which the drawing has been pasted, center: "Carlo Concialini | Sopranist im k[öniglichen] Preuß[ischen] Diensten."; right: "Original Handzeichnung von Stranz | (Berlin)"

Location: D-B, Mus. P. Concialini, Carlo III, 1

Provenance: CPEB's estate—Georg Poelchau—SBB (1841)

References: *GerberL*, 1:294–95; *GerberNL*, 1:767–68

Hermann Conring
(1606–1681)

NV 1790, p. 100: [no. 83] *"Conringius, (Hermannus)* Schriftsteller. Von *Böcklin.* 4." [PLATE 62]

Engraving by Johann Christoph Böcklin; 25 x 20.5 cm

Inscription in oval frame: "HERMANNVS CONRINGIVS, SVEC. DAN. BRVNSV. ET. IVNAEB. CONSILIARIVS, IN ACAD. IVLIA MEDICINAE ET POLITICES PROFESSOR CELEBERRIMVS."; on pedestal, left: "*Natus. Nordæ. Fris.* MDCVI."; on pedestal, right: "*Mortuus Helmstadii MDCLXXXI.*"

Verse below:

> Hic tuus est, tuus est, ingens Germania, Phoenix,
> Consiliis gratus Regibus et Ducibus.
> Masculus assertor veri, seu sacra novaret,

Seu pacem nollet lubrica Roma datam.
Sive nova Harveius post glandes fruge bearet.
Vastaret medicos seu Paracelsus agros.
Teutoniæ decus et priscos defendit honores,
Et fines sacro reddidit Imperio.
Frisia et vitam, de in munia Geulphica tellus,
Famam orbis doctus, qua patet ille, dedit.
        HENRICVS MEIBOMIVS.

Production details at bottom left: "J.C. Böcklin sc"

Location: D-B, Mus. P. Conring, Herm. I, 1

References: Cat. Poelchau no. 140; *GerberL*, 1:296

Arcangelo Corelli
(1653–1713)

NV 1790, p. 100: [no. 84] "*Corelli, (Arcangelo)* Componist und Violinist. Schwarze Kunst von *Smith. Fol.* In schwarzen Rahmen, unter Glas." [PLATE 63]

Mezzotint by John Smith after Hugh Howard, 1704; 36 x 25.5 cm

Inscription below image: "Arcangelvs Corellius de Fusignano dictus Bononiensis. | Liquisse Infernas Iam Credimus Orphea Sedes | Et terras habitare, hujus sub imagine formæ. | Divinus patet Ipse Orpheus, dum numine dignâ | Arte modos fingit, vel chordas mulcet. utramque | Agnoscit Laudem, meritosque Britannus honores."

Production details at lower left: "H. Howard ad vivum pinxit"; at lower right: "I Smith Anglus fecit."

Location: D-B, Mus. P. Corelli, A. II, 1

References: Cat. Poelchau no. 142; *GerberL*, 1:300–301

Nicola Cosimi
(1660–1717)

NV 1790, p. 100: [no. 85] "*Cosimus, (Nic.)* Römischer Violinist. Schwarze Kunst. *Fol.*" [PLATE 64]

Mezzotint by John Smith after Sir Godfrey Kneller, 1706; 35.5 x 26 cm

Inscription below image: "Hic est Romana Cosimus de Gente creatus |Anglica progeniem quem velit esse suam || Non Imitabilibus mulcet concentibus aures | Quos Pater Amphion diceret esse suos || Ne talis volucres vir totus abiret in auras | Sculptura hæc Cosimi non Sinat ora mori. || Illustrissimo Domino Comiti de Baltemore qui Opusculum hoc promovere dignatus est, Hanc Tabulam in perpetuum | Obsequii Sui monumentum dicat consecratque Humillimus Servus J. Smith."

Production details at lower left: "G. Kneller Eques pinx."; at lower right: "I. Smith fec. 1706."

Location: D-B, Mus. P. Cosimi, Nic. II, 1

References: Cat. Poelchau no. 145; *GerberL*, 1:304; *GerberNL*, 1:796–97

Metrophanes Critopulus
(c. 1589–1658)

NV 1790, p. 100: [no. 86] *"Critopulus, (Metrophanes)* Schriftsteller. War ein Neugrieche. Kl. 4." [PLATE 65]

Engraving; 14.5 x 10 cm on sheet 15.5 x 11 cm

Inscription in oval frame: "DN METROPHANES CRITOPULUS BERRCEENSIS MACEDONICUS HIEROMONACHUS et SIGILLIFER ÆT. XXXVIII. A° 1627."; below: "Nil Metra; Nil est mitra, Nil sigillifer, | Nil quod videtur, est: Nae. quem coràm vides, | Est METROPHANES atque CRITOPULUS est!"

Location: A-Wn, PORT 00138115_02

References: *GerberL*, 1:934–35

Gerber lists only one portrait of Critopulus of this size, without artists' names. The image shown here is a likely match with that listed in NV 1790.

Johannes Crüger
(1598–1662)

NV 1790, p. 100: [no. 87] *"Crüger, (Joh.)* Musik-Director in *Berlin.* Von Busch. 4. In schwarzen Rahmen, unter Glas." [PLATE 66]

Engraving by Georg Paul Busch, 1713; 22 x 17 cm

Inscription in oval frame: "IOHANNES CRÜGER DIRECT. MUSIC. NICOL. IST GEBOHREN BEŸ GUBEN. ANNO. M. D. XC IIX. GESTORBEN IST ER IN BERLIN. ANNO. M.DC.LXII."; below left: "SEINES ALTERS IM . LXIV."; below right: "SEINES AMBTS UND DIEN-STES. IM XL IAHR."; below center: "Musa mori Vetuit Cumulatum laude CRÜGERUM; | Et Prolis Pietas hunc Superesse cupit. || Beato Parenti posuit | Joachimus Ernestus Crüger. | Cam. Red. Secret. Reg."

Production details on pedestal at left: "G. P. Busch. del. et. sculpsit."; at right: "Berol. d. 30 Oct. A° 1713."

Location: D-B, Mus. P. Crüger, Joh. I, 1

References: Cat. Poelchau no. 153; *GerberL*, 1:314; Hortschansky 1987, 72; Leaver 2007, 123

Curti

NV 1790, p. 100: [no. 88] "*Curti*. Von *Annib. Carrac.* und *Odoardo Fialetti.* Gr. 8. In schwarzen Rahmen, unter Glas."
[PLATE 67]

Engraving by Odoardo Fialetti after Annibale Carracci, 1598; 13 x 11 cm (corners cut round)

Inscription below image: "à Lettori Odoardo Fialetti."

Verse:

> Si comè t' è di rimirar concesso
> Del CVRTI il uolto dal mio stil' espresso.
> Ti fosse noto il suon de la sua mano.
> A lui ueresti ancor che piu lontano:
> Poi ch' à leggiadri suoi tremuli accenti
> Dorme Amor, tace il Mar, fermási i Venti.

Location: GB-Lbm, Department of Prints & Drawings (registration no. 1944,1014.582)

References: *GerberL*, 1:318

While Fialetti's name is included in the inscription, Carracci's is not and does not appear on the example reproduced here, which has been trimmed close to the edge of the image. CPEB's exemplar may have been more complete, with Carracci's name visible.

Francesca Cuzzoni

(1696–1778)

NV 1790, p. 100: [no. 89] *"Cuzzoni, Sandoni (Mad. Francisca)* Sängerinn aus *Parma*. In Oel gemahlt von *Denner*. 20 Zoll hoch und 16 Zoll breit. In goldenen Rahmen."
Oil painting by Balthasar Denner; c. 51 x 40.5 cm
Lost
References: *GerberL*, 2:380–82 (s.v. "Sandoni")

Louis-Claude Daquin

(1694–1772)

NV 1790, p. 100: [no. 90] *"Daquin, (L. C.) Organiste du Roi.* Von *Desrochers*. 8. In schwarzen Rahmen, unter Glas." [PLATE 68]
Engraving by Étienne Desrochers after Charles Descombes, 1747; 15 x 10 cm on sheet 25 x 16 cm
Inscription below image: "Louis Claude Daquin Parisien | Organiste de la Chapelle | du Roy."
Verse below:

> Il a porté son art jusqu'au dégré suprême
> Du Dieu de l'harmonie il tient tous ses talens.
> Marchand l'a reconnu pour un autre lui même
> Et Paris la nommé le Heros de sons têms.
> > Par Madame ****

Production details at left: "Ch Descombes Pinx."; at right: "Suite de Desrochers"; at bottom: "Gravé par Petit rue S. Jacques près les Mathurins 1747"
Location: D-B, Mus. P. Daquin, Louis-Claude, I, 1
References: Cat. Poelchau no. 157; *GerberL*, 1:322–25; *GerberNL*, 1:849

David

NV 1790, p. 101: [no. 91] *"David*, König und Prophet. Schwarze Kunst von *Bürglen*. Fol."
Mezzotint by Christoph Leonhard Bürglin, c. 1760
Lost

Willem De Fesch
(1687–1761)

NV 1790, p. 101: [no. 92] *"Defesch, (Wm.)* Componist in England. Von *le Cave.* Gr. 4. In schwarzen Rahmen, unter Glas." [PLATE 69]
Engraving by Francois Morellon de la Cave after Andrea Soldi, 1751; 27.5 x 22.5 cm
Inscription below image: "W:ᵐ Defesch."
Production details at left: "A: Soldi pinxit."; at right: "F: Morellon le Cave Sculpsit, 1751."
Location: D-B, Mus. P. Defesch, W. I, 1
References: Cat. Poelchau no. 162; *GerberL*, 1:329

Michael Denis
(1729–1800)

NV 1790, p. 101: [no. 93] *"Denis, (Michael)* Lyrischer Dichter. Von *Adam.* 8." [PLATE 70]
Engraving by Jakob Adam after Ignaz Donner, 1781; 14 x 8 cm on sheet 15 x 8.5 cm
Inscription above image: "MICHAEL DENIS"; on plinth below: "Bardorvm. Citharas. | Patrio. Qvi. Reddidit. | Istro."; on scroll: "FINGAL"
Production details at lower left: "I. Donner fecit."; at lower right: "Jacob Adam sculp. 1781."; at bottom center: "Viennæ apud Artaria Societ."
Location: D-W, Portr. I 3018
References: Mortzfeld, A 4430

Johann Conrad Dieterich
(1612–1667)

NV 1790, p. 101: [no. 94] *"Dietericus, (Joh. Conrad)* Schriftsteller. Von *Thelott.* Fol." [PLATE 71]

Engraving by Johann Philipp Thelott the elder; 19 x 16.5 cm on sheet 27.5 x 18 cm

Inscription in oval frame: "M. Ioh. Conradus Dietericus Græcæ Linguæ et Historiarum in Academia Marpurgensi et Giessensi Professor Publicus. natus 19 Ian. 1612. obiit 24 Iunii 1667."; above, left corner: "Sÿmbol. | Prudenti"; right corner: "Matt. 10. v. 16. | simplicitate."

Verse below:

> Qui nuper Græcæ reseravit mÿstica lingvæ,
> Historiæ laudes asseruitqve suas,
> Magnus Ditrichius maiorque Platone vel ipso,
> Atque Hippocratici gloria magna chori,
> Pingitur hâc facie, sed candida munera mentis,
> Pingere nex Zeuxis Parrhasiusve potest.
> Quam pietate gravem & meritis dum reddidit Astris,
> Serius, heu! tantum flet pia Gissa Virum.

Dedication: "Sic immortalitati nominis Diterichiani erigebat | indelebilem statuam, eiusdem Diterichii p[iae] m[emoriae] | dum viveret individuus amicitiae Comes, Com= | pater, Cognatus et Collega. Joh. Tackius | Prof. & Archiater Hass."

Production details at lower left: "J. Phi: Thelott scul."

Location: D-W, Portr. I 3178

References: *GerberL*, 1:340; Mortzfeld, A 4856

Aelius Dionysius of Halicarnassus
(c. 60 bce–after 7 ce)

NV 1790, p. 101: [no. 95] "*Dionysius, (Aelius) von Haiicarnass*, ein vortrefflicher Musikus und Schriftsteller. Von *Krüger* nach einer alten Büste. Fol."

Engraving by Andreas Ludwig Krüger, 1769; plate 7 in Krüger 1769

Location: D-B, 2° Ns 4811

Étienne Dolet
(1509–1546)

NV 1790, p. 101: [no. 96] "*Doletus, (Steph.)* Es heißt von seinem Tode: *Musica turba dolet.* Holzschnitt. 8." [plate 72]

Woodcut from Reusner 1589; 10 x 8 cm on sheet 15 x 9 cm

Inscription above image: "STEPHANVS DOLETVS AV- | RELIVS GALLVS.";
below image: "Cuncta dolans ad amußim, examino cuncta Doletus: | Me tamen &
rursus Musica turba dolat. || N. R."

Location: US-I, Petrarch N7575.R44 1589

References: *GerberNL*, 1:914–15

Friedrich Ludwig Dülon
(1769–1826)

NV 1790, p. 101: [no. 97] *"Dulon, (Friedlieb Lud.) ein blinder Flötenist. Gezeichnet
von Karstens. 8. In schwarzen Rahmen, unter Glas."*

Drawing by Asmus Jakob Carstens

Lost

References: C.M. Wieland, *Dülons des blinden Flötenspielers Leben und Meynungen
von ihm selbst bearbeitet*, 2 vols. (Zurich, 1807–8), 1:319–21, 326ff; *GerberL*, 1:357–58;
GerberNL, 1:949–50

Dülon's autobiography includes a detailed account of CPEB commissioning
his portrait (see introduction). Other portraits of Dülon as an adult are known.

Josefa Dušková (Duschek)
(1754–1824)

NV 1790, p. 101: [no. 98] *"Duscheck, (Mad.) Sängerinn und Clavierspielerinn in Prag.
In trocknen Farben von E. H. Abel. Gr. Fol. In goldenen Rahmen, unter Glas."*

Pastel by Ernst Heinrich Abel

Lost

References: *GerberL*, 1:366

Christoph Daniel Ebeling
(1741–1817)

NV 1790, p. 101: [no. 99] *"Ebeling, (Christ. Dan.)* Professor in Hamburg und Schriftsteller. Gemahlt von *Kniep,* gestochen von Beyel. Kl. 4." [PLATE 73]
Engraving by Daniel Beyel after Christoph Heinrich Kniep; frontispiece to *Allgemeine Deutsche Bibliothek,* 39/1 (Berlin and Stettin, 1786); 14.5 x 9.5 cm
Inscription below image: "CHRISTOPH DANIEL EBELING | Professor zu Hamburg."
Production details at bottom left: "C. H. Kniep del."; at bottom right: "D. Beyel sc."
Location: D-W, Portr. I 3531
References: *GerberL,* 1:367–69; *GerberNL,* 2:3; Mortzfeld, A 5363

Daniel Eberlin
(1647–between 1713 and 1715)

NV 1790, p. 101: [no. 100] *"Eberlin, (Daniel)* Eisenachischer Kapellmeister. Von *Strauch. Fol.* In schwarzen Rahmen, unter Glas." [PLATE 74]
Engraving by Georg Strauch; 29.5 x 19.5 cm
Inscription below image: a setting of the text "Ex ungue Leonem.", with the heading "CANONE. â 10."
Verse below:

> Es adelt das Gemüth der Degen und ein Kiel,
> Dergleichen edlen Geist uns dieses Kupfer drücket
> Rom, dem Er dankt die Kunst, zählt alter Götter viel
> Hier wird Minerva gar in Mannsgestalt erblicket.

Attribution and dedication: "Zu freundwilligen Ehr=andencken setzte es | in Nürnberg Joh: Ludw: Faber Käjserl. Gek: Poet. || Und in der Löblichē BlumGenossschaft | beÿgenamt, Ferrando."
Production details at bottom center: "Daniel Eberlin"; at bottom right: "Strauch sculps"
Location: D-B, Mus. P. Eberlin, Daniel II, 1

Provenance: CPEB's estate—Georg Poelchau—SBB (1841)

References: *GerberL*, 1:371; *GerberNL*, 2:7–8; *Musiker im Porträt*, 2:118–19

Johannes Eccard
(1553–1611)

NV 1790, p. 102: [no. 101] *"Eccardus, (Joh.)* Kapellmeister in Preussen. Von *Herrmann. Fol.* In schwarzen Rahmen, unter Glas." [PLATE 75]

Engraving by Johann Herman, 1642; from Johann Eccard and Johann Stobaeus, *Preußische Festlieder*, 2. Teil (Königsberg, 1644); 13 x 13 cm

Inscription in oval frame: "JOHANNES ECCARDVS MVLHVSINVS THVRING. NATVS ANN: MDLIII. OBIIT MDCXI."

Verse below, in cartouche:

> En hanc ECCARDI faciem gravitate decoram,
> Quam forsan potuit sculpere docta manus.
> Sed quantus fuerit Musurgus, quantus in arte.
> Quâ melos accentat, sculpere nulla potest.
> Si tamen illius cupias novisse sat artem,
> Hanc in STOBAEO noscere sat poteris.
> Georgius Lothius D.

Production details at lower right: "Johann Herman sculpsit"

Location: F-Pn, Mus Est Eccard 001

References: *GerberL*, 1:371; *GerberNL*, 2:11–12; *Musiker im Porträt*, 1:172–73

Johann Jakob Engel
(1741–1802)

NV 1790, p. 102: [no. 102] *"Engel, (Joh. Jac.)* Professor in Berlin, Schriftsteller. Gezeichnet von *Chodowiecki,* Schwarze Kunst von *Haid.* 8." [PLATE 76]

Engraving by Johann Elias Haid after Daniel Chodowiecki, 1781; 22.5 x 14 cm on sheet 24.5 x 17 cm

Inscription below image: "IOHANN IACOB ENGEL | Professor in Berlin."
Production details at bottom left: "D. Chodowiecki del."; at bottom right: "J. E. Haid
sc. A. V. 1781."
Location: A-Wn, PORT 00135116_01
References: *GerberL*, 1:380–81

Epicurus
(341–270 BCE)

NV 1790, p. 102: [no. 103] *"Epicur.* Von *Krüger* nach einer alten
Buste. Fol." [PLATE 77]
Engraving by Andreas Ludwig Krüger, 1768; plate 5 in Krüger
1769; 26 x 20.5 cm
Inscription on plinth (in pseudo-Greek): "ΕΠΙΣΟΥΡΟΣ:";
below image: "Epicure d'Athene | Marbre Salin. Ouvrage Grec, du seconde rang. |
Dans la collection de Sa Majesté le Roy de Prusse à Sanssouci."
Production details at lower left: "Krüger del. et sculpsit. 1768."
Location: A-Wn, PORT 00135317_02

Desiderius Erasmus
(1469–1536)

NV 1790, p. 102: [no. 104] *"Erasmus, (Desiderius Roterod.)*
Schriftsteller. Holzschnitt. 8." [PLATE 78]
Woodcut from Reusner 1587; 10 x 8 cm on sheet 15 x 9 cm
Inscription above image: "DESIDERIVS ERASMVS |
Roterodamus."; below image: "Quid Batauos rides? Batauus sum magnus Erasmus: |
Magnus & ingenio, magnus & eloquio. | M. D. XXXVI."
References: Lemmer 1973, 460; Leaver 2007, 129

Hans Adolf Friedrich von Eschstruth

(1756–1792)

NV 1790, p. 102: [no. 105] *"Eschstruth, (Hans Adolph Freyh. von)* Componist und Schriftsteller. In Oel. 14 Zoll hoch, 11 Zoll breit. In goldenen Rahmen."
Oil painting
Lost

* * *

NV 1790, p. 102: [no. 106] "Derselbe von *Geyser.* 8." [PLATE 79]
Engraving by Christian Gottlieb Geyser after Specht; 15 x 18.5cm
Inscription below image: "H. A. F. v. Eschstruth."
Production details at lower left: "Specht pinx."; at lower right: "Geyser sc."
Location: D-B, Mus. P. Eschstruth, H. A. F. I, 1
References: Cat. Poelchau no. 184; *GerberL*, 1:386–88

Michael Ernst Ettmüller

(1673–1732)

NV 1790, p. 102: [no. 107] *"Ettmüller, (Mich. Ernst) Dt. Med.* Schriftsteller. 8." [PLATE 80]
Engraving [by Martin Bernigeroth]; 14 x 9 cm on sheet 16 x 9 cm
Inscription below image: "Michael Ernst Ettmüller | Phil. et Med. D. Phÿsiol. P. P. | et Facult. Med. Assessor."
Location: D-W, Portr. I 3992
References: *GerberL*, 1:389; Mortzfeld, A 6173

Correspondence in size, the absence of the artist's name, and the similar information given on the print and in NV 1790 suggest that this is a concordant print.

Euclid of Megara

(c. 435–c. 365 BCE)

NV 1790, p. 102: [no. 108] *"Euclides, (Margarean)* Mathematikus, Schriftsteller. Kl. 8." [PLATE 81]

Engraving from André Thevet's *Les vrais portraits et vies des hommes illustres* (Paris, 1584); 17.5 x 13.5 cm on sheet 20 x 13.5 cm

Inscription above image: "EVCLIDE MARGAREAN | Chap. 24."

Location: US-NYp, PC-WON P. A-Z (digital ID 1624775)

NV 1790 gives relatively little information on this portrait. The image shown here is a possible match, based on the portrait inscription.

Leonhard Euler

(1707–1783)

NV 1790, p. 102: [no. 109] *"Euler, (Leonhard)* Schriftsteller. Von *Küttner.* Fol."* [PLATE 82]

Engraving by Samuel Gottlob Kütner after Joseph Friedrich August Darbes, 1780; 27.5 x 20 cm on sheet 28 x 20.5 cm

Inscription below image: "LEONHARD EULER"

Production details at bottom left: "J. Darbes pinxit."; at bottom right: "S. Kütner scul. Mitau. 1780."

Location: A-Wn, PORT 00121267_01

References: *GerberL*, 1:390–91; *GerberNL*, 2:56–57; *Bach-Dokumente* IV, 405; Andreevna and M. P. Vikturina, "An Unknown Portrait of Euler by J. F. A. Darbès," in *Euler and Modern Science*, ed. N. N. Bogolyubov, G. K. Mikhailov and A. P. Yushkevich (n.p.: Mathematical Association of America, 2007)

Werner Fabricius

(1633–1679)

NV 1790, p. 102: [no. 110] *Fabricius, (Werner)* Organist in Leipzig. Gestochen von *Kilian.* Fol. In schwarzen Rahmen, unter Glas." [PLATE 83]

Engraving by Philip Kilian after Samuel Bottschild; 29 x 23.5 cm

Inscription in frame: "WERNER FABRICIUS, Academiæ et ad D. Nicolai Lipsiensium Musicus. Ætatis suæ XXXUIII. M.D.C.LXXI."; on plinth: "FABRICII *facies hôc vivida sistitur ære:* | *Nescia sed sisti fama per ora volat.* | *Lipsia miratur dextramque pedemque sonantem:* | *Orbem at per totum Cantica scripta sonant.* || *L. Val. Alberti. Prof. publ.*"

Production details at bottom left: "Samuel Bottschild pinxit."; at bottom right: "Philip Kilian sculps."

Location: D-B, Mus. P. Fabricius, W. I, 1

References: Cat. Poelchau no. 189; *GerberL*, 1:396; *GerberNL*, 2:69; Leaver 2007, 124

Johann Albert Fabricius
(1668–1736)

NV 1790, p. 102: [no. 111] "*Fabricius, (Joh. Alb.) Dt. Theol.* und Professor zu Hamburg, Schriftsteller. Von *Wolfgang.* Gr. *Fol.*" [PLATE 84]

Engraving by Gustav Andreas Wolffgang, 1749; 36 x 22.5 cm

Inscription in oval frame: "IOANNES ALBERTVS FABRICIVS S. S. THEOL. D. ET PROF. P. HAMBVRG."; below, in cartouche: "QVI VETERA ILLVSTRI NOVITATIS LVCE RESPERGIT | ATQVE VETVSTATIS MACTAT HONORE NOVA | FABRICIVS VETERVM GNARISSIMVS ATQVE NOVORVM | NONNE APVD DOCTOS PAGINAM VTRAMQVE FACIT. || Io. Christoph Wolfius. P."

Production details at bottom right: "Gustav Andreas Wolffgang Sculps. Aug. Vind. 1749."

Location: D-W, Portr. II 1513

References: *GerberL*, 1:395–96; *GerberNL*, 2:68; Mortzfeld, A 6271

Farinelli (Carlo Broschi)
(1705–1782)

NV 1790, p. 102: [no. 112] "*Farinelli, (Carlo Broschi)* Sänger. Schwarze Kunst von van *Hæcken. Fol.* In schwarzen Rahmen, unter Glas." [PLATE 85]

Mezzotint by Alexander van Haecken after Charles Lucy, 1735; 35 x 26 cm

Inscription in oval frame: "CARLO BROSCHI FARNELLI. [*sic*] | CH: LUCY PINXIT. ALEX: VANHAECKEN FE. 1735."; title on open score resting on plinth: "Artaxerxes."

Location: D-B, Mus. P. Broschi, Carlo II, 1

References: *GerberL*, 1:209–12

Carl Friedrich Christian Fasch
(1736–1800)

NV 1790, p. 103: [no. 113] "*Fasch, (Carl)* Königl. Preußischer Musikus. Gezeichnet von *Wagner*. Gr. 4. In schwarzen Rahmen mit goldenem Stäbchen, unter Glas." [PLATE 86]

Drawing by Friedrich Erhard Wagener, in black chalk on white paper; 26 x 20.5 cm

Signed by artist at lower right: "Wagener del: Berol."

Location: D-B, Mus. P. Fasch, Karl Friedr. Chr. I, 2

Provenance: CPEB's estate—Georg Poelchau—SBB (1841)

References: Cat. Poelchau no. 194a; *GerberL*, 1:399

Faun

NV 1790, p. 103: [no. 114] "*Faune*, mit der Flöte. Von *J. D. Hertz. Fol.*"

Drawing or engraving in folio by Johann Daniel Herz

Lost

Ferdinand I
(1503–1564)

NV 1790, p. 103: [no. 115] "*Ferdinandus, I. Rom. Imp. 4.*" [PLATE 87]

Engraving [by Sebastian Furck]; 15.5 x 12 cm on sheet 17.5 x 12.5 cm

Inscription in oval frame: "FERDINANDVS I. DEI. GRATIA ROMANORVM IMPERATOR SEMPER AVGVSTVS."; at upper right corner: "Christo Duce."; monogram at lower right: "SF fec."

Verse:

> Romulidum Caesarque potens fortisque Monarcha
> Hic fuerat, pictum quem tibi charta refert.
> Bello alij vincunt hic vicit Pace, quietum
> Seruans, quam dudum rexerat, imperium.

Location: D-W, Portr. II 1097

References: *GerberL*, 1:404; Mortzfeld, A 4525

NV 1790 gives little identifying information, beyond the size of this engraving. The portrait included here is a possible candidate: approximately the correct size, it has an inscription close to that in NV 1790 and no clearly visible artist's name.

Ferdinand III
(1608–1657)

NV 1790, p. 103: [no. 116] *"Ferdinandus, III. Rom. Imp. 8."* [PLATE 88]

Engraving; 15.5 x 9.5 cm

Inscription below image: "FERDINANDUS.III | der | Fried-Liebende."

Location: D-B, Mus. P. Ferdinand III I, 1

References: Cat. Poelchau no. 199; *GerberL*, 1:404

The item included here, from the Poelchau collection, is an approximate match for size and inscription.

Marsilio Ficino
(1433–1499)

NV 1790, p. 103: [no. 117] *"Ficinus, (Marsilius)* Schriftsteller. Holzschnitt. 8." [PLATE 89]

Woodcut from Reusner 1589; 10 x 8 cm on sheet 15 x 9 cm

Inscription above image: "MARSILIVS FICINVS | Philosophvs."; below image: "Sum Plato, tam vitâ, quàm cognitus arte, Latinus: | Hoc melior, melior quò mea relligio."

Location: US-I, Petrarch N7575.R44 1589

References: *GerberL*, 1:409

Ignazio Fiorillo
(1715–1787)

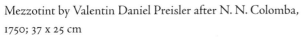

NV 1790, p. 103: [no. 118] *"Fiorillo, (Joh.)* Kapellmeister in Kassel. Schwarze Kunst von *Preisler. Fol.* In schwarzen Rahmen, unter Glas." [PLATE 90]

Mezzotint by Valentin Daniel Preisler after N. N. Colomba, 1750; 37 x 25 cm

Inscription:

IGNATIVS FIORILLO. | NATVS NEAPOLI D. XI MARTII A. O. R. MDCCXII SINGV-LARI MVNIFICENTIA COMITIS ILLVSTRISSIMI FERDINANDI OTTONIS DE TRAVN MVSICAM EDOCTVS ARTEM IN CIVITATE PATRIA. PEREGRINATVS ANNO AETATIS DVODEVIGESIMO IN SICILIAM MESSANAEQVE COMMORATVS MVLTOS ELABORAVIT CONCENTVS MVSICOS IN VSVM SACRORVM HABEN-DORVM. VENETIIS ET MEDIOLANI PATAVIIQVE ET BONONIAE MIRA FELICIS INGENII EX COMPOSITIONIBVS LVDORVM MVSICORVM IN SCENAM PROD-VCTIS SPECIMINA EDIDIT. FACTO IN GERMANIAM ITINERE VINDOBONAE ET ALIBI PASSIM IN CVLTIORIBVS GERMANICI IMPERII CIVITATIBVS ET REGIIS SVAM ARTIS SYMPHONIACAE DEXTERITATEM CONCINNATIS LV-DORVM CONCENTVVMQVE MVSICORVM EXEMPLIS PVBLICE PRIVATIMQVE COMPROBAVIT. TANDEM A. O. R. MDCCXXXXVIIII BRVNSVIGAM PROFECTVS EDITISQVE IN SCENAM LVDORVM SYMPHONIACORVM COMPOSITIONIBVS IN AVLAM PRINCIPALEM RECEPTVS CHORO MVSICO PRAEFICIEBATVR.

Publication details at bottom left: "N. N. Colomba pinxit."; at bottom right: "Val. Dan. Preisler sculpsit | et excudit Norib. A. C. MDCCL"

Location: D-B, Mus. P. Fiorillo, II, 1

References: Cat. Poelchau no. 202; *GerberL*, 1:414; *GerberNL*, 2:129–31

John Abraham Fischer

(1744–1806)

NV 1790, p. 103: [no. 119] *"Fisher, Dt. Mus.* In Miniatur. In goldenen Rahmen, unter Glas."
Miniature
Lost
References: *GerberL*, 1:418; *GerberNL*, 2:140

Robert Fludd

(1574–1637)

NV 1790, p. 103: [no. 120] *"Fludd, (Rob.)* Schriftsteller. *Dt. Med.* in *Oxfurt.* 16." [PLATE 91]
Engraving; c. 8 x 4 cm
Inscription below image: "ROBERTUS FLVDD. | *Medicinæ D. Oxonij.*"
Location: A-Wn, PORT 00073037-01
References: Cat. Poelchau no. 204; *GerberL*, 1:421–22; Leaver 2007, 128

Abbate Folega

NV 1790, p. 103: [no. 121] *"Folega, (Abbate)* Sänger. In *Carricatur* von *Tiepolo.* Fol. In schwarzen Rahmen, unter Glas."
Caricature (drawing?) by Tiepolo
Lost
References: *GerberL*, 1:423; Schmid 1988, 516, 518

This portrait was bought by Ernst Florens Friedrich Chladni.

Margaret Fordyce

(1753–1814)

NV 1790, p. 103: [no. 122] *"Fordyce, (Miss) Lautenistinn.*
Schwarze Kunst. 4. In goldenen Rahmen, unter Glas."
[PLATE 92]

Mezzotint by Richard Purcell (Philip Corbutt) after Sir Joshua
Reynolds, 1762–63; 31.5 x 24.5 cm

Inscription below image: "Miss Fordyce."

Production details at bottom left: "J. Reynolds pinx.ᵗ"; at bottom right: "Philip
Corbutt fecit"

Location: D-B, Mus. P. Fordyce, II, 1

References: *GerberL*, 1:424; Edward Hamilton, *A Catalogue Raisonné of the Engraved
Works of Sir Joshua Reynolds* (London: Colnaghi, 1884), 100

Girolamo Fracastoro

(c. 1478–1553)

NV 1790, p. 103: [no. 123] *"Fracastorius, (Hieron.) Musicorum flos.*
Holzschnitt. 8." [PLATE 93]

Woodcut from Reusner 1589; 10 x 8 cm on sheet 15 x 9 cm

Inscription above image: "HIERONYMVS FRACASTO-
RIVS | POETA & MEDICVS."; below image: "Tam medica, melica quàm clarus in arte
triumpho: | Phœbo par: Phœbus ni magis alter eram. || HIERO."

Location: US-I, Petrarch N7575.R44 1589

References: *GerberL*, 1:431–32; *GerberNL*, 2:173

Franciscello (Francesco Alborea)

(1691–1739)

NV 1790, p. 103: [no. 124] *"Franciscello, Kaiserl. Violoncellist.*
Schwarze Kunst von *Haid. Fol.* In schwarzen Rahmen, unter
Glas." [PLATE 94]

Mezzotint by Johann Jakob Haid after Martin van Meytens; 36 x 26.5 cm on sheet 44.5 x 33.5 cm

Inscription below image: "Musica curarum multis est suave levamen | Perque aures animos illa beare valet. | Fama melos, quo non in terris dulcius ullum, | Nam spargit laudis post quoque fata sonum."

Production details at bottom left: "Martinus de Meitens pinxit."; at bottom right: "Joh. Jacob Haid excud. Aug. Vind."

Location: A-Wn, PORT 00155552_01

References: *GerberL*, 1:434

Michael Franck
(1609–1667)

NV 1790, p. 104: [no. 125] *"Francke (Michael) Musikus und Poet. Von Brühl. 8.*" [PLATE 95]

Engraving by Johann Benjamin Brühl; 21 x 17 cm

Inscription below image: "MICHAEL FRANCKE, Schleusingensis, | P. L. C. im Elbischen Schwanen-Orden Staurophilus. | nat. MDCIX. d. 16. Mart. ob. MDCLXVII. d. 24. Sept."; motto along upper edge of oval frame: "Deus meus in te confido, non erubescam."

Production details at lower right: "Brühl sc. Lips."

Location: D-F, Sammlung Manskopf S36_G00849

References: *GerberL*, 1:434

Georg Frank von Franckenau
(1643–1704)

NV 1790, p. 104: [no. 126] *"Franckenau (Georg Francus de) Schriftsteller. 8.*" [PLATE 96]

Engraving [by Johann Georg Mentzel]; frontispiece to *Neue Bibliothek Oder Nachricht und Urtheile von neuen Büchern und allerhand zur Gelehrsamkeit dienenden Sachen*, 22. Stück (Frankfurt and Leipzig, 1714); 14.5 x 8.5 cm

Inscription below image:"Georgius Francus de Frankenau | Eques et Archiater Regius etc."

Location: D-W, Portr. I 4389a

References: *GerberL*, 1:435; *GerberNL*, 2:183; Mortzfeld, A 6818

Benjamin Franklin
(1706–1790)

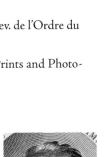

NV 1790, p. 104: [no. 127] *"Francklin, (Benj.) Dt. Med.* Erfinder der Harmonika. Schwarze Kunst von *Cochin*. Gr. 4." [PLATE 97]

Mezzotint by Charles Nicolas Cochin the younger, 1777

Inscription below image:"D. Beniamin Fræncklin. | Grand Cōmissaire plenipotentiaire du Congres d'Amerique en France | né à Boston 1706. en 17. Janvier."

Production details above inscription:"desine par C. N. Cochin Chev. de l'Ordre du Roi a Paris 1777."

Location: US-NYp, Miriam and Ira D. Wallach Division of Art, Prints and Photographs (digital ID 1240192)

Girolamo Frescobaldi
(1583–1643)

NV 1790, p. 104: [no. 128] *"Frescobaldi, (Hieron.)* Organist in Rom. Von *Gallus*. Gr. 8. In schwarzen Rahmen, unter Glas." [PLATE 98]

Engraving by Claude Mellan; 22.5 x 15 cm

Inscription in oval frame:"HIERONYMVS FRESCOBALDVS FERRARIENSIS ORGANISTA BASILICÆ S. PETRI IN VRBE ROMA ÆTATIS SVÆ 36."

Production details below:"*Cl. Mellan Gallus delin. et. sculp.* | *A Paris chez Odieuvre Marchand d'Estampes, Quay de* | *l'Ecole vis-à vis le côté de la Samaritaine, à la belle Image.*"

Location: D-B, Mus. P. Frescobaldi I, 2

References: Cat. Poelchau no. 216; *Bach-Dokumente* IV, 381, 425; Hortschansky 1987, 53, 87–88

Frederick II
(1712–1786)

NV 1790, p. 104: [no. 129] *"Friedrich*, König in Preußen. Mit trocknen Farben. 4. In goldenen Rahmen, unter Glas."
Pastel
References: *GerberL*, 1:445–53

NV 1790 provides too little information for this image to be conclusively identified.

Barthold Fritz
(1697–1766)

NV 1790, p. 104: [no. 130] *"Fritze, (Barth.)* Instrumentenmacher in Braunschweig. Von *Eberling*. Kl. 8." [PLATE 99]
Engraving by J. C. Eberling; 12 x 7.5 cm on sheet 13 x 9 cm
Inscription in oval frame: "BARTHOLD FRITZE BERÜM-TER CLAVIER MACHER IN BRAUNSCHWEIG IST GEBOREN Aº 1697 IST GESTORBEN ANNO 1766." Production details at bottom right: "J. C. Eberling Sculps."
Location: US-NYp, Muller Collection (digital ID 1166435)
References: *GerberL*, 1:456; *CPEB-Briefe*, 1:343; *CPEB-Letters*, 43

Galileo Galilei
(1564–1642)

NV 1790, p. 104: [no. 131] *"Galilæus Galilæi*, Mathemathikus. Schriftsteller. 4."
References: *GerberL*, 1:467; *GerberNL*, 2:239

NV 1790 provides too little information for this image to be conclusively identified.

Christian Fürchtegott Gellert
(1715–1796)

NV 1790, p. 104: [no. 132] "*Gellert, (C. F.)* Professor in Leipzig, Lyrischer Dichter. Von *Fritsch.* Gr. 8." [PLATE 100]
Engraving by Johann Christian Gottfried Fritzsch; 10.5 x 8.5 cm oval on sheet 18.5 x 12 cm
Inscription below image, in cartouche: "C. F. GELLERT, | Professor in Leipzig | gebohren 1715. gestorben 1769."
Production details at bottom right: "J. C. G. Fritzsch Sc."
Location: US-NYp, Miriam and Ira D. Wallach Division of Art, Prints and Photographs (digital ID 1242505)
References: CPEB:CW, VI/1

Francesco Geminiani
(1687–1762)

NV 1790, p. 104: [no. 133] "*Geminiani, (Francesco)* Componist und Violinist. Schwarze Kunst von *Ardell. Fol.* In schwarzen Rahmen, unter Glas." [PLATE 101]
Mezzotint by James McArdell after Thomas Jenkins; 36 x 26 cm
Location: D-B, Mus. P. Geminiani II, 1
References: Cat. Poelchau no. 229; *GerberL*, 1:486–88

The exemplar from the Poelchau collection, reproduced here, has been severely cropped and no inscription remains. The uncropped portrait bears the title "Mr. Geminiani" along with the following production details: at lower left "Tho.ˢ Jenkins pinxt."; at lower right "Ja.ˢ M.ᶜArdell Fecit."; at bottom "Sold by J. Oswald at his Musick Shop in St. Martins Church Yard."

Martin Gerbert
(1720–1793)

NV 1790, p. 104: [no. 134] *"Gerbert, (Martin)* Fürst und Abt, Schriftsteller. Von Bock. 8." [PLATE 102]

Engraving by Christoph Wilhelm Bock, 1786; frontispiece to *Journal von und für Deutschland* (3 St.), 1786; 15 x 10.5 cm on sheet 18 x 13 cm

Inscription below image: "MARTIN GERBERT. | *des H.R.R. Fürst | und Abbt zu St. Blasii.*"

Production details at bottom center: "C. W. Bock sc. 1786. Norimb."

Location: D-W, Portr. I 4834

References: *CPEB-Briefe*, 2:1237; *CPEB-Letters*, 273; Mortzfeld, A 7606

Heinrich Wilhelm von Gerstenberg
(1727–1823)

NV 1790, p. 104: [no. 135] *"Gerstenberg, (von)* Lyrischer Dichter. 12." [PLATE 103]

Engraving by Johann Friedrich Moritz Schreyer; frontispiece to *Neue Bibliothek der schönen Wissenschaften und der freyen Künste*, 50/1 (Leipzig, 1793); 14 x 9 cm

Inscription below image: "GERSTENBERG"

Production details at bottom center: "Schreyer sculp. Schultze direx. Dresde."

Location: D-W, Portr. I 4876a

References: Mortzfeld, A 7672

This engraving appeared on various title pages and frontispieces, in slightly different sizes and contexts but without significant alteration to the portrait itself. CPEB's exemplar, which NV 1790 lists as duodecimo, may have been cropped to the inner oval frame.

Conrad Gesner

(1516–1565)

NV 1790, p. 104: [no. 136] *"Gesnerus, (Conradus)* Schriftsteller. Holzschnitt. 8." [PLATE 104]

Woodcut from Reusner 1587; 10 x 8 cm on sheet 15 x 9 cm

Inscription above image: "CONRADVS GESNERVS PHI-LOS. | & Medicus."; below image: "Plinius alter eram: per me vis iam liquet omnis | Naturæ, ingenij vi superata mei. | M. D. LXV."

References: *GerberL*, 1:502; Lemmer 1973, 463–64; Leaver 2007, 127

Giovannini (Count of St. Germain)

(c. 1691/92–1782?)

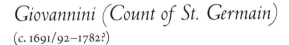

NV 1790, p. 104: [no. 137] *"Giovannini,* (vorgegebner Graf *St. Germain)* Componist und Violinist. Von *Thönert.* 4." [PLATE 105]

Engraving by Medard Thönert after Nicolas Thomas, 1783; 18 x 11 cm

Inscription below image: "LE COMTE | DE S^{T} GERMAIN"

Production details at bottom right: "d'apres Thomas p. Thönert"

Location: A-Wn, PORT 00102396_01

References: *GerberL*, 1:510; *GerberNL*, 2:332

Christoph Willibald Gluck

(1714–1787)

NV 1790, p. 105: [no. 138] *"Gluck, (Christoph)* Ritter, Componist. Von *Miger.* G. 8. In schwarzen Rahmen, unter Glas." [PLATE 106]

Engraving by Simon Charles Miger after Joseph Siffred Duplessis; 30.5 x 23.5 cm

Inscription below image: "CHRISTOPHE GLUCK"

Verse below:

> De l'art d'aller au cœur par les accords touchants
> Nul autre mieux que lui n'a montré la puissance,
> Et de tous ses rivaux c'est le seul dont les chants
> Ayent charmé son pays, l'Italie et la France.

Production details at bottom left: "Peint par J^{ph}. Duplessis Peintre du Roi."; at bottom right: "Gravé par S. C. Miger."; bottom center: "A Paris, chès Miger, Graveur, rue Montmartre, au coin de celle des Vieux Augustins. A. P. D. R."

Location: D-B, Mus. P. Gluck, Ch. I, 9

References: Cat. Poelchau no. 251; *GerberL*, 1:514–18; *CPEB-Briefe*, 1:671; *CPEB-Letters*, 119

Damião de Góis
(1502–1574)

NV 1790, p. 105: [no. 139] "*Goes, (Damianus a)* Componist. 16." [PLATE 107]

Engraving; 7.5 x 4.5 cm

Inscription below image: "DAMIAN^{us} A GOES. | Musicvs Pöeta, Orator et Historicus"

Location: D-B, Mus. P. Goes, Damian a I, 1

References: Cat. Poelchau no. 254; *GerberL*, 1:521; Schmid 1988, 519

Jacques Gaultier
(c. 1600–before 1660)

NV 1790, p. 105: [no. 140] "*Gouterus, (Jac.)* Lautenist. Von *Lævin*. Gr. 4. In schwarzen Rahmen, unter Glas." [PLATE 108]

Engraving by Jan Lievens; 27.5 x 22 cm

Inscription below image:

IACOBO GOVTERO INTER REGIOS MAGNÆ BRITANNIÆ ORPHEOS ET AMPHI-
ONES LYDIÆ DORIÆ PHRYGIÆ TESTVDINIS FIDICINI ET MODVLATORVM
PRINCIPI HANC E PENICILLI SVI TABVLA IN ÆS TRANSSCRIPTAM EFFIGIEM
IOANNES LÆVINI FIDÆ AMICITIÆ MONIMENTVM. L. M. CONSECRAVIT.

Production details at bottom right: "Ioannes Liuius fecit et excudit"

Location: D-B, Mus. P. Gouter, Jac. I, 1

References: Cat. Poelchau no. 256; *GerberL*, 1:528; Hortschansky 1987, 56, 90

Christian Ernst Graf
(1723–1804)

NV 1790, p. 105: [no. 141] *"Graaf, (C. E.) Kapellmeister im Haag. Von ihm selbst gemahlt in Oel. 14 Zoll hoch, 11 Zoll breit. In goldenen Rahmen."*

Self-portrait in oils; c. 33 x 26 cm

Lost

References: *GerberL*, 1:529

Friedrich Hartmann Graf
(1727–1795)

NV 1790, p. 105: [no. 142] *"Graaf, (F. H.) Musik-Director in Augsburg. In Oel gemahlt von C. E. Graaf. 14 Zoll hoch, 11 Zoll breit. In goldenen Rahmen."*

Oil painting by Christian Ernst Graf; c. 33 x 26 cm

Lost

References: *GerberL*, 1:529–30

Johann Friedrich Gräfe
(1711–1787)

NV 1790, p. 105: [no. 143] *"Gräfe, (J. Fr.) Kammer- und Postrath in Braunschweig, Componist. In Porcelain."*

Porcelain relief or bust

Lost

References: *GerberL*, 1:528

Graphaeus (Cornelis Schryver)
(1482–1558)

NV 1790, p. 105: [no. 144] *"Grapheus, (Cornelius)* Musikus und Schriftsteller. Von *N. L. Fe.* 4." [PLATE 109]

Engraving; 17.5 x 13.5 cm on sheet 18 x 14 cm

Inscription below image: "CORNELIVS GRAPHEVS."

Production details at bottom left: "N. L. Fe."

Location: US-NYp, Muller Collection (digital ID 1169021)

References: *GerberL*, 1:532

Marcus Heinrich Graul
(fl. 1742–1798)

NV 1790, p. 105: [no. 145] *"Graul, (Marc. Heinr.)* Königl. Preußischer Violoncellist. Gezeichnet. *Fol.* In schwarzen Rahmen, unter Glas."

Drawing

Lost

References: *GerberL*, 1:533

Johann Gottlieb Graun
(1702/3–1771)

NV 1790, p. 105: [no. 146] *"Graun, (Joh. Gottlieb)* Königl. Preußischer Concertmeister. In Oel. 18 Zoll hoch, 15 Zoll breit. In goldenen Rahmen."

Oil painting; c. 48 x 38 cm

Lost

References: *GerberL*, 1:537–38

Carl Heinrich Graun

(1703/4–1759)

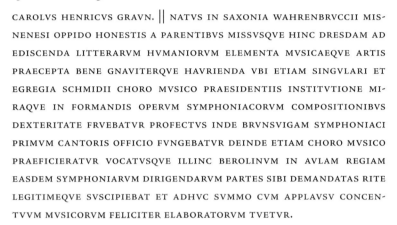

NV 1790, p. 105: [no. 147] *"Graun, (C. H.)* Königl. Preußischer Kapellmeister. Schwarze Kunst von *Preisler. Fol.* In schwarzen Rahmen, unter Glas." [PLATE 110]

Mezzotint by Valentin Daniel Preisler after Andreas Möller, 1752; 34 x 22.5 cm

Inscription below image:

CAROLVS HENRICVS GRAVN. ‖ NATVS IN SAXONIA WAHRENBRVCCII MIS-
NENESI OPPIDO HONESTIS A PARENTIBVS MISSVSQVE HINC DRESDAM AD
EDISCENDA LITTERARVM HVMANIORVM ELEMENTA MVSICAEQVE ARTIS
PRAECEPTA BENE GNAVITERQVE HAVRIENDA VBI ETIAM SINGVLARI ET
EGREGIA SCHMIDII CHORO MVSICO PRAESIDENTIIS INSTITVTIONE MI-
RAQVE IN FORMANDIS OPERVM SYMPHONIACORVM COMPOSITIONIBVS
DEXTERITATE FRVEBATVR PROFECTVS INDE BRVNSVIGAM SYMPHONIACI
PRIMVM CANTORIS OFFICIO FVNGEBATVR DEINDE ETIAM CHORO MVSICO
PRAEFICIERATVR VOCATVSQVE ILLINC BEROLINVM IN AVLAM REGIAM
EASDEM SYMPHONIARVM DIRIGENDARVM PARTES SIBI DEMANDATAS RITE
LEGITIMEQVE SVSCIPIEBAT ET ADHVC SVMMO CVM APPLAVSV CONCEN-
TVVM MVSICORVM FELICITER ELABORATORVM TVETVR.

Production details at bottom center: "A Möller pinx."; at bottom right: "V. D. Preisler sc. et exc. Nov. 1752".

Location: D-B, Mus. P. Graun, C. Heinr. II, 1

References: Cat. Poelchau no. 258; *GerberL*, 1:533–37; *Bach-Dokumente* IV, 381, 425; *Musiker im Porträt*, 3:58–59

Saint Gregory

(c. 540–604)

NV 1790, p. 105: [no. 148] *"St. Gregorius Magnus*, Papst. Ein großer Verbesserer der Musik. Schwarze Kunst von *Bürchlen. Fol."*

Mezzotint by Christoph Leonhard Bürglin

Lost

References: *GerberL*, 1:541

Joseph Legros
(1739–1793)

NV 1790, p. 106: [no. 149] *"Gros, (Joseph le) de l'Acad. Rojale de Musique. Von Macret. Gr. 4. In schwarzen Rahmen, unter Glas."* [PLATE III]

Engraving by Charles François Macret after [Pierre Thomas?] le Clerc; 22.5 x 16 cm on sheet 27 x 20.5 cm

Inscription in oval frame: "JOSEPH LE GROS DE L'ACADEMIE ROIALE DE MUSIQUE. Reçu en 1763."; on plaque: "Ce n'est pas un crime en aimant | D'emprunter un peu d'Art pour plaire. || De l'Acte d'Erosine || Avec Privilège du Roi."

Production details at bottom left: "le Clerc del."; at bottom right: "Macret Sculp."; at bottom center: "A Paris chez Elluin rue St Jacques vis à vis celle des Mathurins. | a present chez Crepy rue S. Jacques a S. Pierre près la rue de la parcheminerie."

Location: US-NYp, Muller Collection (digital ID 1269372)

References: *GerberL*, 1:549–50

Jean-Pierre Guignon
(1702–1774)

NV 1790, p. 106: [no. 150] *"Guignon, (J. P.) Roi de Violons. Von Pinssio 8. In schwarzen Rahmen, unter Glas."* [PLATE 112]

Engraving by Sébastien Pinssio after Vanloo; 25 x 18 cm

Inscription below image: "JEAN PIERRE GUIGNON | de Turin, | *Roy des Violons.*"

Production details at left: "Vanloo Pinxit."; at right: "Pinssio Sculp."

Location: D-B, Mus. P. Guignon, Pierre de I, 1

References: Cat. Poelchau no. 274; *GerberL*, 1:565

Adam Gumpelzhaimer
(1559–1625)

NV 1790, p. 106: [no. 151] *"Gumpelzaimer, (Adam) Musik-Director in Augsburg. Von Kilian. 4. In schwarzen Rahmen, unter Glas."* [PLATE 113]

Engraving by Lucas Kilian, 1622; from Gumpelzhaimer's *Compendium musicae* (Augsburg, 1625); 18 x 12 cm on sheet 20 x 14 cm

Inscription in oval frame: "ADAMVS GVMPELZHAIMER TROSPERGIVS. BOIVS AETAT. A. LXIII. CHR. MDCXXII."; on ledge beneath sitter: "Altissimi Gratia Tantvm | Beat."; on plaque held by sitter: a four-voice musical setting of the text "Pax huic domui," which is rendered "PaXhVICDoMVI. *Luc. 10.*", with the headings "4. voc. A. G. T." and "Cantus. | Altus. | Tenor. | Bassus."

Verse below image:

De Virtute Musica A. Gumpelzhaimeri.
Qvid forma melius? qvid fulvo carius auro?
Quid toto regnis majus in orbe datur?
Iaspide qvid pulchrum magis est? qvid melle tenaci
Dulcius? Hyblæis candidiusque rosis?
Dulcior est virtus sed Musica, pulchrior una
Forma, auro, regnis, jaspide, melle, rosis.
F. Ehinger, Primarius.

Production details: "Lucas Kilian. || sculpsit."

Location: D-B, Mus. P. Gumpelzhaimer, Adam I, 1

References: Cat. Poelchau no. 278; *GerberL*, 1:567; *Musiker im Porträt*, 1:176–77; Hortschansky 1987, 34, 71

Johann Wilhelm Hässler
(1747–1822)

NV 1790, p. 106: [no. 152] "*Hæsler, (Joh. Wilh.)* Organist und Musik-Director in Erfurt. Von *Müller.* 4." [PLATE 114]

Engraving by [Christian?] Müller; 23 x 21 cm

Inscription in oval frame: "IOHANN. WILHELM. HÆSLER."

Production details below: "C. Müller sc."

Location: D-B, Mus. P. Haesler, Joh. Wilh. I, 1

References: Cat. Poelchau 282; *GerberL*, 1:575–78

Friedrich von Hagedorn

(1708–1754)

NV 1790, p. 106: [no. 153] *"Hagedorn (Fried. von) Lyrischer Dichter. Von Fritsch. 8."* [PLATE 115]

Engraving by Johann Christian Gottfried Fritzsch, 1755; frontispiece to *Zuverläßige Nachrichten von dem gegenwärtigen Zustande, Veränderung und Wachstum der Wissenschaften*, 193. Teil (Leipzig, 1756) and *Bibliothek der schönen Wissenschaften und der freyen Künste*, 1. Band, 1. Stück (Leipzig, 1757); 10 x 8.5 cm on sheet 18 x 10.5 cm

Inscription below image: "Friedrich von Hagedorn. | Horatz mein Freund mein Lehrer mein Begleiter"

Production details below: "J. C. G. Fritzsch sc. Lips. 1755."

Location: D-W, Portr. I 5456a

References: Mortzfeld, A 7672

Andreas Hammerschmidt

(1611/12–1675)

NV 1790, p. 106: [no. 154] *"Hammerschmidt, (Andr.) Musik-Director in Zittau. 4. In schwarzen Rahmen, unter Glas."* [PLATE 116]

Engraving by Samuel Weisch, 1646; from Hammerschmidt's *Musicalische Andachten*, 4. Teil (1646); 9 x 7 cm on sheet 28 x 18.5 cm

Inscription at upper left: "Aõ CHRISTI | 1646."; at upper right: "Aõ ÆTATIS | 34."; within frame, on background: "Sam. Weish. fec."; on ledge beneath sitter: "Andreas Hammerschmid | Pontanus Bohe- | mus."; below: *"En HAMMERSCHMIDI faciem, sive Organa pulset, | Sive mele condat flexamina; ARTIFICIS!* || M.C.K.Z."

Location: D-B, Hammerschmidt, Andreas I, 1

References: Cat. Poelchau no. 286; *GerberL*, 1:581–82; *GerberNL*, 2:491–92; Leaver 2007, 123

George Frideric Handel
(1685–1759)

NV 1790, p. 106: [no. 155] *"Händel, (G. F.) Schwarze Kunst von Faber. Fol.* In schwarzen Rahmen, unter Glas." [PLATE 117]

Mezzotint by John Faber the younger after Thomas Hudson, 1749; 39 x 28.5 cm

Inscription below image: "George Frederick Handel."

Production details at left: "T. Hudson pinx.ᵗ"; at right: "I. Faber fecit. 1749."; at bottom center: "Price 2. shill. Sold by J. Faber at the Golden Head in Bloomsbury Square."

Location: D-B, Mus. P. Handel, G. Fr. II, 1a

References: Cat. Poelchau no. 294; *GerberL*, I: 569–574; *Bach-Dokumente* IV, 381, 425; Leaver 2007, 120–21

Jacobus Handl
(1550–1591)

NV 1790, p. 106: [no. 156] *"Handel, (Jacobus,* sonst *Gallus* genannt) Kapellmeister in Olmütz. Holzschnitt. Fol.* In schwarzen Rahmen, unter Glas." [PLATE 118]

Woodcut; from Handl's *Opus musicum IV* (1590); 15.5 x 11 cm

Although no inscription is visible in the exemplar shown here, Gerber cites its inscription as follows: "Contra[factur] des Weitberhümbten MVSICI | *IACOBI GALLI* sonst Handl | genannt, &c."

Verse below image:

> *IACOBVS* Handl ein *MVSICVS*
> Sonst *Gallus* gnandt *Carniolus,*
> Der hat in wenig Jahren viel,
> Zum Singen und zum Seytenspiel,
> Gar nützlich ding verrichtet baldt,
> Dann gleich wie in eim grünen waldt,
> Die Vöglein vntereinander singn,
> Daß eim das Hertz im Leib möcht springn,
> Für grosser Frewd und Lieblichkeit,
> So hat er viel *Motetn* bereit,

Wem solt nu seine *Music* gut.

Erweichen nicht beid Hertz und Muth,

Es müst fürwar gantz steinern sein,

Das sich nicht ließ [be]wegen sein.

Drumb dancken wir und [lo]ben GOTT,

Der uns erfrewt [in] mancher not,

Mit solcher schönen *Harmoney*,

Zu singen, spielen mancherley.

Henric[us Goettin]g. VV. Anno 1593.

Location: A-Wn, PORT 00155023_01

References: *GerberNL*, 2:468

Johann Daniel Hardt
(1696–1763)

NV 1790, p. 106: [no. 157] "*Hard*, (*J. D.*) Würtembergischer Kapellmeister. Schwarze Kunst von *Preisler. Fol.* In schwarzen Rahmen, unter Glas." [PLATE 119]

Mezzotint by Valentin Daniel Preisler, 1750; 47.5 x 33.5 cm

Inscription below image:

IOHANNES DANIEL HARD. | NATVS A. O. R. MDCLXXXXVI AD DIEM VIII MAII FRANCOFVRTI AD MOENVM. FVIT PRIMVM REGIAE MAIESTATIS STANISLAI A CVBICVLO ET AB INSTRVMENTO MVSICO BARBITI MAIORIS INTER GENVA DIRIGENDI PER QVINQVENNIVM BIPONTII. FACTVS INDE REVERENDIS-SIMI EPISCOPI WVRZEBVRGENSIS DVCISQVE FRANCONIAE SERENISSIMI IO. PHILIPPI FRANCISCI SCHOENBORNII MINISTER MVSICVSQVE CVBICVLARIS PER QVADRIENNIVM. POST HAEC AB ANNO MDCCXXV SERENISSIMIS DVCIBVS WVRTEMBERGICIS EBERHARDO LVDOVICO, CAROLO ALEXANDRO ET CAROLO EVGENIO SINGVLAREM FIDEM MIRAMQVE ARTIS MVSICAE DEXTERITATEM COMPROBAVIT. AB ILLO MVSICVS CVBICVLARIS. AB ISTO CONCENTVVM SYM-PHONIARVMQUE MAGISTER ET AB HOC SVPREMVS CHORI MVSICI PRAEFEC-TVS CONSTITVTVS.

Production details at lower right: "Val. Dan. Preisler sc. et. exc. | Norib. A.C. MDCCL."

Location: D-B, Mus. P. Hard, Joh. D III, 1

References: Cat. Poelchau no. 299; *GerberL*, 1:584

Johann Adolf Hasse

(1699–1783)

NV 1790, p. 106: [no. 158] "*Hasse, (Joh. Adolph)* Ober-Kapell-meister in Dresden. Von *Zucchi. Fol.* In schwarzen Rahmen, unter Glas." [PLATE 120]

Engraving by Lorenzo Zucchi after Pietro Rotari; 40 x 28 cm

Inscription below image: "GIO: ADOLFO HASSE DET: IL SASSONE | Primo Maestro di Cappella di S. M. | Il Re di Polo= Elet= di Sas= &c. &c."

Production details at left: "C. P. Rotari pinx."; at right: "L. Zucchi. sc: | Dresda"

Location: D-B, Mus. P. Hasse, Joh. Ad. II, 1

References: Cat. Poelchau no. 304; *Bach-Dokumente* IV, 387, 431; *Musiker im Porträt*, 3:54–55

Faustina Hasse (née Bordoni)

(1697–1781)

NV 1790, p. 108: [no. 159] "*Hasse, (Mad. Faustina Bordoni)* Sängerinn in Dresden. Von *Zucchi. Fol.* In schwarzen Rahmen, unter Glas." [PLATE 121]

Engraving by Lorenzo Zucchi after Stefano Torelli;
41.5 x 28.5 cm

Inscription below image: "Favstina Hasse | Virtuosa di Camera di S. Mtà il Re di | Polonia Elettore di Sassonia &c &c &c"

Production details at bottom left: "Step: Torelli pinx:"; at bottom right: "Laur: Zucchi Sculps"

Location: D-B, Mus. P. Hasse, Faustina II, 1

References: Cat. Poelchau no. 302; *Bach-Dokumente* IV, 387, 431

Joseph Haydn

(1732–1809)

NV 1790, p. 107: [no. 160] *"Haydn, (Jos.)* Fürstl. *Esterhazischer* Kapellmeister. Von *Mansfeld.* 8. In schwarzen Rahmen, unter Glas." [PLATE 122]

Engraving by Johann Ernst Mansfeld, 1783; 16.5 x 14 cm

Inscription in oval frame: "IOSEPHVS HAYDN."; quotation from Horace on plinth: "Blandvs avritas fidibvs canoris | Dvcere qvercvs. || Horat."; name of muse on pedestal: "EVTERPE."

Production details at bottom right: "*J. E. Mansfeld inv. et. sc.*"; at bottom center: "*Viennæ apud Artaria Societ.*"

Location: D-B, Haydn, Jos. I, 24

References: Cat. Poelchau no. 312; *GerberL*, 1:609–12; *CPEB-Briefe*, 2:1098–99

John Hebden

(c. 1705–1765)

NV 1790, p. 107: [no. 161] *"Hebden, (J.)* Violoncellist in England. Schwarze Kunst von *Faber.* Fol. In schwarzen Rahmen, unter Glas." [PLATE 123]

Mezzotint by John Faber the younger after Philippe Mercier, 1741; 35 x 25 cm

Inscription below image: "John Hebden."

Verse:

> The finest Voice that e'er sooth'd mortal Ear
> If lost, thy Accents are so sweetly clear,
> 'Twere needless to regret the melting Sound,
> Since, near thy rival Bon, the like is found.
> Lockman.

Production details at left: "PhP: Mercier pinx^t"; at right: "J. Faber fecit 1741"; at bottom left: "Sold by Faber at the Golden Head in Bloomsbury Square. Price 1^s 6^d"

Location: D-B, Mus. P. Hebden II, 2

References: *GerberL*, 1:613

Paul Hainlein

(1626–1686)

NV 1790, p. 107: [no. 162] *"Heinlein, (P.)* Nürnbergischer Musik-Director. 8. In schwarzen Rahmen, unter Glas." [PLATE 124]

Engraving; 21 x 15 cm

Inscription in oval frame: "PAULUS HEINLEIN DIRECT: CHORI MUSICI & ORGANIS: AD S: SEBALD: IN NÜRNB: *Obijt 1686."*

Verse below, in cartouche:

> Herr Heinlein ist zwar todt, doch wird sein froṁes Leben,
> und edle Music-Kunst so lang die Noris steht,
> stets durch der [*sic*] Tugend Lob≈und≈Fama≈Rhum≈Trompet
> auf froṁer Christenzung und in den Lüfften schweben.
>> Dieses schrieb seinem Seel≈Wehrt geliebten Herrn Schwager, Zu letzt
>> schuldigen Ehren Magnus Daniel Omeis. *Prof: P:* zu Altdorf.

Production details at bottom: "Seinem Seel: H: Schwer Vatter, zur lezten Ehre lies diß verfärtigen. I: F: Schmit."

Location: D-B, mus. P. Heinlein, Paul I, 1

References: Cat. Poelchau no. 321; *GerberL*, 1:616

Helius Eobanus Hessus

(1488–1540)

NV 1790, p. 107: [no. 163] *"Helius, (Eobanus Hessus)* Schriftsteller. Holzschnitt. 8." [PLATE 125]

Woodcut from Reusner 1587; 10 x 8 cm on sheet 15 x 9 cm

Inscription above image: "HELIVS EOBANVS HES[-] | sus Poêta"; below image: "Rex ego sum natum: vatum Sol, Phœbus, Apollo: | Iesseæ fidicen maximus ille lyræ. | M. D. XL."

References: *GerberL*, 1:618; Lemmer 1973, 465

Johann Andreas Herbst
(1588–1666)

NV 1790, p. 107: [no. 164] *"Herbst, (J. A.)* Kapellmeister in
Frankfurt. 4. In schwarzen Rahmen, unter Glas." [PLATE 126]
Engraving by Sebastian Furck, 1635; 18.5 x 14 cm
Inscription in oval frame: "IOHANNES ANDREAS
HERBST, NORIBERG: MUSICUS POETICUS P.t. FRANCOFURTI
MUSICES DIRECTOR. 1635. Natus Aº 1588."; in open book: a musical setting of
the text "Music bleibet ewig." with the heading "Cantio Cancri. 2. vel 3. voc: in perpt:
vox 3 in Decima."; below, in cartouche: "Præclari Autumni facies hîc Musici in ære |
Stat, dona ingenÿ [*sic*] cantica scripta probant. || Hier. Ammon."
Production details at bottom center: "Sebastian Furck ad viuum | delineauit, Aº 1635."
Location: D-B, Mus. P. Herbst, I, 1
References: Cat. Poelchau no. 324; *GerberL*, 1:624; Hortschansky 1987, 35, 71–72;
CPEB-Briefe, 2:1237; *CPEB-Letters*, 273; Leaver 2007, 127

Hermannus of Reichenau
(1013–1054)

NV 1790, p. 107: [no. 165] *"Hermannus, (Contractus)* Componist und Schriftsteller.
Holzschnitt. 8."
References: *GerberL*, 1:617

NV 1790 provides too little information for this image to be conclusively identified.

Johann Adam Hiller
(1728–1804)

NV 1790, p. 107: [no. 166] *"Hiller, (J. A.)* Curländischer
Kapellmeister und Musik-Director in Leipzig. Von *Geyser*. 4.
In schwarzen Rahmen, unter Glas." [PLATE 127]
Engraving by Christian Gottlieb Geyser after Heinrich Füger;
17.5 x 13.5 cm

Inscription below image: "I. A. HILLER"

Production details at bottom left: "Füger del."; at bottom right: "Geyser sc."

Location: D-B, Mus. P. Hiller, J. A. I, 1

References: Cat. Poelchau no. 333; *GerberL*, 1:636–648

Jacob Hintze
(1622–1702)

NV 1790, p. 107: [no. 167] "*Hinze, (J.)* Musikus in Berlin. Von *Bodenehr*. 4. In schwarzen Rahmen, unter Glas." [PLATE 128]

Engraving after Moritz Bodenehr, 1695; 20 x 15 cm

Inscription on scroll: a musical setting of the text "In te Domine speravi non confundar in æternum." with the heading "Canon: â 4. Vocum. in unisono."; below, on plinth: "IACOB HINTZE | Musicus Instrumentalis, Berno= | viensis Marchicus Ætat: 73."

Production details at lower edge of oval frame: "Mauritius Bodenehr del: et sculpeb: Dresdæ 1695."

Location: D-B, Mus. P. Hintze, Jac. I, 2

References: Cat. Poelchau no. 388; *GerberL*, 1:649

Konrad Höffler
(1647–1705)

NV 1790, p. 107: [no. 168] "*Höfler, (C.)* Weissenfelsischer Kammer-Musikus. Von *Romstädt*. 4. In schwarzen Rahmen, unter Glas." [PLATE 129]

Engraving by Christian Romstet; 25.5 x 19.5 cm

Inscription in oval frame: "CONRADVS HOEFFLERVS, NORIMBERGENSIS, SERENIS. PRINC. SAXO-WEISENFELS. MUSICVS IN CAMERA. ÆT. 48."

Verse below:

> Hoffleri facies, quam nunc tua lumina cernunt.
> Perplacet ingenio, sed magis arte manus,

Vertit Grammaticam, plectro dum vinculat aures,
Namque suum (miror!) fingere vicit habet.
Linque posuit Johannes Beer.

Production details at bottom right: "C. Romstet sculpsit."

Location: D-B, Mus. P. Hoeffler, Konrad I, 1

References: *GerberL*, 1:653

Ludwig Christoph Heinrich Hölty

(1748–1776)

NV 1790, p. 107: [no. 169] "*Hölty, (Lud. Hein. Christ.)* Lyrischer Dichter. Von *Chodowiecki*. 12." [PLATE 130]

Engraving by Daniel Chodowiecki; 8.5 x 5 cm on sheet 10.5 x 6 cm

Inscription below image: "HŒLTY"

Production details at lower left, in reverse: "D. Chodowiecki del."

Location: D-W, Port. I 6108

References: Mortzfeld, A 9785

Homer

NV 1790, p. 107: [no. 170] "*Homer*, nach einer alten *Büste* von *Krüger. Fol.*"

Engraving by Andreas Ludwig Krüger, 1769; plate 1 in Krüger 1769

Location: D-B, 2° Ns 4811

Horace

(65–8 BCE)

NV 1790, p. 107: [no 171] "*Horaz*, Lyrischer Dichter. Nach einer alten *Büste* von *Krüger. Fol.*"

Engraving by Andreas Ludwig Krüger, 1768; plate 10 in Krüger 1769

Location: D-B, 2° Ns 4811

Anne-Antoinette Clavel, Mme de Saint-Huberty

(1756–1812)

NV 1790, p. 108: [no. 172] "*Huberti, (Mad. de St.)* Sängerinn in *Paris de l'Academie Rojale de Musique*. Von *Endner*. 8. In schwaren [*sic*] Rahmen, unter Glas." [PLATE 131]

Engraving by Gustav Georg Endner after Jacques Antoine Marie le Moine; 16 x 10 cm

Inscription below image: "M^de. S^t. HUBERTI. | de l'Académie Royale de Musique."

Production details at bottom left: "le Moine del"; at bottom right: "Endner sculp. Lips."

Location: D-B, Mus. P. Saint-Huberty, A. C. I, 2

References: Cat. Poelchau no. 347; *GerberL*, 1:670; *CPEB-Briefe*, 2:1209, 1222; *CPEB-Letters*, 263, 267

Arabella Hunt

(1662–1705)

NV 1790, p. 108: [no. 173] "*Hundt, (Arabella)* Sängerinn und Lautenistinn in England. Schwarze Kunst von *Smith. Fol*. In schwarzen Rahmen, unter Glas." [PLATE 132]

Mezzotint by John Smith after Sir Godfrey Kneller, 1706; 32 x 25 cm on sheet 46 x 29.5 cm

Inscription below image: "M.^RS ARABELLA HUNT Dyed December 26.th, 1705"

Verse below:

> Were there on Earth another Voice like thine,
> Another Hand, so Blest with skill Divine,
> The late afflicted World some hopes might have,
> And Harmony recall thee from the Grave.

Production details at bottom left: "G. Kneller S.R. Imp et. Angl. Eques Aur Pinx."; at bottom right: "I. Smith fec. et ex. 1706."

Location: D-W, Portr. III 787

References: *GerberL*, 1:675; Mortzfeld, A 10329

James I
(1566–1625)

NV 1790, p. 108: [no. 174] "Jacobus, König von Grosbrittannien. Von Kilian. Fol." [PLATE 133]

Engraving by Wolfgang Kilian; 18 x 12 cm

Inscription in oval frame: "IACOBVS D. G. MAGNÆ BRITANNIÆ FRANCIÆ ET HIBERNIÆ REX."

Verse below:

> En tibi, Rex; suprâ, cum Pallade doctus Apollo,
> In laudes meritò, Magne Iacobe, tuas:
> Infrâ te posita est Pax alma et Copia rerum,
> Quam felix populus, Magne Iacobe, tuus?

Production details at left: "Wolf. Kilian."; at right: "Augus. exc."

Location: London, National Portrait Gallery, NPG D25694

Johannes Jeep
(1581/2–1644)

NV 1790, p. 108: [no. 175] *"Jeep, (J.)* Componist in Braunschweig. Von *Ullrich.* 4. In schwarzen Rahmen, unter Glas." [PLATE 134]

Engraving by Heinrich Ullrich, 1613; 18.5 x 14.5 cm

Inscription in oval frame: "IOHANNES IEEP, DRANS-FELDENSIS SAXO-BRUNSWIGUS."

Verse below, in cartouche:

> Magistrum honestæ lætitiæ spectare vis,
> Qui mille vocum in promptu habet discrimina,
> Sacris, profanis, serijsque apta & iocis?
> Brunswigium Orphea hic videsis IEEPIUM:
> Cui mitia apprecare fata ac mollia.

Production details at left: "Heinrich Vllrich sculpsit, 1613."; at right: "Conradus Rittershusius. I. C."

Location: D-B, Mus. P. Jeep, Joh. I, 1

References: Cat. Poelchau no. 353; *GerberL*, 1:688; Leaver 2007, 123

Johann Georg II
(1613–1680)

NV 1790, p. 108: [no. 176] *"Johann George II*, Churfürst zu Sachsen. Componist. Von E. N. 4."
Engraving
Location unknown
References: *GerberL*, 1:692

Niccolò Jommelli
(1714–1774)

NV 1790, p. 108: [no. 177] *"Jomelli, (Nic.)* Würtembergischer Kapellmeister. In *Carricatur* von *Oesterreich. Fol.* In schwarzen Rahmen, unter Glas." [PLATE 135]
Engraving by Matthias Oesterreich after Pier Leone Ghezzi, 1751; from *Raccolta de vari disegni dell Cavalliero Pietro Leone Ghezzi Romano è di Giovan Battista Internari Romano e di alcuni altri maestri Incise in rame da Matteo Oesterreich Hambourghese* (Potsdam, 1766); 36 x 27 cm
Inscription below image: *"MAESTRO DI CAPPELLA DI S. PIETRO IN VATICANO"*
Verse:

> Venne un giorno ad Apollo in fantasia
> Di premiare un Maestro di cappella,
> E quindi dato l'ordine à Talià
> Si fece innanzi comparir Jomella:
> Poi per un tubo, tutta l'Armonia
> Di Pindo, gli cacciò ne le budella,
> È si l'empiè d'armonioso fiato,
> Che l'fè restare in ogni parte enfiato.

Below verse: "Il Disegno Originale si conserva nel Gabinetto di Sua Maestà | IL RÈ DI POLONIA ELETTORE DI SASSONIA"
Production details at left: "Cavallier, Piet: Leone Ghezzi disegnò"; at right: "Matteo Oesterreich incise: Roma 1751."; in lower right corner of image, in reverse: "Oesterreich=scuplsit=li=10=Augusto=1751=Roma."

Location: D-B, Mus. P. Jomelli, Nic. II, 3

References: Cat. Poelchau no. 360; *GerberNL*, 1:693–96; *CPEB-Briefe*, 2:1151; *CPEB-Letters*, 247; Rostirolla, 185, 224–25, 381–82, 411–12

CPEB owned other caricatures by Ghezzi/Oesterreich, as he reported to Forkel in a letter of 13 May 1786: "Of the caricatures by Oesterreich I have only the Bresciani, Jommelli (under which is written Maestro in Vaticano) and Annibali sub No. XIX." (Von Carricaturen Oesterreichs habe ich nur die Bresciani, Jomelli (wo drunter steht Maestro in Vaticano) u. Annibali sub No. XIX.)

Françoise Journet
(d. 1720)

NV 1790, p. 108: [no. 178] *"Journet, de l'Academie de Musique a Paris 4.* In schwarzen Rahmen, unter Glas." [PLATE 136]

Engraving by Étienne Desrochers; 14 x 10 cm on sheet 14.5 x 20 cm

Inscription below image: "Mlle. JOURNET | de l'Academie Royale de Musique | à Paris, Née à Lyon en [...]"

Verse:

> Journet d'une Déesse a le port et les yeux,
> Qui nous fit mieux sentir les charmes que rassemble
> La Poésie unie aux Sons Melodieux
> Elle enchante les sens lésprit le coeur ensemble.

Production details: "E. Desrochers Seul. à Paris chés Daumont rue St Martin."

Location: D-B, Mus. P. Journet, I, 1

References: *GerberL*, 1:698–99

Giovanni Pontano
(1429–1503)

NV 1790, p. 108: [no. 179] *"Jovianus, (Joh. Pontanus)* Schriftsteller. Holzschnitt. 8." [PLATE 137]

Woodcut from Reusner 1589; 10 x 8 cm on sheet 15 x 9 cm

Inscription above image: "IOAN. IOVIANVS PONTANVS | Poeta & His-
toricvs."; below image: "Patria mî Pons est: nomen Iouianus: at altrix | Parthenope:
cecini sidera, rura, Duces. || Ioan."

Location: US-I, Petrarch N7575.R44 1589

References: *GerberL*, 2:171–72; *GerberNL*, 2:809

Johann Christian Jürgensen
(1744–1823)

NV 1790, p. 108: [no. 180] *"Jürgensen*, Clavierist, ein Däne.
Gezeichnet von *Kniep*. 4. In schwarzen Rahmen mit goldenem
Stäbchen, unter Glas." [plate 138]

Drawing by Christoph Heinrich Kniep, in black chalk with
white highlights on white paper, 1779; 18 x 17 cm

Inscription below image, in the hand of the artist, in gray pencil: "C. Kniep fec. Ao
1779"; on verso, in pencil: "Gezeichnet von Kniep Aus der [Bachschen?] Sammlung";
below, in pencil: "Jurgensen Instrumentenmacher in Hollstein"

Location: D-B, Mus. P. Jürgensen I, 1

Provenance: CPEB's estate—Georg Poelchau—SBB (1841)

References: Georg Striehl, *Der Zeichner Christoph Heinrich Kniep (1755–1825)*
(Hildesheim: Georg Olms, 1998)

The D-B catalogue annotation "aus d. Sammlung Hollstein" is an incorrect
reading of the inscription on the reverse of the drawing. The inscriptions are
similar to those on items from the Poelchau collection, and this drawing likely
entered the SBB via that collection, although it is not listed in Cat. Poelchau.
The drawing, which has suffered some water damage and tearing, is similar
in style and format to Kniep's drawing of another Dane, the painter Jens Juel,
made in 1780 (currently in the Statens Museum for Kunst, Copenhagen): both
present the artist's face in profile, as if on a relief medallion. This image of Jürgensen appears to be unknown; it is not mentioned in the literature on Kniep,
and has not been previously reproduced.

Hadrian Junius
(1511–1575)

NV 1790, p. 108: [no. 181] *"Junius, (Hadrianus) Med. Dt.* Schriftsteller. Holzschnitt. 8."
Woodcut
References: *GerberL*, 1:701–2

NV 1790 provides too little information for this image to be conclusively identified.

Juno

NV 1790, p. 108: [no. 182] *"Juno, Jupiters* Gemahlinn und Beschützerinn der Grazien. 8."

NV 1790 provides too little information for this image to be conclusively identified.

Jupiter

NV 1790, p. 109: [no. 183] *"Jupiter,* Vater der Grazien und Unterrichter seines Sohnes *Amphion* in der Musik. 8."

NV 1790 provides too little information for this image to be conclusively identified.

Philipp Christoph Kayser
(1755–1823)

NV 1790, p. 109: [no. 184] *"Kaiser, (P. C.)* Musikus in Zürich. 4."
[PLATE 139]
Engraving by J. O. Berndt; from Johann Caspar Lavater's
Physiognomische Fragmente zur Beförderung der Menschenkenntnis und Menschenliebe, 3 (Leipzig and Winterthur, 1777); 20.5 x 18 cm on sheet 29 x 23 cm
Production details at lower left: "J. O. Berndt fec. Zürich 17[76?]"
Location: US-NYp, Muller Collection (digital ID 1258033)
References: Lavater, *Physiognomische Fragmente,* 2:111, 3:202; *GerberL,* 1:705

Johann Christoph Kellner
(1736–1803)

NV 1790, p. 109: [no. 185] *"Kellner, (J. C.)* Hoforganist in Cassel. Von *Schwenter.* 8." [PLATE 140]

Etching by Christian Heinrich Schwenterley; 11.5 x 8.5 cm on sheet 10 x 13 cm

Inscription below image: "I. C. Kellner"

Production details below right: "Schwenterley del."

Location: D-B, Mus. P. Kellner, Joh. Chris. I, 1

References: Cat. Poelchau no. 368; *GerberL,* 1:715; *CPEB-Briefe,* 2:1221–22; *CPEB-Letters,* 267

According to Gerber, this portrait was published in Kellner's *Orgel-Stücke von verschiedener Art,* Op. 14 (1787), and was a late addition to CPEB's collection. CPEB mentions it in a letter to Westphal written on 4 August 1787: "Now something about the portraits. I will take Kellner's. You have made me very embarrassed by your far too great kindness. I thank you most respectfully for Mme de Saint-Huberty and Herr Professor Engel." (Nun etwas von den Portraits. Kellners kriege ich. Durch Ihre allzugroße Gutheit haben Sie mich sehr verlegen gemacht. Für M. d. St. Huberti und H. P. Engeln danke ich ganz ergebenst.)

Johannes Kepler
(1571–1630)

NV 1790, p. 109: [no. 186] *"Keppler, (Joh.)* Schriftsteller. Kl. 4." [PLATE 141]

Engraving [by or after Argentina?]; 26.5 x 17 cm

Inscription in oval frame: "IOANNES KEPPLERVS S. CÆS. MAIEST. ET ORDD. SVP. AVSTRIÆ MATHEMATICVS. &c."

Verse below:

> KEPPLERI quæ nomen habet, cur peccat imago?
> Quæ tanto errori caussa subesse potest?
> Scilicet est TERRÆ, KEPPLERI regula, CVRSVS:

Per vim hic sculptoris traxerat erro manum.

Terra utinam nunquam currat, sempérque quiescat:

Quô sic KEPPLERI peccet imago minùs.

Th. Lans.

Production detail at bottom left: "Argentina"

Location: D-B, Mus. P. Keppler, Joh. I, 1

References: Cat. Poelchau no. 369; *GerberL*, 1:717–18; Leaver 2007, 128

Although NV 1790 does not specify an artist for this engraving, the spelling of Kepler's name and the provenance of this item suggest possible concordance with the item in CPEB's collection.

Johann Erasmus Kindermann
(1616–1655)

NV 1790, p. 109: [no. 187] *"Kindermann, (J. E.)* Organist in Nürnberg. Von *Fleisch*. 4. In schwarzen Rahmen, unter Glas."
[PLATE 142]

Engraving by Johann Friedrich Fleischberger after Daniel Preisler; 24.5 x 17.5 cm

Inscription around image: "Johannes Erasmus Kinderman Norimbergensis, Melo-poëticus und Organist zu St. Egidien, ward gebohren A°. 1616, den 29, Martj starb. 14. April, 1655."; below image: "Dein Blut Herz Jesu soll mich laben | Nichts bessers kan und will ich haben."

Production details at bottom left: "Dan. Preisler pinx."; at bottom right: "Joh. F. Fleischb. Sculps."

Location: D-B, Mus. P. Kindermann, Joh. Erasm. I, 1

References: Cat. Poelchau no. 372; *GerberL*, 1:721–22; Hortschansky 1987, 53, 88–89; *Musiker im Porträt*, 2:84–85

Athanasius Kircher

(1601–1680)

NV 1790, p. 109: [no. 188] *"Kircherus, (Athanas.)* Schriftsteller.
Fol. In schwarzen Rahmen, unter Glas." [PLATE 143]

Engraving by Cornelis Bloemaert, 1664; published in Kircher's
Mundus subterraneus, vol. 1 (Amsterdam, 1665); 33 x 21.5 cm on
sheet 36 x 23.5 cm

Inscription in oval frame: "IHS P. ATHANASIUS KIRHERUS FULDENSIS
E SOCIETATE IESU ANNO ÆTATIS LXII ANNO M D C LXIV."; below:
"Frustrà vel Pictor, vel Vates dixerit, Hɪᴄ ᴇsᴛ: | Et vultum, et nomen terra scit An-
tipodum. || Jacobus Albanus Ghibbesim, M.D. | in Rom: Sapientia Eloq: Prof."

Location: D-W, Portr. II 2835. I

References: *GerberL*, 1:723–24; Mortzfeld, A 11047; Leaver 2007, 127–28

The engraving shown here bears no artist name and is printed on a folio sheet,
thus offering a likely correspondence with the item listed in NV 1790.

Johann Philipp Kirnberger

(1721–1783)

NV 1790, p. 109: [no. 189] *"Kirnberger, (J. Ph.)* Componist.
In Oel. 18 Zoll hoch, 15 Zoll breit. In goldenen Rahmen."
[PLATE 144]

Oil painting by Schaup after Christian Friedrich Reinhold
Lisiewski; 95 x 80 cm

Location: D-B, Mus P. Kirnberger, Joh. Ph. V, 1

References: *GerberL*, 1:726; Biehahn 1961, 19

NV 1790 gives no information as to the painter of this portrait. The now-lost
painting by Lisiewski (1776) was commissioned by Princess Anna Amalia; it
hung in her library (alongside a portrait of JSB) and then, after her death, in the
library of the Joachimstal Gymnasium. The portrait shown here is too large to
have been the item listed in NV 1790, but is likely a copy of the Lisiewski original. The attribution to the otherwise unknown "Schaup" is written on the verso.

Friedrich Gottlieb Klopstock

(1724–1803)

NV 1790, p. 109: [no. 190] *"Klopstock, (Friedr. Gottl.) 12."*
[PLATE 145]
Engraving; 9 x 7 cm oval on sheet 12.5 x 8 cm
Inscription below image: *"KLOPSTOK."*
Location: Us-NYp, Miriam and Ira D. Wallach Division of Arts, Prints and Photographs (digital ID 1549771)
References: CPEB:CW, VI/4

Franziska Koch

(1748–after 1796)

NV 1790, p. 109: [no. 191] *"Koch, (Francisca Romana)* Sängerinn und *Actrice.* Von *Berger.* 8." [PLATE 146]
Engraving by Daniel Berger; from *Litteratur und Theater-Zeitung,* vol. 3 (1781); 14 x 9 cm on sheet 18.5 x 12.5 cm
Inscription below image: *"*FRANCISKA ROMANA KOCH | *geb. Giraneck."*
Production details at lower left: *"*D. Berger, Sculpsit."
Location: D-B, Mus. P. Koch, Francisca Romana I, 1
References: *GerberL,* 1:741

Jakob Kremberg

(c. 1650–1715)

NV 1790, p. 109: [no. 192] *"Kremberg, (Jac.)* Churfürstl. Sächsischer Musikus. Von *Bodenehr.* 8. In schwarzen Rahmen, unter Glas." [PLATE 147]
Engraving by Moritz Bodenehr after Samuel Bottschild; frontispiece to Kremberg's *Musicalische Gemüths-Ergötzung oder Arien* (Dresden, 1689); 32 x 39 cm
Inscription: *"*Jacob Krembergs | Churf: Sachl: Kam̄er= und Hoff=*Musici.* | Musicalische Gemüths Ergötzung | Oder | Arien | Samt deren unterlegten hochdeutschen

Gedichten | Theils hoher Standes Bersohnen u. Vortrefflicher Leuthe | Theils eigener Erfindung | Welche also eingerichtet | Daß Sie entweder mit einer Stiṁe allein zu singen benebenst dem *General Bass* | Oder aber | Zugleich und besonders |Auf der Lauthe, *Angelique, Viola di Gamba*, u: *Chitarra* | können gespielet werden. | Alles nach der neusten *Italiänisch*⸗ und *Französischen Manier* | Mit grosser Mühe ünd Fleisse verfertiget | Und | Nach eines Jeden *Instruments Natur* und Eigenschafft | gantz bequehm in die Hand gesezzet. || Mit Römischer Kaÿserl: *Majestät* | und Churfürstl: Durchl: Zu Sachsen | allergnädigsten *Privilegiis.* | Dresden | In Verlegung des *Authoris.*"

Production details at lower right, on spinnet: "Samuel Bottschild inven."; at lower right edge: "Mauritz Bodenehr sculps. | Dresden."

Location: D-B, Mus. P. Kremberg, I, 1

References: Cat. Poelchau no. 380; *GerberL*, 1:757–58

Adam Krieger
(1634–1666)

NV 1790, p. 109: [no. 193] *"Krieger, (Adam)* Hoforganist in Dresden. *Fol.* In schwarzen Rahmen, unter Glas." [PLATE 148]

Engraving by Christian Romstet after Johann Caspar Höckner; from *Neue Arien* (Dresden, 1667); 28.5 x 16.5 cm on sheet 30 x 18 cm

Inscription in oval frame: "NOBIL: & PRÆEX: DN: ADAMUS KRIEGERUS. POETA & MUSICUS. NRI: SECULI EXCELLENTIS: SERENIS: SAX: ELECT: ORGAN: IN. CAM: PRIM."; at upper left: *"Nat. A*$^{\underline{o}}$ M.DC.XXXII"; at upper right: *"Denat. A*$^{\underline{o}}$ M.DC.LXVI."; below, on plaque: *"Ade sacra Digitis clarus lauruque coruscus | KRIEGERUS tali Fronte tuendus erat. | Non ita Saxonicam traxit Dulcedine RUTAM | Qui Melete ma canit qvique Poema facit. | Hinc Ejus Vitam Parnassus inumbrat & Astra | Cingunt æterno Lumine Cæsariem. | Quam benejam Victrix superat Mens ardua Famam. | Quippe Sibi semper nil nisi Fama fuit. || Amico desiderabili P. Dresdæ. | David Schirmerus. Sereniss: Sax: Elect: Bibliothecarius."*

Production details at bottom left: "Joh. Casp. Höckner. et"; at bottom right: "Christian Romstedt sculp."

Location: D-B, Mus. P. Krieger, Adam I, 1

References: Cat. Poelchau no. 384; *GerberL*, 1:759; *Musiker im Porträt*, 2:126–27

Johann Kuhnau
(1660–1722)

NV 1790, p. 109: [no. 194] *"Kuhnau, (Joh.)* Musik-Director in
Leipzig. *Fol. oblongo.* In schwarzen Rahmen, unter Glas."
[PLATE 149]

Engraving; title page to Kuhnau's *Neue Clavierübung* (Leipzig,
1689); 13 x 20 cm

Inscription on pedestal: *"Johann Kuhnau= | ens Neue |* CLAVI^ER=UBUNG. |
LEIPZIG."

Production details below: "Zu finden bey Joh. Herbert Klosen."

Location: D-B, Mus. P. Kuhnau, Joh. I, 1

References: Cat. Poelchau no. 392; *GerberL,* 1:761–64; *Bach-Dokumente* IV, 374, 417;
Musiker im Porträt, 2:160–61; Leaver 2007, 122

Christoph Johann Frideric Kupecký
(1716–1733)

NV 1790, p. 109: [no. 195] *"Kupetzky, (C. J. Fr.)* ein junger
Musikus. Schwarze Kunst. *Fol.* In schwarzen Rahmen, unter
Glas." [PLATE 150]

Mezzotint by Bernhard Vogel after Jan Kupezky; 35 x 23.5 cm

Inscription below image: "Christoph. Johann. Frideric. Kupezkÿ. | Nat. Viennæ Austr.
A.C. 1716. Octobr. 19. Denat. Norimbergae. A.C. 1733. | Novembr. 6. Aetat. 17. Ann. et
2. Hebdom."

Verse:

> Ein Jüngling denkt mit Recht vollkommen hier zu werden;
> doch die Vollkommenheit erreicht das Stück-Werk nicht:
> drum eilt der Edle Geist zum Himmel von der Erden,
> weil Ihm die Ewigkeit vollkommnen Werth verspricht.

Motto on scroll in sitter's hand: "Τετέλεσται" (It is finished)

Location: D-B, Mus. P. Kupezky, Chr. Joh. Fr. II, 1

Gaetano Latilla

(1711–1788)

NV 1790, p. 110: [no. 196] *"Ladilla*, Kapellmeister in Italien. In einer satyrischen *Carricatur. Fol.* In schwarzen Rahmen, unter Glas."

Caricature

Lost

References: *GerberL*, 1:787–88; cf. Rostirolla, 171, 370–71

NV 1790 does not indicate whether the portrait is a drawing or an engraving. Gerber's listing adds the name "Oesterreich," which suggests that the portrait was an engraving by Matthias Oesterreich, possibly after Pier Leone Ghezzi, like those of Annibali and Jommelli.

Michel-Richard de Lalande

(1657–1726)

NV 1790, p. 110: [no. 197] *"Lalande, (M. A.) Ecuyer, Chev. Surintend. de la Musique du Roi. Von Desrochers.* 8. In schwarzen Rahmen, unter Glas." [PLATE 151]

Engraving by Étienne Desrochers; 21.5 x 16.5 cm

Inscription below image, in cartouche: "Michel Richard de la Lande | Ecuyer Chevalier de l'Ordre de S.ᵗ Michel Surinten[-] | dant de la Musique du Roy, Maitre de Musique de | la Chambre et de la Chapelle, né à Paris le 15 Decembre | 1656, mort à Versaille le 18. Juin 1726."

Verse:

> Mortels, cest de ce beau Délire
> Que sont nez parmy vous ses accords si touchants,
> A deux divinitez la Lande doit ses chants.
> Appollon le forma, c'est Louis qui l'inspire.

Production details in middle: "Suite de Desrochers"; at bottom margin: "a Paris chez Petit rue S. Jacques pres les Mathurins"

Location: D-B, Mus. P. Lalande, Mich. Rich. De I, 1

References: Cat. Poelchau no. 395a; *GerberL*, 1:781–82

Jean François Lallouette
(1651–1728)

NV 1790, p. 110: [no. 198] *"Lalouette, (J. F.) Maitre de Musique de notre Dame a Paris*. 8. In schwarzen Rahmen, unter Glas." [PLATE 152]

Engraving by J[acques Nicholas] Tardieu after Ferdinand; 23 x 14.5 cm

Inscription below image: "JEAN FR. LALOUETTE | M.ᵉ de Musique et Benéficier | de Nôtre Dame de Paris. | Mort le 1.ᵉʳ Septemb. 1728 Age de 77. ans."

Production details at left: "Ferdinand pinx."; at right: "J. Tardieu filius sculp."; at lower right: "C. P. R."; at bottom: "A Paris chez Odieuvre M.ᵈ d'Est. rue d'Anjou le derniere P. Coch. à gauche entrant par la rue Dauphine."

Location: D-B, Mus. P. Lalouette, Jean Fr. I, 1

References: Cat. Poelchau no. 396; *GerberL*, 1:776

Friedrich Adolph Lampe
(1683–1729)

NV 1790, p. 110: [no. 199] *"Lampe, (Friedr. Adolph)* Schriftsteller. Von *Haas*. 8." [PLATE 153]

Engraving by Jonas Haas, 1751; 20 x 13 cm

Inscription below image: "Frid. Adolph Lampe. | Theol. D. et in Lyceo | Bremensi Prof. Publ."

Production details: "gestochen von J. Haas in Hamburg, 1751."

Location: D-B, Mus. P. Lampe, Friedrich Adolph I, 1

References: Cat. Poelchau no. 397; *GerberL*, 1:778

John Frederick Lampe
(1702/3–1751)

NV 1790, p. 110: [no. 200] *"Lampe, (J. F.)* Englischer Kirchen-Componist. Schwarze Kunst von *Ardell. Fol.* In schwarzen Rahmen, unter Glas." [PLATE 154]

Mezzotint by James McArdell after S. Andrea; 35.5 x 25.5 cm
Inscription below image: "John Frederick Lampe."
Production details at left: "S. Andrea Pinx.ᵗ"; at right: "Js. M. Ardell fecit"
Location: D-B, Mus. P. Lampe, J. Frd. II , 1
References: *GerberL*, 1:778–79

Aloysia Lange (née Weber) with her husband
(1759/61–1839)

NV 1790, p. 110: [no. 201] "*Lange, (Mad. Mar. Antonia, mit ihrem Manne) Sängerinn in Wien. Von Berger. 8.* In schwarzen Rahmen, unter Glas." [PLATE 155]
Engraving by Daniel Berger after Joseph Lange; 18 x 12 cm
Inscription below image: "HERR UND MADAME LANGE | *Mitglieder des K. K. National | Hoftheaters in Wien.*"
Production details at bottom left: "Lange del."; at bottom right: "D. Berger Sculp. 1785."
Location: D-B, Mus. P. Lange, Weber Aloysia I, 2
References: Cat. Poelchau no. 403; *GerberL*, 1:785

This double portrait depicts the Viennese court actor and painter Joseph Lange and his second wife, Aloysia, whom he married in 1780; the woman shown here is not Lange's first wife, Maria Antonia (née Schindler), as NV 1790 states.

Orlando di Lasso
(1532–1592)

NV 1790, p. 110: [no. 202] "*Lasso, (Orlando) Bayerscher Ka-pellmeister. Von Sadeler. 8.* In schwarzen Rahmen, unter Glas." [PLATE 156]
Engraving by Johann Sadeler; 15 x 10 cm
Inscription above image: "POVR REPOS TRAVAIL."; within frame, at upper left

of background: "ÆTAT. SVÆ LXI | OBIIT AN°. 94."; at upper right of background: "AN°. D̄NO 1593."; below image: "*Hic ille Orlandus qui Lassum recreat orbem* | *Discordemque sua copulat harmonia.* | NOBILI & EXIMIO VIRO DNO ORLANDO | DE LASSVS, SERNISS.*mi* VTRIVSQVE BAVARIAE | DVCIS GVILIEL.*mi* MVSICI CHORI PRE-FECTO, | *Johān. Sadeler eiusdē Principis chalcographus obseruāt. ergô scalpsit & dedicauit.* || *Monachij.*"; below this: "cum privelegio Sac. Cæs. M."

Location: D-B, Mus. P. Lasso, Orlando di, I, 2

References: Cat. Poelchau no. 409; *GerberL*, 1:786–87

Gottfried Wilhelm Leibniz
(1646–1716)

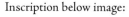

NV 1790, p. 110: [no. 203] "*Leibnitz, (Gottfried Wilh.)* großer *Philosophus* und Schriftsteller. Von *Boetius*. Gr. 8." [PLATE 157]

Engraving by Christian Friedrich Boetius after Gottfried Leygeben; 17.5 x 12 cm

Inscription below image:

> Si nescis, docti ciuis qui diceris orbis,
> Ista tabella refert praesidis ora tui.
> Nomina si quaeras, norunt ea Gallus, Iberus,
> Anglus et Ausonius, nec minus Antipodes.
> Nouit, doctrinis nisi quis sit in omnibus hospes.
> Hospitis in nulla, nomina LEIBNITII.
> > Sebastianus Kortholtus. | Eloq. et Poet. in Acad. Holsat. | Prof. ordin.

Production details at left: "G. Leygeb. del."; at right: "C. F. Boetius sculp."

Location: D-B, Mus. P. Leibnitz, Gottfr. Wilh. I, 1

References: Cat. Poelchau no. 419; *GerberL*, 1:794

Leopold I
(1640–1705)

NV 1790, p. 110: [no. 204] "*Leopoldus, I. Rom. Imperator.* Von *Bernigerot. Fol.*" [PLATE 158]

Engraving by Martin Bernigeroth; 30.5 x 18.5 cm

Inscription below image: "LEOPOLDUS I. | ROMANORUM IMPERATOR | SEMPER AUGUSTUS."

Production details at lower left: "M. Bernigeroth sculps. Lips."

Location: A-Wn, PORT 00046865_01

References: *GerberL*, 1:801

Gotthold Ephraim Lessing
(1729–1781)

NV 1790, p. 110: [no. 205] *"Lessing, (G. E.) Lyrischer Dichter. Von Fritsch.* 8." [PLATE 159]

Engraving by Johann Christian Gottfried Fritzsch after Anton Graff; 15 x 9 cm on sheet 15.5 x 9 cm

Inscription below image: "G. E. LESSING"

Production details: "J. C. G. Fritzsch, sc."

Location: A-Wn, PORT 00004184_02

Richard Leveridge
(1670–1758)

NV 1790, p. 110: [no. 206] *"Leveridge, (Richard) Englischer Componist. Schwarze Kunst von Pether. Fol.* In schwarzen Rahmen, unter Glas." [PLATE 160]

Mezzotint by William Pether after Thomas Frye; 33 x 26 cm on sheet 38 x 28 cm

Location: US-NYp, Muller Collection (digital ID 1269344)

References: *GerberL*, 1:803–4

The exemplar shown here presents the engraving in its first state, before inscription. The engraved inscription gives the name "Mr. Leveridge", along with production details: "T. Frye pinxit"; "Wm. Pether fecit"; and "Sold by Wm. Pether, in Great Newport Street, Leicester Fields | Pr. 2s."

Hendrik Liberti

(c. 1610–1669)

NV 1790, p. 111: [no. 207] *"Liberti, (H.)* Organist in *Antwerpen.*
Gemahlt von *van Dyck,* und gestochen von *Lode* nach dem
Original zu Potsdamm. Gr. 4. In schwarzen Rahmen, unter
Glas." [PLATE 161]

Engraving by Pieter de Jode II after Anthony Van Dyck; 28.5 x 21 cm

Inscription below image: "HENRICVS LIBERTI. | GROENINGENSIS CATHED.
ECCLESIÆ. ANTVERP. ORGANISTA."

Production details at bottom left: "Anton. van Dijck pinxit."; at bottom right: "Petrus
de Iode sculpsit."

Location: D-B, Mus. P. Liberti, Hendrik I, 1

References: Cat. Poelchau no. 425; *GerberL,* 1:804–5; Constance Richardson, "The
Van Dyck Portraits of Liberti," *Music & Letters* 39/1 (1958): 13–15

At least eight copies of the Van Dyck portrait on which this engraving is based
are known; according to NV 1790, one of them hung in the royal palace at
Potsdam and would likely have been known to CPEB.

Georg Friedrich Lingke

(1697–1777)

NV 1790, p. 111: [no. 208] *"Lingke, (G. F.)* Bergrath, *Membr.
Acad. Mus.* 8. In schwarzen Rahmen, unter Glas." [PLATE 162]

Engraving by Johann Christoph Sysang; 18 x 12 cm

Inscription below image: "Georg: Frider: Lingke | Potentiss: ac
Sereniss: Polon: Regis | rerum metallicarum Consil: Societ: scien: | music: in
Germania florentis Socius."

Production details at bottom left: "Sysang sc. Lips."

Location: D-B, Mus. P. Lingke, Georg Friedr. I, 1

References: Cat. Poelchau no. 428; *GerberL,* 1:810

Johann Jakob Löwe

(1629–1703)

NV 1790, p. III: [no. 209] *"Löwe, (J. J.)* Kapellmeister in Zeiz. Von *Dars.* 4. In schwarzen Rahmen, unter Glas." [PLATE 163]

Engraving by Johann Dürr after Christian Schäffer, 1663; 17.5 x 13 cm

Inscription in oval frame: "JOH: JACOB Löwe AB Eisenach. SERENISS. | DUCIS SAX. MAURITII ADMINIST. NUMB. CAPEL. Mag."; below: *"Fertur homo** [f.n. **Orpheus.*] *quondam cantu mulsisse leones:* | *Hîc hominem suavi permovet ore LEO.* | *Austria adhuc resonat, modulis repleta Leonis;* | *Saxoniæ tractus, Misnia dulce sonat.* || *Honoris & amoris ergo adjecit* | *J. G. A. P. O."*

Production details at bottom left: "Christ. Schäffer pinx."; at bottom right: "Joh. Dürr sculp."; center: "Anno 1663"

Location: D-W, Portr. II 3267.2

References: Mortzfeld, A 12780

Antonio Lolli

(c. 1725–1802)

NV 1790, p. III: [no. 210] *"Lolli, (Anton)* Violinist. Gezeichnet von *Hardrich.* 4. In goldenen Rahmen, unter Glas." [PLATE 164]

Pastel drawing by Hardrich, in colored chalk on vellum; 20 x 16.5 cm

Inscription in pencil in CPEB's hand: "Antonio Lolli"

On verso, in Poelchau's hand: "Antonio Lolli beruhmter Violinspieler aus Venedig †zu Neapel 1802 | gezeichnet von Hardrich, in Hamburg. Aus der Bachschen Sammlung. | Georg Poelchau | Hamburg 1832."

Location: D-B, Mus. P. Lolli, Antonio I, 1

Provenance: CPEB's estate—Georg Poelchau—SBB (1841)

References: Cat. Poelchau no. 435; *GerberL,* 1:820–21

CPEB's portrait collection contains two other drawings by the Hamburg artist Hardrich: of F. A. Benda (no. 47) and T. C. Walther (no. 363); the latter is similar in format and medium to Lolli's portrait and was perhaps executed at the same time.

Santa Stella Lotti
(c. 1703–1759)

NV 1790, p. III: [no. 211] *"Lotti, (Mad. Santa Stella)* Sängerinn in Dresden. Gezeichnet. *Fol.* In schwarzen Rahmen, unter Glas."
Drawing
Lost
References: *GerberL*, 2:576

Matthäus Ludecus
(1527–1606)

NV 1790, p. III: [no. 212] *"Ludecus, (Matthæus)* Schriftsteller. 4."
[PLATE 165]
Engraving from M.F. Seydel's *Bilder-Sammlung, in welcher hundert gröstentheils in der Mark Brandenburg gebohrne . . . Männer vor gestellet werden . . .* (Berlin 1751); 13.5 x 11 cm
Inscription below image: "MATTHÆUS LUDECUS WILSNA= | CENSIS EPISCOPALIS ECCLESIÆ IN | HAVELBERG CANONICUS ET CAPITU= | LI IBIDEM DECANUS. VIR INGENIO= | SUS ET HONESTISSIMUS. OBIIT ANNO | 1606."
Location: D-B, Mus. P. Ludecus, M I, 2
References: Cat. Poelchau no. 436; *GerberL*, 1:827; Leaver 2007, 130

NV 1790 gives no details as to medium or artist for this portrait, relating only that the image is in quarto format. Gerber lists the quarto-sized image shown here, taken from the collection of Georg Poelchau, and identified in his handwritten catalogue as "Seydel, 54."

Jean-Baptiste Lully
(1632–1687)

NV 1790, p. III: [no. 213] *"Lully, (J. B. de)* Componist in Frankreich. Von *Desrochers.* 8. In schwarzen Rahmen, unter Glas."
[PLATE 166]

Engraving by Étienne Desrochers after Paul Mignard; 15 x 10.5 cm on sheet 16 x 11 cm

Inscription below image: "Jean Baptiste de Lully | Secretaire du Roy et Surintendant | de la Musique de sa Majesté, né a Flo= | rence et mort a Paris le 22. mars 1687. agé de 54 ans."

Verse:

> I'ay fait chanter les Dieux, ainsy que les Heros,
> Mes airs ont exprimé le murmure des flots,
> Le Someil, les Zéphirs, la pluye et le tonnere.
> I'ay même fait oüir les ombres des enfers:
> Et pour vn Roy fameux, dans la paix dans la guerre
> D'immortelles chansons I'ai rempli l'vnivers.

Production details: "Gravé par E. Desrochers et se vend chez lui a Paris rue S.ᵗ Iacques au Mecænas."

Location: A-Wn, PORT 00155191_01

References: *GerberL*, 1:829–35

Martin Luther
(1483–1546)

NV 1790, p. 111: [no. 214] *"Lutherus, (Martinus) Reformator.* Componist vieler feiner Lieder. Von *Pachwill*. Gr. 8. In schwarzen Rahmen, mit goldenem Stäbchen, unter Glas." [PLATE 167]

Engraving by August Joseph Pechwell; 17 x 11 cm

Inscription below image: "Martinus Lutherus"

Production details at lower left: "A. Pechwill del."

Location: Kupferstichkabinett, Staatliche Museen zu Berlin, Luther, Martin; A. Pechwill del., K D A, Inv. 774–124

References: Leaver 2007, 128–29

Johann Balthasar Lutter
(1698–1757)

NV 1790, p. 111: [no. 215] *"Lutter, (J. B.)* Hannoverscher Kapellmeister. Schwarze Kunst von *Preisler. Fol.* In schwarzen Rahmen,
unter Glas." [PLATE 168]

Mezzotint by Valentin Daniel Preisler, 1751; 33 x 21.5 cm

Inscription below image:

> IO. BALTHASAR LVTTER. | *NATUS A. C. MDCLXXXXVIII POSTRIDIE KALEND.*
> *MARTIAS HANNOVERAE. IAM A PVERO MVSICAM EDOCTVS ARTEM DIVI-*
> *NAQVE MVNIFICENTISSIMI REGIS ET ELECTORIS GEORGII I. LIBERALITATE*
> *SIMI MACTATVS FELICISSIMAE VENTVRINII CHORO MVSICO PRAEFECTI FIDI-*
> *VMQVE PVLSANDARVM PERITISSIMI DOCTRINAE INSTITVTIONIQVE TRADE-*
> *BATVR MIRABILITERQVE IN COMPOSITIONE SYMPHONIARVM MVSICARVM*
> *FIDIVMQVE PVLSANDARVM FACILITATE PROFICIEBAT. INDE A. C. MDCCXLV*
> *IN LOCVM PRAECEPTORIS FIDISSIMI, CVIVS VICES IAM SVBIIT, SVMMA RE-*
> *GIAE MAIESTATIS INDVLGENTIA SVFFECTVS EXIMIO DIRECTORIS SYMPHO-*
> *NIARVM CONCENTVVMQVE MVSICORVM OFFICIO BENE LAVDABILITERQVE*
> *FVNGITVR.*

Production details at bottom right: "Val. Dan. Preisler sc. et exc. | Norib. A. C.
MDCCLI"

Location: US-NYp, Muller Collection (digital ID 1270232)

References: *GerberL*, 1:841; Mortzfeld 1987

Gertrud Elisabeth Mara (née Schmeling)
(1749–1833)

NV 1790, p. 111: [no. 216] *"Mara, (Mad. Elis.)* Sängerinn.
Gezeichnet von *L. A. Abel.* Kl. 4. In schwarzen Rahmen, mit
goldenem Stäbchen unter Glas." [PLATE 169]

Drawing by Leopold August Abel, in black chalk and India ink
on cream paper; 21 x 18 cm

Inscription below image, in the hand of Leopold August Abel, in brown ink: "Mademoiselle Schmelling:· ou Madame Mara:· 1779:·"

At bottom left, in Poelchau's hand: "Gezeichnet von Leopold Aug. Abel. | für die
Bachsche Sammlung"

Location: D-B, Mus. P. Mara, G. El. I, 8

Provenance: CPEB's estate—Georg Poelchau—SBB (1841)

References: Cat. Poelchau no. 451; *GerberL*, 1:856–65

Louis Marchand
(1669–1732)

NV 1790, p. 112: [no. 217] *"Marchand, (L.) Organiste du Roi.* Von
Dupuis. 8. In schwarzen Rahmen, unter Glas." [PLATE 170]

Engraving by Charles Dupuis after Nicolas Robert; 21 x 15.5 cm

Inscription below image: "LOUIS MARCHAND | *Organiste
du Roy | Né à Lion, Mort à Paris le 17 Février | 1732. Agé de 61 ans"*

Production details at left: "Robert Pinx."; at right: "Ch. Dupuis Sculp."; at bottom: "A
Paris chez Odieuvre M^d. d'Estampes quai de l'Ecole vis à vis la Samarit^e. ala belle
Image C.P.R."

Location: D-B, Marchand, Louis, I, 1

References: Cat. Poelchau no. 457; *GerberL*, 1:871–72; *Bach-Dokumente* IV, 371, 414;
Musiker im Porträt, 2:172–73; Leaver 2007, 124–25

Maria Antonia Walpurgis
(1724–1780)

NV 1790, p. 112: [no. 218] *"Maria Antonia,* Churfürstinn von
Sachsen. Von *Zucchi. Fol. oblongo.* In goldenen Rahmen, unter
Glas." [PLATE 171]

Engraving by Lorenzo Zucchi after Stefano Torelli; 20 x 14.5 cm

Inscription in oval frame: "MARIA ANTONIA PRIN. REG. PO. ELECT. SAX.
NATA PRINC. IMP. DUX. BAV."; on plaque below: "ERMELIND. TAL. |
P.A."

Production details at lower left: "Steph: Torelli del:"; at lower right: "Lau: Zucchi
sculp:"

Location: D-B, Mus. P. Maria Antonia, I, 2

References: Cat. Poelchau no. 464; *GerberL*, 1:879–80; *CPEB-Briefe*, 1:251; *CPEB-
Letters*, 25; Heartz 2003, 336–38

Breitkopf provided this portrait for CPEB's collection (see his letter of 2 January 1772). The portrait is relatively unelaborated, and is similar in style to the Zucchi engraving of Hasse, also in Bach's collection. The NV 1790 entry lists the format as oblong folio; CPEB's exemplar of the Torelli/Zucchi portrait may have been in oblong format with different decoration from that shown here, or, more likely, the sheet had been cropped to the oval, with wide margins on left and right.

Clement Marot
(1496?–1544)

NV 1790, p. 112: [no. 219] "*Marot, (Clement)* Schriftsteller. Von *Duflos le jeune.* 8." [PLATE 172]

Engraving by Claude Augustin Duflos after [Giovanni Battista?] Carlone; 13 x 8 cm on sheet 14.5 x 8.5 cm

Inscription below image: "CLÉMENT MAROT | Né à Cahors en 1484. Mort à Turin en 1544."

Production details below left: "Peint par Carlone a turin"; below right: "Gravé par Duflos le Jeune"

Location: A-Wn, PORT 00092362_01

Friedrich Wilhelm Marpurg
(1718–1795)

NV 1790, p. 112: [no. 220] "*Marpurg, (F. W.)* Kriegsrath, Schriftsteller. Von *Kauke.* 4. In schwarzen Rahmen, unter Glas." [PLATE 173]

Engraving by Johann Friedrich Kauke, 1758; 19 x 13 cm

Inscription below image: "*Amicum Amicus* | Fredr: Guil: Marpurgium"

Production details: "*Fredericus Kauke del: ad viv: et Sculp: Berol.* | *MDCCLVIII.*"

Location: D-B, Mus. P. Marpurg, Fr. Wilhel. I, 1

References: Cat. Poelchau no. 466; *GerberL*, 1:882–84; *Musiker im Porträt*, 3:88–89

Charlotte-Jeanne Béraud de la Haye de Riou, Marquise de Montesson

(1738–1806)

NV 1790, p. 112: [no. 221] *"Marquise ***, (Adrienne Sophie) Von Balchow. Fol. In schwarzen Rahmen, unter Glas."* [PLATE 174]
Engraving by Augustin de Saint-Aubin, c. 1779; 26 x 18 cm on sheet 30 x 20 cm
Inscription below image: "A.^{driene} S.^{ophie} MARQUISE DE ***"
Verse:

> Sage ou folle à propos, tendre, enjouée ou grave,
> Apollon est son maître et l'Amour son Esclave.

Production details at bottom: "aug. de St Aubin ad vivum delin. et sculp."
Location: Art Institute of Chicago, Accession number 1926.990
References: Gaston Schéfer, "Deux portraits d'Augustin de Saint-Aubin: La Baronne d'Andlau—La Marquise de Montesson," *Bulletin de la Société de l'histoire de l'art français* (1907): 95–100

This is one of the more enigmatic portraits in CPEB's collection. The caption and the size of the exemplar shown here correspond exactly with the NV 1790 entry; this image, however, bears no sign of the name "Balchow" (an otherwise unknown artist); rather, the artist of both painting and engraving is Augustin de Saint-Aubin.

Giovanni Battista Martini

(1706–1784)

NV 1790, p. 112: [no. 222] *"Martini, (G. B.) Pater. Gezeichnet von Joh. Seb. Bach. Gr. 4. In schwarzen Rahmen, unter Glas."*
Drawing by Johann Sebastian Bach the younger
Lost
References: *GerberL*, 1:889–92; *CPEB-Briefe*, 2:1151; *CPEB-Letters*, 247 (modified); Leisinger 1991, 119–20; *NBR*, 385

CPEB sent a copy of this portrait drawing, accompanied by a letter, to Forkel on 13 May 1786: "You are receiving herewith Pater Martini. The artist did his work rather well. It is said to resemble Martini well, as he was when he was younger; that is what Herr Capellmeister Naumann, who studied with him, told me." (Hierbeÿ erhalten Sie Pater Martini. Der Zeichner hat seine Sachen ziemlich gut gemacht. Es soll Martini, wie er jünger war, gut gleichen; so sagte mir H. C. Mstr. Naumann, welcher beÿ ihm studirt hat.) It is possible that the drawing was made by the artist, while he was in Italy in 1777–78, but more likely that it was a copy of the famous portrait in pastels (1770) by Angelo Crescimbeni (1734–1781). According to CPEB's letter, the drawing was less detailed and less difficult (hence cheaper) to copy than his son's drawings of Buffardin and Mingotti.

Johann Mattheson
(1681–1764)

NV 1790, p. 112: [no. 223] "*Matheson, (Joh.)* Kapellmeister und Legations-Rath in Hamburg. Von *Wahl* in schwarzer Kunst. *Fol.* In schwarzen Rahmen, unter Glas." [PLATE 175]

Mezzotint by Johann Jakob Haid after Johann Salomon Wahl; 21 x 15 cm

Inscription below image: "IOANNES MATTHESON | Celsitudinis Imperialis Magni Russiæ Princip. | Supremi Holsatiæ Ducis | Legationum Consiliarius.| cet. | nat. Hamburg d. 28. Sept. A. 1681."

Production details at bottom left: "Wahll pinxit."; center: "V. Dec."; at right: "Ioh. Iac. Haid sc. et exc. Aug. Vind."

Location: D-B, Mus. P. Mattheson, II, 1

References: Cat. Poelchau no. 472; *GerberL*, 1:903–12; *Bach-Dokumente* IV, 370, 414; *Musiker im Porträt*, 3:28–29

Johann Friedrich Mayer
(1650–1712)

NV 1790, p. 112: [no. 224] "*Mayer, (Joh. Fr.)* Pastor zu St. Jacobi in Hamburg, schrieb sein Bedenken über die Opern. 8."
[PLATE 176]
Engraving by Johann Georg Mentzel; 17.5 x 17 cm on sheet 32.5 x 23 cm

Inscription below image: "D. Johannes Fridericus Mayer. | Augustiss. Reg. Sveciæ per Germaniæ Provincias, et Reverend. Abbatissæ | Quedlinb. Consil. in Sacris Primar Pomer. citer. et Rüg. Superinten. General. | Univ. Grÿpsw. Procanc. Profess. Primar. et Consistorii Reg. Præs. etc."
Production details at bottom left: "Mentzel sc. Lips."
Location: D-W, Portr. II 3472
References: *GerberL*, 1:917; Mortzfeld, A 13706; Leaver 2007, 131

Lorenzo di Medici
(1449–1442)

NV 1790, p. 112: [no. 225] "*Medices, (Laurentius)* Großherzog in Florenz, guter Musikus und Patron. Holzschnitt. 8." [PLATE 177]
Woodcut from Reusner 1589; 10 x 8 cm on sheet 15 x 9 cm
Inscription above image: "LAVRENTIVS MEDICES, MVSA- | RVM PATRONVS incomparabilis."; below image: "Musarum Pater en, decorat quem laurea Phœbi | Quàm benè Laurentis nomina digna gero! || LAVREN."
Location: US-I, Petrarch N7575.R44 1589
References: *GerberL*, 1:922

Jacob Meiland
(1542–1577)

NV 1790, p. 112: [no. 226] "*Meilandus, (Jac.)* Kapellmeister in Anspach. Holzschnitt. *Fol.* In schwarzen Rahmen, unter Glas."
[PLATE 178]

Woodcut; title page verso to *Neuwe ausserlesene Teutsche Gesäng . . .* (Frankfurt, 1575);
14 x 15 cm

Inscription above image: "IACOBVS MEILANDVS, ÆTATIS | SVÆ XXXIII."

Location: F-Pn, Mus. Est. Meiland J. 001

References: *GerberL*, 2:923; Hortschansky 1987, 44, 81; Leaver 2007, 122

Philipp Melanchthon
(1497–1560)

NV 1790, p. 113: [no. 227] "*Melanchton, (Phil.)* Schriftsteller.
Holzschnitt nach *Lucas Cranach. Fol.*" [PLATE 179]

Woodcut based on Lucas Cranach, 1561; from Melanchthon's
Omnium operum . . . Pars secunda (Wittenberg: Johannes Crato,
1582); 25 x 15 cm on sheet 27.5 x 16 cm

Inscription above image: "EFFIGIES REVERENDI VIRI, D. PHI= | LIPPI
MELANTHONIS, EXPRESSA VVITEBER= | GÆ, ANNO M. D. LXXXII"; at lower left of
image: "1561." and Cranach's dragon insignia

Location: D-W, Portr. I 8828

References: *GerberL*, 1:925; Mortzfeld, A 13855; Leaver 2007, 129

NV 1790 lists a woodcut "after" rather than "by" Cranach. Many versions of the
Cranach portrait of this important figure were in circulation.

Maria Anna de Mena

NV 1790, p. 113: [no. 228] "*Mena, (Maria Anna de)* Italienische Sängerinn. Gr. 8. In
schwarzen Rahmen, unter Glas."

References: *GerberL*, 1:927

NV 1790 provides too little information for this image to be conclusively identified.

Moses Mendelssohn

(1729–1786)

NV 1790, p. 113: [no. 229] *"Mendelsohn, (Moses)* Schriftsteller.
Von *Müller. Fol."* [PLATE 180]

Engraving by Johann Gotthard Müller after Johann Christoph
Frisch, 1787; 26.5 x 18.5 cm on sheet 35 x 27 cm

Inscription below image: "MOSES MENDELSSOHN. | *Dem Könige Friedrich
Wilhelm II.* | *unterthænigst gewidmet* | *von der Jüdischen Freÿschule zu Berlin 1787."*

Production details above image: "Müller sc. 1786."; at bottom left: "p. par J. C. Frisch.";
at bottom right: "Gravé à Stoutgard par J. G. Müller Prof. à l'Acad. Carol. | De l'Acad.
Royale de Peinture &c. à Paris."

Location: D-W, Portr. II 3513

References: *GerberL*, 1:974; Mortzfeld, A 13935

Mercury

NV 1790, p. 113: [no. 230] *"Mercur,* Erfinder der Lyre. Von *Annib.
Caracci.* Quer 8." [PLATE 181]

Engraving [by Jean le Blond?] after Annibale Carracci, c. 1657–
66; 9.5 x 15 cm

Inscription at bottom center: "ann. Carac. jn."

Location: GB-Lbm, Department of Prints & Drawings (registration no. 1980, U. 1410
AN818176001)

References: Evelina Borea, et al., *Annibale Carracci e i suoi incisori* (Rome: Ecole fran-
çaise de Rome, 1986), 150

This print is from a series of 41 plates, published by the French printmaker
Jean le Blond as *Gallerie que l'eccelent Annibal Carrache a peinte a Rome dans le
Palais de Farnese*, after Carlo Cesio's series *Galeria nel Palazzo Farnese in Roma.
del Sereniss. Duca di Parma etc. dipinta da Annibale Carracci intagliata da Carlo
Cesio* (1657).

Claudio Merulo
(1533–1604)

NV 1790, p. 113: [no. 231] *"Merulus, (Claudius)* Organist in *Parma* und Schriftsteller. Holzschnitt. 12. In schwarzen Rahmen, unter Glas." [PLATE 182]

Woodcut; title page to Merulo's *Libro secondo di canzoni d'intavolatura d'organo . . . a quattro voci* (Venice, 1606)

Inscription in oval frame: "CLAVDIVS MERVLVS CORRIGIENSIS, ANNO ÆTATIS SVÆ LXXII, 1604."

Location: F-Pn, RES F-184

References: *GerberL*, 1:932; *Musiker im Porträt*, 1:158–59

Several portraits of Merulo were made during his lifetime. The image that corresponds to the small woodcut described in NV 1790 appeared on publications by Merulo after 1604.

Pietro Metastasio
(1698–1782)

NV 1790, p. 113: [no. 232] *"Metastasio, (Pietro)* Lyrischer Dichter. Von *Gregory.* 8." [PLATE 183]

Engraving by F. Gregory after Johann Nepomuk Steiner; frontispiece to Johann Adam Hiller's *Über Metastasio und seine Werke* (Leipzig, 1786); 16 x 10.5 cm

Inscription below image: "PIETRO METASTASIO | *ROMANO* | *Poeta Cesarco.*"

Production details at bottom left: "Joh. Steiner pinx."; at bottom right: "F. Grögorÿ sculps. Lips. 1786"

Location: D-B, Mus. P. Metastasio, P. I, 2

References: Cat. Poelchau no. 482; *GerberL*, 1:933–34

Johannes Meursius

(1579–1639)

NV 1790, p. 113: [no. 233] "*Meursius, (Joh.)* Schriftsteller. 4."
[PLATE 184]

Engraving by Theodor de Bry from *Bibliotheca Chalcographica*
(Frankfurt, 1669); 14.5 x 10 cm

Inscription in oval frame: "· ÆTERNITATEM COGITA · IOANNES MEUR-
SIUS I.C. ET HISTORIÆ GRÆCÆ PROFESSOR"; below: "Talis erat famam
cui pristina tempore debent | Meursius et debent tempora nostra, suam"

Location: D-B, Mus. P. Meursius Joh. I, 1

References: Cat. Poelchau no. 486; *GerberL*, 1:936; *GerberNL*, 3:411–12

NV 1790 gives too little information for the sitter, or the image itself, to be
definitively identified. But the provenance of the image shown here, from Poelchau, suggests that it may have been the item in CPEB's collection.

Caterina Regina Mingotti

(1722–1808)

NV 1790, p. 113: [no. 234] "*Mignotti, (Cathar.)* Eine deutsche
Sängerinn. Gezeichnet von *Joh. Seb. Bach* nach dem Original von
Mengs in der Dresdner Gallerie. Gr. Fol. In goldnen Rahmen,
unter Glas." [PLATE 185]

Drawing by Johann Sebastian Bach the younger after Anton
Raphael Mengs, in black chalk with white highlights on white paper; 38.5 x 31.5 cm

On verso, at lower edge, in Poelchau's hand: "Catharina Mingotti (geb. in Neapel 1726
†1807 in Neuburg am Donau), nach dem pastell Gemälde von Mengs in Dresden, von
Joh. Sebast. Bach (Sohn von Emanuel B.) aus der Sammlung der Hamburger Bach.
G. Poelchau, 1805."

Location: D-B, Mus. P. Mingotti, Cath. III, 1

Provenance: CPEB's estate—Georg Poelchau—SBB (1841)

References: Cat. Poelchau 490a; *GerberL*, 1:948–51; Heartz 2003, 337–38, 351;
Fröhlich, 163–64

This is a copy of the pastel portrait by Mengs, c. 1747 (Staatliche Kunstsammlungen Dresden, Gemäldegalerie Alte Meister, Gal. Nr. P 170).

John Milton
(1608–1674)

NV 1790, p. 113: [no. 235] *"Milton, Poet.* Von *Fritsch.* 8."
[PLATE 186]
Engraving by Christian Fritsch, 1762; 19 x 12.5 cm
Inscription below image: "MILTON"
Production details at bottom right: "C. Fritzsch sculps. 1762."
Location: A-Wn, PORT 00092134_02
References: *GerberL*, 1:944

Minerva

NV 1790, p. 113: [no. 236] *"Minerva,* (oder *Pallas)* Erfinderinn der Flöte. 8."

NV 1790 provides too little information for this image to be conclusively identified.

Jean-Joseph Cassanéa de Mondonville
(1711–1772)

NV 1790, p. 113: [no. 237] *"Mondonville, (J. J. Cassanea de) Maitre de Musique* in Frankreich. Von *Delatre.* 4. In schwarzen Rahmen, unter Glas." [PLATE 187]
Engraving by Jean Marie Delâtre after Charles Nicolas Cochin the younger; 20.5 x 14.5 cm
Inscription below image: "JEAN JOSEPH CASSANEA | DE MONDON-VILLE | Maitre de musique de la Chapelle du Roi | *Né a Narbonne*"
Production details at bottom left: "Dessiné par C. N. Cochin 1768"; at bottom right: "Gravé par Delatre"; bottom center: "A Paris chés Esnauts et Rapilly rue St Jacques a la Ville de Coutance A. P. D. R."
Location: D-B, Mus. P. Mondonville, J. J. Cass. De I, 2
References: *GerberL*, 1: 961–63

Francesco Montanari
(1676–1737)

NV 1790, p. 113: [no. 238] *"Montanari, (Franc.)* Violinist. Schwarze Kunst von *Vaillant. Fol.* In schwarzen Rahmen, unter Glas."
Mezzotint by [Jacques?] Vaillant
Lost
References: *GerberL,* 1:964

Philippe de Monte
(1521–1603)

NV 1790, p. 114: [no. 239] *"Monte, (Phil. de) Mus. Cæs. Canon & Thesaur. Camer.* Kaiser. Kapellmeister. 8. In schwarzen Rahmen, unter Glas." [PLATE 188]
Engraving [by Theodor de Bry?] after Robert Boissard, 1592;
14 x 10.5 cm
Inscription in oval frame: "PHILIPPUS DE MONTE Belga DD Max & Rod II Jmpp Musici Canon & Thesaur Cameracencis"; below: "Clarior ut supero resonaret in æthere Psaltes | Fixit in hoc Montis vertice Diva pedem."
Location: A-Wn, PORT 00154433-01
References: *GerberL,* 1:964–65; Hortschansky 1987, 43, 80

Although the NV 1790 entry lists no artists' names and the print cannot be identified conclusively, it was likely similar to the anonymous print shown here, whose inscription matches that in CPEB's annotation.

Angelo Maria Monticelli
(c. 1712–1758?)

NV 1790, p. 114: [no. 240] *"Monticelli, (Angelo Maria)* Sänger in Dresden. Schwarze Kunst von *Faber. Fol.* In schwarzen Rahmen, unter Glas." [PLATE 189]
Mezzotint by John Faber the younger after Andrea Casali; 35.5 x 25.5 cm

Inscription below image: "Angelo Mar:ᵃ Monticelli"

Production details at left: "Equ.ˢ Adr.ᵃˢ Casali pint. et delin.ᵗ"; at right: "J. Faber fecit.";
bottom center: "Printed for John Bowles, at Nº. 13 in Cornhill."

Location: D-B, Mus. P. Monticelli, II, 1

References: Cat. Poelchau no. 495; *GerberL*, 1:967–68

Daniel Georg Morhof
(1639–1691)

NV 1790, p. 114: [no. 241] "*Morhof, (Dan. George)* Schriftsteller.
Von Lemküs. 4." [PLATE 190]

Engraving by Diederich Lemkus; 21.5 x 15 cm

Inscription below image: "DANIEL GEORG | MORHOF."

Production details below right: "D. Lemküs fec:"

Location: D-B, Mus. P. Morhof, Daniel I, 2

References: Cat. Poelchau no. 497; *GerberL*, 1:971–72; *CPEB-Briefe*, 2:1209; *CPEB-Letters*, 262

CPEB had a duplicate copy of the Morhof portrait that he sent to J. J. H. Westphal on 8 May 1787.

Sir Thomas More
(1478–1535)

NV 1790, p. 114: [no. 242] "*Morus, (Thomas)* Kanzler, ein guter Musikus. Kl. 8."

References: *GerberL*, 1:973

An engraving by Theodor de Bry from *Bibliotheca Chalcographica* (Frankfurt,
1650) might be concordant to the item in CPEB's collection, but it is impossible to identify with certainty given the limited information in NV 1790. The
Bibliotheca Chalcographica was widely available and a likely source for other engravings in CPEB's collection.

Leopold Mozart with his children

(1719–1787)

NV 1790, p. 114: [no. 243] *"Mozard (Leop.) mit
seiner Musikalischen Familie, Salzburgischer
Concertmeister. Von de la Fosse. Fol. In schwarzen
Rahmen, unter Glas."* [PLATE 191]

Engraving by Jean Baptiste Delafosse after Louis
Carmontelle, 1764; 39 x 22 cm

Inscription below image: "LEOPOLD MOZART, Père de MARIANNE
MOZART, Virtuose âgée de onze ans | et de J. G. WOLFGANG MOZART,
Compositeur et Maître de Musique | âgé de sept ans."

Production details at left: "L. C. De Carmontelle del."; at right: "Delafosse sculps.
1764"

Location: D-B Mus. P. Mozard, Leop. II, 1

References: Cat. Poelchau no. 504; *GerberL*, 1:976–77

Christian Müller

(1570–after 1635)

NV 1790, p. 114: [no. 244] *"Müller, (Christian) Mathem. Optic. und Musikus in Berlin.
8. In schwarzen Rahmen, unter Glas."*

References: *GerberL*, 1:981

NV 1790 provides too little information for this image to be conclusively identified. An engraving by Albrecht Christian Kalle (see Mortzfeld, A 14524) might
be a concordant print to the item in CPEB's collection.

Carolina Fredrika Müller

(1755–1826)

NV 1790, p. 114: [no. 245] *"Müller, (Mad. Car. Fried. geschiedene
Walther, verehlichte) Sängerinn und Actrice in Stockholm. Von
Kleve. Fol. In schwarzen Rahmen, unter Glas."* [PLATE 192]

Engraving by Terkel [Johan T.] Kleve after Cornelius Høyer, 1777; 34 x 26 cm

Inscription below image: "M^{dm} CAROLINE WALTER."

Verse:

> Qu'a t'elle besoin d'art? l'illusion est sure:
> elle est ce qu'elle joue, elle pleure, elle rit.
> Sa beauté prete encore un charme à la nature
> et c'est le coeur qui l'applaudit.

Production details at bottom left: "Dessiné par C. Höyer"; center: "à Coppenhague, 1777."; bottom right: "Gravé par J. Kleve."

Location: D-B, Mus. P. Walter, Karoline II, 1

References: Cat. Poelchau no. 747; *GerberL*, 1:980–81

Wolfgang Musculus
(1497–1563)

NV 1790, p. 114: [no. 246] *"Musculus, (Wolfgang)* Musikus und Schriftsteller. Holzschnitt. 8." [PLATE 193]

Woodcut from Reusner 1587; 10 x 8 cm on sheet 15 x 9 cm

Inscription above image: "VVOLFGANGVS MVSCVLVS | Theologus."; below image: "Corde pius, grauis ore, sacro sermone disertus, | Præco Dei, pariter voce styloque potens. | M. D. LXIII."

References: *GerberL*, 1:990–91; Lemmer 1973, 472; Leaver 2007, 129

Pietro Nardini
(1722–1793)

NV 1790, p. 114: [no. 247] *"Nardini, (Pietro)* Violinist. Von *Cecchi.* Gr. 4. In schwarzen Rahmen, unter Glas." [PLATE 194]

Engraving by Giovanni Battista Cecchi after Marco Vestri; 26.5 x 23.5 cm

Inscription below image: "PIETRO NARDINI"

Production details at bottom left: "Marco Vestri del."; at bottom right: "G. Battā Cecchi Sc."

Location: D-B, Mus. P. Nardini, P. I, 2

References: *GerberL*, 1:3–4; *GerberNL*, 3:544; Schmid 1988, 520

Christian Gottlob Neefe
(1748–1798)

NV 1790, p. 114: [no. 248] *"Neefe, (Christ. Gottlieb) Von Liebe. 12."* [PLATE 195]

Engraving by Christian Gottlob August Liebe after [Johann Georg?] Rosenberg; published in *Taschenbuch für die Schaubühne*, 1780; 7 x 8.5 cm

Inscription below image: "C. G. NEEFE."

Production details at lower left of frame: "Rosenberg del."; at lower right of frame: "Liebe sc."

Location: D-B, Mus. P. Neefe, Chr. Gottlieb I, 3

References: Cat. Poelchau no. 522; *GerberL*, 2:13–16; *Musiker im Porträt*, 3:144–45

Erdmann Neumeister
(1671–1756)

NV 1790, p. 214: [no. 249] *"Neumeister, (Erdmann)* Lyrischer Dichter, Von *Fritsch*. Gr. 4." [PLATE 196]

Engraving by Christian Fritsch after Johann Salomon Wahl, 1721; 17.5 x 14 cm on sheet 21 x 15.5 cm

Inscription below image: "Effigiem, Venerande, Tuam, NEUMEISTER, et ora, | Artificum certet reddere docta manus. | Doctrinam, ingenium, svadam, zelumque fidemque | Non dabit. Illa libris exprimis ipse Tuis. || Jo. Albertus Fabricius. D."

Production details at left: "Wahl pinx:"; at right: "1721. Christian Fritzsch Sculps: Hamb:"

Location: D-W, Portr. I 9525

References: Mortzfeld, A 15008; Wolff 2000, 160–61, 255, 334; Leaver 2007, 132

Marie Sophie Niklas
(fl. late eighteenth century)

NV 1790, p. 115: [no. 250] *"Nicklas, (Sophie)* Sängerinn in Berlin.
Von *Berger.* Gr. 8. In schwarzen Rahmen, unter Glas."
[PLATE 197]
Engraving by Daniel Berger, 1779; 11 x 16 cm
Inscription below image: "SOPHIA NIKLAS."
Production details at bottom: "D Berger del. et. sculp. 1779."
Location: D-B, Mus. P. Niklas, Sophie I, 1
References: Cat. Poelchau no. 532; *GerberL,* 2:27

Georg Noëlli
(1727–1789)

NV 1790, p. 115: [no. 251] *"Noelly,* Pantalonist in Meklenburg-Schwerin. In Gips auf
Schiefer. In vergoldeten gipsernen Rahmen, unter Glas."
Plaster relief on slate in gilded plaster frame
Lost
References: *GerberL,* 2:32–33; Clemens Meyer, *Geschichte der Mecklenburg-Schweriner
Hofkapelle* (Schwerin: Davids, 1913), 144; *CPEB-Briefe,* 2:1278–80; *CPEB-Letters,*
282–83

This item was bought by J. J. H. Westphal and is listed in the draft catalogue of
his collection (B-Bc, 34.734 H.P., p. 100) as one of four items from the CPEB
collection: "In plaster, to be found in my collection, are: . . . Noelly in plaster."
(Aus der Gipsischen befinden sich in meiner Sammlung: . . . Noelly in Gips.)
The item may later have been sold to Fétis along with the rest of Westphal's
large portrait collection and library, but there is now no trace of it.

Sybrandus van Noordt
(1659–1705)

NV 1790 (p. 115): [no. 252] "*Noordt, (Sybrand van)* Organist und Glockenist in Holland. Von *Schenck.* Fol. In schwarzen Rahmen, unter Glas." [PLATE 198]

Mezzotint by Pieter Schenck, 1702; 24.5 x 17 cm

Inscription below image: "SYBRANDUS van NOORD, | *Grootmeester in de Musykkunde, en Vermaart voortreffelyk Organist*"

Verse:

> Schenks snykunst maalt can Noord de Roem der Kunstenaaren,
> Wiens doorgeleerd Musyk de Kunstekenners streelt,
> Als hy, door Lust genoopt, op 't Orgel gaad' loos speelt,
> En toont, hoe zyn vernuft voor and'ren is ervaaren.
> Doch deze Prent verbeeld slegs d' ommetrek en leest
> Des grooten Meesters, wydbefaamt door kunst en geest.
> Men moet 's mans gaaven in zyn Orgelspeelkunst hooren,
> Of Clavicimbelklank, of Klokspel op den Tooren.
>   A: ALEWYN. A° 1702

Location: D-B, Mus. P. Noordt, Sybr. van. I, 1

References: Cat. Poelchau no. 533; *GerberL*, 2:33

Jacob Nozemann
(1693–1745)

NV 1790, p. 115: [no. 253] "*Nozemann, (J. A. C.)* Von *Fritsch.* Fol. In schwarzen Rahmen, unter Glas." [PLATE 199]

Engraving by Christian Friedrich Fritsch; 30 x 20 cm

Inscription below image: "JACOBUS NOZEMAN. Natus Hamburgi | 3.^{tio} ante Calend. Septemb: 1693. denatus AMSTELODAMI, 6. Id. Octob: 1745."

Verse:

> Orphea ab Elysiis revocatum *FRITSCHIUS* oris
> Artifici voluit sistere in ære manu;
> Fata negant reditum, Stygias nî leniat umbras

Nozeman Orpheæ, quam tenet, arte lyræ:
Ære Nozemanni faciem citharamque canoram
Condidit, Odrysium restituitque senem.

Production details at bottom left: "C. F. Fritsch, ad vivum Delineavit et Sculpsit. 1745."; at bottom right: "Prostat apud Vid: P: de Coup & G. Kuyper."

Location: D-B, Mus. P. Nozemann, I, 1

References: *GerberL*, 2:36

Sebastian Ochsenkuhn
(1521–1574)

NV 1790, p. 115: [no. 254] "*Ochsenkuhn, (Sebastian)* Lautenist. 8. In schwarzen Rahmen, unter Glas." [PLATE 200]

Engraving; title page to Ochsenkuhn's *Tabulaturbuch auff die Lauten von Motetten . . .* (Heidelberg, 1558); 16 x 10.5 cm

Inscription below image: "Sebastian, Ochsenkun."

Location: D-B, Mus. P. Ochsenkhun, I, 2

References: Cat. Poelchau no. 534; *GerberL*, 1:37; Hortschansky 1987, 55, 89

Johannes Olearius
(1611–1684)

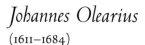

NV 1790, p. 115: [no. 255] "*Olearius, (Joh.)* D. Lyrischer Dichter. Von *Romstædt.* 8." [PLATE 201]

Engraving by Christian Romstet; 15 x 9 cm on sheet 16.5 x 9

Inscription below image: "Johannes Olearius D. | Fürstl: S. M. Ober=Hoff=Prediger, Kirchen= |Rath und General Superintendens | *Ætatis LIX Anno 1671.*"

Production details at bottom right: "Christian Romstet sculp."

Location: D-W, Portr. I 9789

References: Mortzfeld, A 15421; Wolff 2000, 81; Leaver 2007, 131

The NV 1790 entry gives insufficient information to identify the portrait by sitter (numerous engravings of members of the Olearius family whose first names were Johann or a variant were in circulation), but the reference to the artist "Romstædt" (Romstet) is indicative.

Benjamin Orting
(1717–?)

NV 1790, p. 115: [no. 256] *"Orting, (Benj.)* Musik-Director in Augsburg. Von *Hess.* 4. In schwarzen Rahmen, unter Glas."
References: *GerberL*, 2:48

Gerber lists the portrait as an engraving by Hess after Maucher, but explains that the name of the sitter is not inscribed on the print. In the absence of the sitter's name, the portrait remains difficult to identify.

Jakob Paix
(1556–1623)

NV 1790, p. 115: [no. 257] *"Paix, (Jac.)* Organist in Lauingen. Holzschnitt. *Fol.* In schwarzen Rahmen, unter Glas."
[PLATE 202]
Woodcut; 13 x 10 cm (oval cut out from larger sheet)
Inscription in oval frame: "IACOBVS PAIX AVGVSTANVS. ORGANICVS ET SYMΦONETES. ANN. ÆTA. SVÆ XXXIII. XPI M D XIC."
Location: D-B, Mus. P. Paix, Jac. I, 1
References: *GerberL*, 2:64

Giovanni Pierluigi da Palestrina
(1525/26–1594)

NV 1790, p. 115: [no. 258] *"Palestrina, (Giov. Piet. Alois.)* Päpstlicher Kapellmeister. Gezeichnet in Italien. Gr. 4. In schwarzen Rahmen, unter Glas."
Drawing
Lost

References: *GerberL*, 2:65–69; *Musiker im Porträt*, 1:148–49; *Iconografia palestrina. Giovanni Pierluigi da Palestrina: immagini e documenti del suo tempo*, ed. Lino Bianchi and Giancarlo Rostirolla (Lucca: Libreria Musicale Italiana, 1994), plates 239–40; Leaver 2007, 121

Leonhard Paminger
(1495–1567)

NV 1790, p. 115: [no. 259] *"Paminger, (Leonh.)* Componist, *Lutheri Amicus.* Holzschnitt. 12. In schwarzen Rahmen, unter Glas." [PLATE 203]

Woodcut; 8.5 x 7.5 cm on sheet 10 x 9.5 cm

Inscription in frame: "ISTA LEONARTI PAMINGERI EFFIGIES EST | CORPORE PRÆSTANTIS INGENIOQVE VIRI | QVI BENE CHRIS-TICOLA DE POSTERITATI MERENDO | VESTIIT HARMONICIS DOGMATA SACRA MODIS."

Location: D-B, Mus. P. Paminger, Leonh. I, 1

References: Cat. Poelchau no. 549; *GerberL*, 2:73; Hortschansky 1987, 32, 70; Leaver 2007,121

Pan

NV 1790, p. 115: [no. 260] *"Pan,* vortrefflicher Flötenspieler. Gemahlt von *Carrache,* gestochen von *Aubert.* Breit 4." [PLATE 204]

Engraving by Michel Aubert after Annibale Carracci; 21.5 x 16 cm

Inscription below image: "PAN INSTRUIT PAR L'AMOUR"

Verse: *"Que Pan soit l'inventeur de la Flûte Champêtre, | C'est une fable il eut un Maître."*

Production details at left: "A. Carache Pinx. Romæ."; at right: "M.Aubert Sculp."; at bottom: "à Paris, chez L. Surugue, Graveur du Roi, rue des Noyers, attenant le Maga-sin de pap.ʳ vis-à-vis le mur de S.Yves. C.P.R."

Location: GB-Lbm, Department of Prints & Drawings (registration no. 1873,0809.34)

References: Evelina Borea et al., *Annibale Carracci e i suoi incisori* (Rome: Ecole fran-
çaise de Rome, 1986), 286

The visible ascription to Carache and Aubert, as well as the verse which draws
attention to Pan's flute-playing (while disavowing the legend that he was the inventor of the instrument), make this print a likely candidate for the item listed
in NV 1790. It has been questioned, however, whether Carracci was the creator
of the painting on which the print is based.

Guido Panciroli
(1523–1599)

NV 1790, p. 116: [no. 261] *"Pancirolus, (Guido),* Schriftsteller. 4."
[PLATE 205]
Engraving; 17.5 x 12 cm
Inscription below image: "GVIDVS PANCIROLVS | REGINVS |
IVRIS CONSVLTOR CLARISS."
Location: D-B, Mus. P. Pancirolus, Guidus I, 1
References: Cat. Poelchau no. 308; GerberL, 2:74

No engraver's name is visible and NV 1790 gives none, but Gerber lists the
engraver of the quarto-sized portrait print of Panciroli as "H. David." Given its
provenance from the Poelchau collection, the plate is included here.

Maria Theresia Paradis
(1759–1824)

NV 1790, p. 116: [no. 262] *"Paradis, (Mar. Theres.)* blinde Clavierspielerin. Gezeichnet
von *Schubart.* In goldenen Rahmen, unter Glas."
Pastel by Schubart
Lost
References: GerberL, 2:76–78; Tobias Biehler, *Über Miniaturmalereien. Mit Anga-
ben vieler Künstler und Hofbibliotheken* (Vienna: Zamarski & Dittmarsch, 1861), 80;
Schmid 1988, 524

The presence in CPEB's collection of a drawing of Paradis suggests a personal connection; Bach's daughter, Anna Carolina Philippina, had herself met Paradis, and could attest to the likeness when she sold the portrait to J.J.H. Westphal in 1804: "If the good Mademoiselle Paradis knew that she had found herself in such good hands, she would be glad. Her portrait is a speaking likeness." (Wenn die gute Dem. Paradis wüßte, daß sie in so gute Hände gekommen wäre: sie würde sich freuen. Sprechend ähnlich ist ihr Bildniß.) This portrait is one of several that were bought by Westphal after CPEB's death; in the draft pages that Westphal prepared for a catalogue of his collection (extant but incomplete in B-Bc, 34.734 H.P) this image is listed with three other unique items from the CPEB collection, with the added detail that it is a pastel: "NB: not drawn, but painted in pastel by Schubart." (NB: nicht gezeichnet, sondern in Pastell gemahlt von Schubart.)

Giovanni Battista Passeri
(1694–1780)

NV 1790, p. 116: [no. 263] "*Passerius, (Joh. Bapt.)* Musikus und Schriftsteller. Schwarze Kunst von *Haid. Fol.*" [PLATE 206]

Mezzotint by Johann Jakob Haid; from Jacob Brucker's *Bildersal heutiges Tages lebender und durch Gelahrtheit berühmter Schrifftsteller . . . Siebentes Zehend.* (Augsburg, 1748); 32 x 20 cm

Inscription below image: "IOANNES | BAPTISTA | PASSE= | RIVS, | Protonotarius Apostol. | Episcopi Pisaurensis | Vicar. general. So= | ciet. regiæ Londin. | aliarumque Itali=| carum membrum | nat. d. 10. Novembr. | MDCXCIV."

Production details at bottom left: "Dec. VII."; at bottom right: "I. Iac. Haid. sc. et exc. A.V."

Location: D-W, Portr. II 4021

References: *GerberL*, 2:82–83; Mortzfeld, A 15977

The NV 1790 entry may have been based on Walther's entry for Passeri's namesake, the artist Giovanni Battista Passeri (c. 1610–1679), who is described as a famous painter and musician. The subject of Haid's portrait, however, was not a musician but rather an eighteenth-century archaeologist, antiquarian, and scholar. Although confusing him with the earlier Passeri, Gerber does give the correct information that this portrait depicts the author of a discussion of the music of the Etruscans in his *Picturae Etruscorum in Vasculis*, 3 vols. (1767–75), 2:73.

Johann Christoph Pepusch
(1667–1752)

NV 1790, p. 116: [no. 264] *"Pebusch, (J. C.) Doct. Mus.* in England. 8. In schwarzen Rahmen, unter Glas." [PLATE 207]
Engraving; 15 x 10 cm on sheet 17 x 10.5 cm
Inscription above image: "Engraved for the Universal Magazine."; in plinth below image: "D.ᴿ PEPUSCH."
Production details at bottom: "Printed for J. Hinton, at the Kings Arms, in Paternoster Row."
Location: US-NYp, Muller Collection (digital ID 1541167)
References: Cat. Poelchau no. 556; *GerberL*, 2:91–102

Louis Guillaume Pécour
(1651?–1729)

NV 1790, p. 116: [no. 265] *"Pecour, (Louis) Compos.* der *Ballets.* Von *Cheron.* Gr. *Fol.* In schwarzen Rahmen, unter Glas." [PLATE 208]
Engraving by François Chéreau after Robert Le Vrac Tournières; 38 x 29 cm
Annotation, written below image in ink in an unknown hand: "Louis Pecour, Compos: de Ballet."
Production details at left: "Peint par R. Tourniere."; at right: "Gravé par F. Chereau."
Location: D-B, Mus. P. Pecour, Louis III, 1
References: Cat. Poelchau no. 553; *GerberL*, 2:88

This exemplar, from the Poelchau collection, has been trimmed to the edge of the image itself, and the name of the sitter has been written in below. The complete inscription on the untrimmed print, on which the NV 1790 entry is based, reads: "LOUIS PECOUR | Pensionnaire du Roy, Compositeur des Balets de l'Academie Royalle | de Musique, et Maitre a Danser de Made la Duchesse de Bourgogne".

Lorenzo Penna
(1613–1693)

NV 1790, p. 116: [no. 266] *"Penna, (L.) Dt. Theol.* und Professor, Musikus in *Bologna.* 4. In schwarzen Rahmen, unter Glas."
[PLATE 209]

Engraving; 21 x 15 cm

Inscription in oval frame: "EFFIGIE DEL P. LORENZO PENNA DA BOL.ᴬ CARM.ᴺᴼ DELLᴬ CONG.ᴺᴱ DI MANT.ᴬ MR̄O E DOTT. COLLEG. DI SAC. TEOL. PROFES. DI MVSICA D'ETA D AN. 65."

Location: D-B, Mus. P. Penna, Lorenzo I, 1

References: Cat. Poelchau no. 555; *GerberL*, 2:90

David Perez
(1711–1778)

NV 1790, p. 116: [no. 267] *"Perez, (David)* Portugiesischer Kapellmeister. In *Carricatur.* Gr. 4. In schwarzen Rahmen, unter Glas."

Caricature

Lost

References: *GerberL*, 2:104; *CPEB-Briefe*, 2:1151–52; *CPEB-Letters*, 247; Rostirolla, 191, 385–86

CPEB mentions this portrait in a letter to Forkel, 13 May 1786; the letter concludes with Bach's listing of the three Oesterreich caricatures (Annibali, Bresciani, and Jommelli) that he owns, all from the Ghezzi/Oesterreich *Raccolta.* In a marginal comment he wrote: "Westphal wants to sell the complete work, together with Perez's portrait." (Westphal will durchaus das ganze Werk mit Perez Portrait zusammen verkaufen.) The Perez portrait is listed in NV 1790 as a caricature, as are the other three portraits mentioned here; no artist is given, and the paper size is smaller than in the *Raccolta*, but Gerber lists this caricature as being by Oesterreich. The Perez portrait may indeed have been a print made by Oesterreich, based on a copy of the extant caricature by Ghezzi, and perhaps issued separately, like one of the two Annibali caricatures.

François-André Danican Philidor
(1726–1795)

NV 1790, p. 116: [no. 268] *"Philidor. (A. D.)* Französischer Componist. Von *St. Aubin.* 4. In schwarzen Rahmen, Unter Glas."
[PLATE 210]
Engraving by Augustin de Saint-Aubin after Charles Nicolas Cochin the younger, 1772; 19.5 x 14 cm
Inscription in round frame: "André Danican PHILIDOR, M.^tre de Chapelle de son Al.^se S.^me Mgr le Duc Règnant des Deux Ponts."
Verse below:

> Aux Français étonnés, de sa Mâle Harmonie,
> Il montra dans son art des prodiges nouveaux:
> Dans ses délassemens admirant son Génie,
> On voit qu'en ses jeux même il n'a point de Rivaux.
> Par M. Davesne.

Production details at bottom left: "C. N. Cochin filius delin."; at bottom right: "Aug. de S^t. Aubin sculp. 1772."
Location: D-B, Mus. P. Philidor I, 2
References: *GerberL*, 2:126–29

Niccolò Piccinni
(1728–1800)

NV 1790, p. 116: [no. 269] *"Piccini, (Nic.)* Componist. Von *Cathelin. Fol.* In schwarzen Rahmen, unter Glas." [PLATE 211]
Engraving by Louis-Jacques Cathelin after Charles Jean Robineau; 34 x 26 cm

Inscription below image: "NIC. PICCINI."
Verse:

> Avec une grace divine
> Tour à tour comique et touchant
> S'il est le Moliere du chant
> Il n'en est pas moins le Racine.

Production details at bottom left: "*Peint par Robineau.*"; center: "*A Paris, chez Basan, M.^d d'Estampes, Rue et Hôtel Serpente, N.°14.*"; right: "*Gravé par Cathelin, Graveur du Roi.*"

Location: D-B, Mus. P. Piccini, Nicol. II, 1

References: Cat. Poelchau no. 560; *GerberL*, 2:133–41; *Musiker im Porträt*, 3:110–11

Giovanni Pico della Mirandola
(1463–1494)

NV 1790, p. 116: [no. 270] "*Picus, (Joh.) Graf in* Mirandula. *Componist. Holzschnitt. 8.*" [PLATE 212]

Woodcut from Reusner 1589; 10 x 8 cm on sheet 15 x 9 cm

Inscription above image: "IOANNES PICVS MIRAND-VLA, | PHOENIX cognominatus."; below image: "Corporis haud, animique deest vis; sola sed ætas: | Quid tum? me facit ars ingeniumque senem. || IOAN."

Location: US-I, Petrarch N7575.R44 1589

References: *GerberL*, 2:143

Johann Georg Pisendel
(1687–1755)

NV 1790, p. 116: [no. 271] "*Pisendel, (J. G.) Concertmeister in* Dresden. *Gezeichnet von* Franke, *sehr ähnlich. 4. In goldenen Rahmen, unter Glas.*" [PLATE 213]

Drawing by [Johann Heinrich Christian?] Franke, in black chalk and India ink with white highlights and wash on cream paper; 25 x 18.5 cm

On verso: "aus der Bachschen Sammlung. Georg Poelchau, 1832. Handzeichnung von Frank."

Location: D-B, Mus. P. Pisendel, Joh. Georg I, 1

Provenance: CPEB's estate—Georg Poelchau—SBB (1841)

References: Cat. Poelchau no. 564; *GerberL*, 2:150–55; *Bach-Dokumente* IV, 387–88, 431; *Musiker im Porträt*, 3:44–45; Leaver 2007, 125–26

NV 1790 lists only "Franke" as the artist (as with Quantz, no. 282), probably referring to Johann Heinrich Christian Franke, who moved to Berlin from Braunschweig in 1765. The Pisendel and Quantz portrait drawings were likely made around the same time, presumably before the death of Pisendel in 1755, when Franke was at the most 17 years old—unless the drawing is a copy of a portrait in oils, mentioned by Gerber as being in the possession of "Herr Transchel in Dresden," who was likely the JSB student Christoph Transchel (1721–1800).

Plato

(c. 429–347 BCE)

NV 1790, p. 117: [no. 272] *"Plato*, Von *Krüger* nach einer alten marmornen *Büste. Fol."* [PLATE 214]

Engraving by Andreas Ludwig Krüger, 1768; plate 4 in Krüger 1769; 26 x 20.5 cm

Inscription below image: "Platon, Elêve de Socrate | Colossal de marbre de Carara, Ouvrage Romain du prémier rang. | Dans la Collection de sa Majesté le Roy de Prusse à Sanssouci."

Production details at left: "Krüger del. et Sculpsit. 1768."

Location: A-Wn, PORT 00135269_02

References: *GerberL*, 2:159

Angelo Poliziano

(1454–1494)

NV 1790, p. 117: [no. 273] *"Politianus, (Angellus) Ling. Græc. & Lat. Prof. Flor.* Schriftsteller und guter Musikus. Holzschnitt. 8." [PLATE 215]

Woodcut from Reusner 1589; 10 x 8 cm on sheet 15 x 9 cm

Inscription above image: "ANGELVS POLITIANVS | Poeta."; below image: "Qui colui Musas, & quem coluêre viciẞim | Musæ, Phœbus eram, Flora superba, tuus."

Location: US-I, Petrarch N7575.R44 1589

References: *GerberL*, 2:169–70

Porphyry
(c. 232/3–c. 305 BCE)

NV 1790, p. 117: [no. 274] *"Porphire, Sophiste,* Schriftsteller. 8."

Engraving

References: *GerberL*, 2:173

NV 1790 provides too little information for this image to be conclusively identified. The rubric suggests that the image was taken from a French translation of Porphyry.

Guillaume Postel
(1510–1581)

NV 1790, p. 117: [no. 275] *"Postellus, (Guillielmus)* Schriftsteller. Von *Gründler.* 8." [PLATE 216]

Engraving by Gottfried August Gründler; 14.5 x 9 cm on sheet 17 x 10 cm

Inscription below image: *"Guillelmus Postellus"*

Production details at lower right: "Gründler sc. Halae"

Location: A-Wn, PORT 00149736_02

References: *GerberL*, 2:180–81

Michael Praetorius

(1571–1621)

NV 1790, p. 117: [no. 276] *"Prætorius, (Mich.)* Kapellmeister in Braunschweig. Holzschnitt. 4. In schwarzen Rahmen, unter Glas." [PLATE 217]

Woodcut; from Praetorius's *Musae Sioniae: geistliche Concert Gesänge über die fürnembste deutsche Psalmen und Lieder . . .*, 4. Teil (Helmstadt, 1607); 15 x 13 cm

Inscription in outer four corners of image: "SALVUM ME | FAC DN̄E, | DEUS SALU: | :TIS MEÆ."; in oval frame: "F. I. A. MICHAEL PRÆTORIUS Creutzb. Thür. apud DUCEM BRUNSVIG Organ. et chori Müsici Magister. Aō, ætat. XXXV. C̄HRI. M. DC. IVX."; in book under sitter's hand: "In Deo speravit cor meum"; above image: a canonical five-voice setting ("V. *Voc*:") with the text "Non moriar sed vivam & narrabo opera Dn̄i, sed vi: & nar: opera Do-mini; | Cum [moriar] da mihi mori morte pia & placida, da m: m: mo: pia & pla-cida."; at right of image: "*Me IOVA castigat, necis haud tamen obruit umbra, | Gaudeo quod Dominus me premit atque juvat.*"; at left of image: "*Me quatiunt passim, sed opem fers CHRISTE vocanti, | Gratia quod me humilem reddis, & addis opem.*"; below image: "Cui chorus assurgit Musarum & Musica tota, | Hac Michaël Prætor Musicus est facie."; monogram at lower right: "SFA"

Location: US-CA, Mus 786.1.550

References: *GerberL*, 2:186–88; Hortschansky 1987, 45, 81–82; *Musiker im Porträt*, 2:34–35; Leaver 2007, 127

Gerber had difficulty locating Praetorius' portrait, and appears to have known of it only from NV 1790. He wrote: "His portrait in woodcut is extremely rare, and is perhaps to be found before one of the volumes of his Syntagma." (Sein Bildniß in Holzschnitt ist höchst selten, und befindet sich vielleicht vor einem Bande seines Syntagm.) The portrait was in fact printed with the fourth part of the *Musae Sioniae* (1607).

Ptolemy

(after 83–161 CE)

NV 1790, p. 117: [no. 277] *"Ptolomæus, (Claud. Alexandrinus)* Schriftsteller. Holzschnitt. 8." [PLATE 218]

Woodcut from Reusner 1589; 10 x 8 cm on sheet 15 x 9 cm

Inscription above image: "CLAVDIVS PTOLEMAEVS ALE- | XANDRINVS Mathematicus."; below image: "Per me doctrinæ totum diuina Mathesis | Corpus habet: cuius glorior esse parens."

Location: US-I, Petrarch N7575.R44 1589

References: *GerberL*, 2:199–200

Gaetano Pugnani
(1713–1798)

NV 1790, p. 117: [no. 278] *"Pugnani, Violinist. Gezeichnet in Carricatur. Kl. 4. In schwarzen Rahmen, unter Glas."*

Caricature drawing

Lost

References: *GerberL*, 2:200–201; *GerberNL*, 3:774, 4:740–41; Daniel Heartz, "Portrait of a Court Musician: Gaetano Pugnani of Turin," *Imago musicae* 1 (1984), 103–20; Rostirolla, 222, 258, 410–11

Gerber cites a caricature of Pugnani in quarto in Ernst Florens Friedrich Chladni's collection, describing it as "probably by Tiepolo" and as having come from the CPEB collection ("aus Em. Bachs Nachlasse"). Three caricatures of Pugnani by Pier Leone Ghezzi are extant today.

Giovanni Punto (Johann Wenzel Stich)
(1746–1803)

NV 1790, p. 117: [no. 279] *"Punto, (J.) Waldhornist. Gezeichnet von Cochin, gestochen von Miger. 12."* [PLATE 219]

Engraving by Simon Charles Miger after Charles Nicolas Cochin the younger, 1782; 7.5 x 7 cm on sheet 12 x 11 cm

Inscription above image: " J. PUNTO."

Production details: "Dessiné par C. N. Cochin 1782. Gravé par S. C. Miger."

Location: D-B, Mus. P. Punto, J. I, 1

References: Cat. Poelchau no. 580; *GerberL*, 2:201

Erycius Puteanus
(1574–1646)

NV 1790, p. 117: [no. 280] *"Puteanus, (Ericius) Eloq. Prof. Mediolani. 4."* [PLATE 220]

Engraving; 14 x 9.5 cm

Inscription in oval frame: "ERYCIUS PUTEANUS INSIGNIS POETA NATUS ANNO M DL XXV."; below: "Qui negat historicum PUTEANUS quique, Poêtam | Helleboro cerebrum purget et esse sciet."

Location: D-B, Mus. P. Puteanus, I, 2

References: *GerberL*, 2:201–2

Although a very beautiful quarto-sized engraving of Puteanus by Pieter de Jode II after Anthony Van Dyck was available to collectors, NV 1790 lists no artists; it is unlikely that the names of these two well-known artists would have been omitted had they been visible on CPEB's copy of the print. Gerber lists only one other portrait of Puteanus available in quarto, one without artists' names. It is likely, then, that CPEB's portrait corresponded to the image shown here.

Pythagoras
(second half of sixth century BCE)

NV 1790, p. 117: [no. 281] *"Pythagoras, Inventor Intervallorum. Gr. 4."*

Engraving

References: *GerberL*, 2: 204

NV 1790 provides too little information for this image to be conclusively identified.

Johann Joachim Quantz
(1697–1773)

NV 1790, p. 117: [no. 282] *"Quanz, (Joh. Joach)* Preußischer Flötenist und Componist. Gezeichnet von *Frank.* 4. In goldenen Rahmen, unter Glas." [PLATE 221]

Drawing by [Johann Heinrich Christian?] Franke, in black chalk and India ink with white highlights and wash; 24.5 x 18.5 cm

Location: D-B, Mus. P. Quantz, J. J. I, 1

Provenance: CPEB's estate—Georg Poelchau—SBB (1841)

References: Cat. Poelchau no. 584; Biehahn 1961, 26–27

NV 1790 lists only "Frank" as the artist of the drawing (see also Pisendel, no. 271), likely referring to Johann Heinrich Christian Franke.

* * *

NV 1790, p. 117: [no. 283] "Derselbe. Von *Schleuen*. 8."

[PLATE 222]

Engraving by Johann David Schleuen after Johann Heinrich Christian Franke; frontispiece to *Allgemeine Deutsche Bibliothek*, 4 (Berlin, 1767); 15 x 9 cm

Inscription below image: "IOHANN IOACHIM | QUANZ"

Production details at bottom right: "Schleuen sc."

Location: D-B, Mus. P. Quantz, J. J. I, 2

References: Cat. Poelchau no. 585; GerberL, 2:206–17; *Bach-Dokumente* IV, 391, 435; *Musiker im Porträt*, 3:52–53; Charles Walthall, "Portraits of Johann Joachim Quantz," *Early Music* 14 (1986): 500–18

The date of publication of this print (1767) has been taken to imply that the portrait was made late in Quantz's life and represents the musician close to the age of 70 (see Walthall). However, the portrait surely represents a younger man, and while the engraving may have been made close to 1767, the drawing on which it was based was likely made much earlier. If, as seems likely, the drawing was made around the same time as Franke's drawing of Pisendel (see no. 271), then this was almost certainly before Pisendel's death in 1755 (when Franke was only 17). The drawing and engraving would then both represent Quantz in his 50s, rather than at the age of 70.

Johann Quiersfeld

(1642–1686)

NV 1790, p. 117: [no. 284] "*Qviersfeld, (M. Joh.)* Cantor zu Pirna. Von *Menzel*. 8."

Engraving by Menzel

References: *GerberL*, 2:220; *GerberNL*, 3:785

The identification of the engraving referred to in NV 1790 is uncertain. None of the extant engravings of Quiersfeld bears the artist's name "Menzel."

Jean-Philippe Rameau
(1683–1764)

NV 1790, p. 118: [no. 285] *"Rameau, (J. Ph.) Organist, Componist und Schriftsteller. Von St. Aubin. 4. In schwarzen Rahmen, unter Glas."* [PLATE 223]

Engraving by Augustin de Saint-Aubin after J.J. Cassieri; 18.5 x 12.5 cm

Inscription below image: "J. PH. RAMEAU | *Né à Dijon le 25 Septembre 1683.* | *Mort le 12 Septembre 1764.*"

Production details at bottom left: "fait par J. J. Cassieri S. D. R. 1760."; at bottom right: "Gravé par Aug. St. Aubin."; bottom center: "Se Vend à Paris chez Joulain Quai de la Megisserie."

Location: D-B, Mus. P. Rameau, Jean Phil. I, 7

References: Lavater, *Physiognomische Fragmente*, 1:266; *GerberL*, 2:226–31; *CPEB-Briefe*, 1:647; *CPEB-Letters*, 113

Karl Wilhelm Ramler
(1725–1798)

NV 1790, p. 118: [no. 286] *"Ramler, (C. W.) Professor in Berlin, Lyrischer Dichter. Von K. 8."* [PLATE 224]

Engraving by Johann Friedrich Kauke; 15 x 9 cm

Inscription below image: "Karl Wilhelm Ramler."

Production details at bottom center: "FJK fecit."

Location: D-W, Portr. I 10750

References: *GerberL*, 2:231–32; Mortzfeld, A 17197

Jean-Fery Rebel
(1666–1747)

NV 1790, p. 118: [no. 287] *"Rebel, (J. B.) Ober-Kapellmeister und Componist in Frankreich. Von Mogreau. Fol. In schwarzen Rahmen, unter Glas."* [PLATE 225]
Etching by Jean Moyreau after Antoine Watteau, 1726/31; 33 x 26 cm on sheet 38.5 x 28.5 cm
Inscription below image: *"J. B. REBEL | Compositeur de la Chambre du Roy, | Et Maître de Musique de l'Académie Royale."*
Production details: *"Gravé d'après un dessein de Wateau de même grandeur, par I. Moyreau, rue gallande vis à vis la Chapelle St Blaise."*
Location: D-B, Mus. P. Rebel, J. B. II, 1
References: Cat. Poelchau no. 593; *GerberL*, 2:246; Louis-Antoine Prat and Pierre Rosenberg, *Antoine Watteau 1684–1721: Catalogue raisonné des dessins* (Paris: Gallimard, 1996), 1122

Nicolò Reginelli
(1710–1751)

NV 1790, p. 118: [no. 288] *"Reginelli, (Nic.)* Sänger in Berlin. Gezeichnet von *Tiepolo* in *Carricatur. Fol."*
Caricature drawing by Tiepolo
Lost
References: *GerberL*, 2:248

Johann Friedrich Reichardt
(1752–1814)

NV 1790, p. 118: [no. 289] *"Reichard, (J. F.)* Preußischer Kapellmeister. Eine italienische Zeichnung. 12." [PLATE 226]
Drawing in red pencil on cream paper; 9.5 x 8 cm
Inscription below image, in red pencil: *"J. F. Reichard"*

Location: D-B, Mus. P. Reichardt, J. Fr. I 2

Provenance: CPEB's estate—Georg Poelchau—SBB (1841)

References: Cat. Poelchau no. 595; *GerberL*, 2:251–58

Although Poelchau gave no indication on the picture itself that it came from the Bach collection, this small unsigned (and hitherto unpublished) drawing corresponds in size to the NV 1790 entry. It depicts a younger Reichardt than that shown in the 1791 drawing by Henry (engraved by Bendix in 1796). Listed in NV 1790 as an Italian drawing, it could have been made during Reichardt's single journey to Italy, on operatic business, in 1783.

Gottfried Reiche
(1667–1734)

NV 1790, p. 118: [no. 290] *"Reiche, (Gottfr.) Rathsmusikus in Leipzig, ein guter Componist. Von Rosbach. 4. In schwarzen Rahmen, unter Glas."* [PLATE 227]

Engraving by Johann Friedrich Rosbach after Elias Gottlob Haußmann, 1727; 29.5 x 22.5 cm

Inscription below image: "GOTTFRIED REICHE. | Leucopetra Misnicus. | natus d. v Februarii MDCLXVII. | Musicorum Senatus Lipsiensis | Senior."

Production details at bottom left: "E. G. Hausmañ Reg. Pol: pict: pinx:"; at bottom right: "Rosbach sculps: Lips: 1727."

Location: D-B, Mus. P. Reiche, G I, 1

References: Cat. Poelchau no. 597; *GerberL*, 2:258; *Bach-Dokumente* IV, 383, 427; *Musiker im Porträt*, 2:166–67; Wolff 2000, 361

Johann Adam Reincken
(1623–1722)

NV 1790, p. 118: [no. 291] *"Reincken, (J. A.) Organist in Hamburg. Fol. In schwarzen Rahmen, unter Glas."* [PLATE 228]

Engraving; 32.5 x 22 cm

Inscription below image: *"In Effigiem* MUSICI *et* ORGANICI *sæculi hujus longe præstantissimi* | Domini Iohannis Adami Reinken. | *Quem probet Auditus quid surdis pingitur Oclis? Si vis hunc dingne [sic]* | *pingere pinge Melos: Mæandros. quin cum rectâ ratione furores. Certosque* | *Errores suspice Phoebe lÿrâ. Dædala Dextra jubet linguamque stilumque* | *Silere. Auribus attonitis hanc stupor ipse stupet. Græcia si mendax* | Reinecco *Amphiona præfers. Auriculas Referes præmia digna Midæ.* || *Joannis Bambamius D.*"

Location: D-B, Mus. P. Reincken, Joh. Adam II, 1

References: Cat. Poelchau no. 599; *GerberL*, 2:261–62; *Bach-Dokumente* IV, 372, 416; Leaver 2007, 124

Nikolaus Reusner

(1545–1602)

NV 1790 (p. 118): [no. 292] *"Reusner, (Nic.) Scrips. Icones viror illustr. Holzschnitt. 8."* [PLATE 229]

Woodcut from Reusner 1587; 10 x 8 cm on sheet 15 x 9 cm

Inscription above image: "IMAGO NICOLAI REVSNERI IVRISC. | Consiliarij Saxonici."; below image: "Effigies homo parva tua est, DEVS: effigiem fac | Me quoque, dum vivo, semper habere tuam."

References: Lemmer 1973, 430ff.

Andreas Reyher

(1601–1673)

NV 1790, p. 118: [no. 293] *"Reyher, (Andreas) Schriftsteller. Von Walch. 4."* [PLATE 230]

Engraving by Georg Walch, 1638; 15.5 x 11 cm

Inscription in oval frame: "M. ANDREAS REYHER HEINRICHS. HENNEBERGICUS | ILLUST. GYMNASII HÉNEBERGICI RECTOR. Æt. An. 37¼."; in cartouche above: "Psal. 27, 1. | הְוִהי ,רֹוא" [Dominus lux mea]; in cartouche below: "Psal. 25, 21. | סֹמ-ןיִשֶׁר יִצְרוּנְי" [Simplicitas et aequitas servabunt me]

Production details at bottom center: "Georg Walch fecit."

Location: A-Wn, PORT 00094594_01

Beatus Rhenanus

(1485–1547)

NV 1790, p. 118: [no. 294] *"Rhenanus, (Beatus)* Schriftsteller. Holzschnitt. 8." [PLATE 231]

Woodcut from Reusner 1587; 10 x 8 cm on sheet 15 x 9 cm

Inscription above image: "BEATUS RHENANVS | Historicus."; below image: "Multum se Germana mihi historia, atque Latina | Debet: me Patriæ vindice claret honos. || M, D. XLVII."

References: Lemmer 1973, 454

Michael Richey

(1678–1761)

NV 1790, p. 118: [no. 295] *"Richey, (Michael)* Professor in Hamburg und Secretär der dasigen musikal. patriotischen Gesellschaft, Lyrischer Dichter. Von *Fritsch.* Kl. 4." [PLATE 232]

Engraving by Christian Fritsch, 1753; 16.5 x 9.5 cm on sheet 41 x 27.5 cm

Inscription below image: "MICHAEL RICHEY | HISTOR. ET GR. L. IN GYMNASIO HAMBVRGENSI PROF. P. ORDINIS SVI SENIOR. | ANNO MDCCLII. AETAT. LXXIV."

Verse:

> Hac facie RICHEIVS erat, quum viuida nondum
> Oscula desineret figere Musa seni.
> Cynthius ingenium gravitate iocoque venustum
> Rugosas tarde iussit habere vices.
> Spirat adhuc candor, doctrinae gratia spirat,
> Postque Deum Patriae proximus ardet amor.
> O! sibi dulce diu pergant decus esse vicissim
> Vir Patria dignus, Patria digna Viro!
>   Amico veteri ac vero *IOHANNES HENRICVS A SEELEN. TH. L.*

Production details at bottom right of image: "C. Fritzsch sc. Hamb. 1753."

Location: D-B, Mus. P. Richey, Michael, I, 1

References: Cat. Poelchau no. 601; *GerberL,* 2:281–82

Johann Rist
(1660–1667)

NV 1790, p. 119: [no. 296] "*Rist, (Joh.)* Schriftsteller und Lyrischer Dichter. Von *Streuheld*. 8." [PLATE 233]

Engraving by Franz Steürhelt; from Rist's *Sabbahtische Seelenlust* (Lüneburg, 1651); 12 x 8.5 cm on sheet 14.5 x 8.5 cm

Inscription in oval frame: "IOHANNES RIST, PREDIGER ZV WEDEL AN DER ELBE, RÖMISCHER KAISERLICHER MAIESTÂTT HOF AUS EDEL GE-KROHNTER POET. GEBOHREN IM. 1607 IAHR. †"

Verse:

> Rüstig ist der grosse Rist. Rüstig, wen Sein Geist Sich reget,
> Rüstig, wen Er Seinen Ruhm in gelehrte Bücher preget
> Vnd dadurch daß Sterngerüste mehr als Rüstig überfleügt,
> Wunder! wird den dises alles durch diß blosse Bild bezeügt?

Dedication below: "dem grossen Risten Zu längst verdienten Ehren geschriben | in Helmstätt von Enoch Gläsern, Kaiserl. | Gekröhnten Poéten."

Production details at bottom right: "F. Steürhelt delineavit et sculp."

Location: D-W, Port. I 11066

References: *GerberL*, 2:294; *CPEB-Briefe*, 2:1151; *CPEB-Letters*, 247; Hortschansky 1987, 68; Mortzfeld, A 17715; Leaver 2007, 123

CPEB sent a copy of Rist's portrait to J. N. Forkel in May 1786, along with a copy of a drawing of Padre Martini: "I have enclosed a lyrical poet, the honorable Rist. <u>I make of the two of them a small present for you.</u>" (Ich habe einen lÿrischen Dichter, den ehrlichen Rist beÿgelegt. <u>Mit beÿden mache ich Ihnen ein kleines Präsent.</u>)

Johann Heinrich Rolle
(1716–1785)

NV 1790, p. 119: [no. 297] "*Rolle, (Joh. Heinr.)* Musik-Director in Magdeburg. Kl. 8. In schwarzen Rahmen, unter Glas." [PLATE 234]

Engraving by Christian Gottlieb Geyser after [Jacob Adolph?] Fischer; frontispiece to *Bibliothek der schönen Wissenschaften*, 27 (Leipzig, 1782);

18 x 11 cm

Inscription below image: "I. H. ROLLE."

Production details at bottom left: "Fischer pinx."; at bottom right: "Geyser sc."

Location: D-B, Mus. P. Rolle, J. H. I, 1

References: Cat. Poelchau no. 614; *GerberL*, 2:314–17

NV 1790 supplies no identifying information beyond size for this portrait. The only portrait of Rolle (according to Gerber) was widely available from the *Bibliothek der schönen Wissenschaften*.

Jean-Jacques Rousseau
(1712–1778)

NV 1790, p. 119: [no. 298] *"Rousseau, (J. J.) Componist und Schriftsteller in Frankreich. Schwarze Kunst. Fol. In schwarzen Rahmen, unter Glas."* [PLATE 235]

Mezzotint by David Martin after Allan Ramsay, 1766; 39 x 27.5 cm on sheet 40 x 28.5 cm

Inscription below image: "*Jean Jacques Rousseau.* | VITAM IMPENDERE VERO. | *From an Original Picture by M.ʳ Ramsay, in the Possession of David Hume Esq.ʳ*"

Production details at left: "A. Ramsay Londini pinx.ᵗ | 1766."; at right: "D. Martin fecit"; lower right corner: "Pr. 5.ˢ"

Location: A-Wn, PORT 00134945_01_1

References: *GerberL*, 2:334–39

NV 1790 lists a mezzotint in folio. No artists' names are given. Since Gerber lists only one mezzotint of this size—the Martin/Ramsay portrait—it is likely that this corresponds to the item listed in CPEB's collection. Bach's copy may have been cropped to the frame of the portrait image itself, removing the artists' names.

Hans Sachs

(1494–1576)

NV 1790, p. 119: [no. 299] *"Sachse, (Hans)* Meistersänger. Von *Knorr.* 4. In schwarzen Rahmen, unter Glas." [PLATE 236]

Engraving by Georg Wolfgang Knorr, c. 1730; 11 x 9.5 cm on sheet 14.5 x 10.5 cm

Inscription below image: "HANNS SACHS | Norimbergensis | *Sutor. Poëta et Phonascus | famigeratissimus.* | *Nat. A. 1494. d. 5. Nov. Den. A. 1576. d. 19. Januarij.* | *Ex collectione Friderici Roth-Scholtzii Norimberg."*; upper right: "*Sic humiles animos | respicit orbe DEVS."*

Production details at bottom center: "Knorr fecit."

Location: D-W, Portr. I 11417a

References: *GerberL,* 2:364; Mortzfeld, A 18283; Leaver 2007, 128

Felice Salimbeni

(c. 1712–1751)

NV 1790, p. 119: [no. 300] *"Salimbeni, (Felix)* Sänger in Berlin. Von *G. F. Schmidt.* Gr. 4. In schwarzen Rahmen, unter Glas." [PLATE 237]

Engraving by Georg Friedrich Schmidt, 1751; 23.5 x 18.5 cm

Inscription below image: "ΜΟΥΣΑΙΣ ΑΠΓΑΡΟΤΤΟΣ." [Muse of Algarotti]

Production details at bottom center: "G. F. Schmidt ad vivum del. et sculp. Berolini 1751."

Location: D-B, Mus. P. Salimbeni I, 1

References: Cat. Poelchau no. 636b; *GerberL,* 2:372–73

Julius Caesar Scaliger

(1484–1558)

NV 1790, p. 119: [no. 301] *"Scaliger, (Jul. Gæs.)* Schriftsteller. 4."

References: *GerberL,* 2:399–400

NV 1790 provides too little information for this image to be conclusively identified.

Joseph Justus Scaliger
(1540–1609)

NV 1790, p.119: [no. 302] *"Scaliger, (Josephus) Schriftsteller. 4"*
References: *GerberL*, 2:399

NV 1790 provides too little information for this image to be conclusively identified.

Paul Scalichius
(1534–1575)

NV 1790, p. 119: [no. 303] *"Schalichius, (Paulus) Schriftsteller. Holzschnitt. 8."* [PLATE 238]
Woodcut from Reusner 1587; 10 x 8 cm on sheet 15 x 9 cm
Inscription above image: "PAVLVS SCALICHIVS COMES HVN- | norum, Marchio Veronæ, S. Th. D."; below image: "Regulus Hunnorum, Scalæ hæres glorior esse | Gentis: Sacrificus Cæsaris, inde Papæ."
References: *GerberL*, 2:398–99; Lemmer 1973, 477

Heinrich Scheidemann
(c. 1595–1663)

NV 1790, p. 119: [no. 304] *"Scheidemann, (Heinr.) Organist in Hamburg. Von Fleischberger. Fol. In schwarzen Rahmen, unter Glas."* [PLATE 239]
Engraving by Johann Friedrich Fleischberger, 1652; 23.5 x 14.5 cm
Inscription above image: "IN VERAM EFFIGIEM MUSICI ET OR= | GANICI LONGÈ PRÆSTANTISSIMI CELEBER= | RIMIQVE, HENRICI SCHEIDEMANNI."

Verse:

> Musarum ocelli illius, et verecati,
> Suavis canorique modulatus arbitri,
> Hæc sculpta vultum Scheidemāni vividū,
> Refert tabella. Quem semel si quis virū,
> Summâ accinentem. Pegaseium melos,
> Arte, lepidisque tot modis, audiverit:
> Plane Orphea, vel Amphionem stupens novū:
> Coram videre protinus quàm gestiet,
> Mirabiturque in eo unicè, quæ nullius,
> Pictoris aut sculptoris exprimit manus.
>   H. I. ML.

Production details at bottom center: "J. F. Fleischberger. Delineavit et Sculpsit. Anno 1652."

Location: D-B, Mus. P. Scheidemann, Heinr. I, 1

References: Cat. Poelchau no. 642; *GerberL*, 2:418–19; *Musiker im Porträt*, 2:56–57

Samuel Scheidt
(1587–1654)

NV 1790, p. 119: [no. 305] "*Scheidt, (Sam.)* Kapellmeister und Organist in Halle. 4. In schwarzen Rahmen, unter Glas."
[PLATE 240]

Engraving; frontispiece to *Tabulatura Nova* (1624); 17.5 x 13 cm on sheet 28.5 x 11.5 cm

Inscription below image, on a sheet of music: canon on the text "In te Domine speraui non confundar in æternum"

Verse:

> In effigiem SAMVELIS SCHEITI Musicorū principis
> Hic ille est SAMVEL cuius vultū ænea cernis.
> SCHEITIVS organici gloria prima chori
> O numeris natam liceat quoque sculpere mentem
> Pegaseas liceat sculpere posse manus?
> Nil tibi laudo virum sat eum tibi publica laudant
> Scripta: sat artificem nobile laudat opus.
>   Ioach. Cæsar

Location: US-NYp, Muller Collection (digital ID 1713155)
References: *GerberL*, 2:417–18; Hortschansky 1987, 88

Samuel Schelwig
(1643–1715)

NV 1790, p. 119: [no. 306] *"Schelguigius, (Sam.) Dt.* Professor und
Rector zu Danzig, Schriftsteller. 8." [PLATE 241]
Engraving by Johann Christoph Böcklin; frontispiece to
Schelwig's *Synopsis controversiarum sub pietatis praetextu
motarum* . . . 2nd ed. (Danzig, 1703); 14 x 8 cm on sheet 15.5 x 8.5 cm
Inscription below image: "SAMUEL SCHELGUIGIUS | S. THEOL. D. ET PROF. P. ATHE= |
NÆI GEDANENSIS RECTOR ET AD | SS. TRINIT. PASTOR. *Natus* MDCXLIII. |
Depictus MDCCIII. C. G. Ludwig fieri curavit."
Production details at bottom center: "J. C. B. Sc."
Location: D-W, Portr. I 11800a
References: *GerberL*, 2:423; Mortzfeld, A 19012

Johannes Schenck
(1660–after 1710)

NV 1790, pp. 119–120: [no. 307] *"Schenck, (Joh.)* Churpfälzischer
Violdigambist in Amsterdamm. Schwarze Kunst von *Schenck.
Fol.* In schwarzen Rahmen, unter Glas." [PLATE 242]
Mezzotint by Pieter Schenck; 25 x 18.5 cm
Inscription below image: "JOHAN SCHENCK, *apud Amstelædamenses Musicus famig-
eratissimus.* | *Manuque sustinet læva chelyn, Qui saxa dulci traxit Amphion sono. Seneca.
Oedip.*"
Production details at bottom left: "Pet: Schenk fec: et exc: Amstelod:"; at bottom
right: "cum Privil: Ord: Holl: et West-Frisiæ"
Location: D-B, Mus. P. Schenck, Joh. I, 2
References: Cat. Poelchau no. 645; *GerberL*, 2:424; Jonathan Dunford with Pierre-
Gille Girault, trans. Robert A. Green, "A Portrait of the Musician Marin Marais by
Jean Dieu dit Saint-Jean in the Museum in the Chateau of Blois," *Journal of the Viola
da Gamba Society of America,* 44 (2007–8): 5–12

Niels Schiørring
(1743–1798)

NV 1790, p. 120: [no. 308] *"Schiörring, (Nils)* Königl. Musikus in Copenhagen. Gezeichnet von *Bruhn.* Gr. 4. In goldenen Rahmen, unter Glas." [PLATE 243]

Drawing by T. Bruhn, in black chalk, India ink, and watercolor on cream paper, 1770; 22.5 x 18 cm

Inscription, signed in ink, in frame at bottom left: "T. Bruun, 1770"

On verso, in Poelchau's hand: "Nils Schiörring Königl. Musicus in Copenhagen. †1800. | Gezeichnet von Bruhn. Aus der Bachschen Sammlung. G. Poelchau 1832."

Location: D-B, Mus. P. Schiörring, Nils I, 1

Provenance: CPEB's estate—Georg Poelchau—SBB (1841)

References: Cat. Poelchau no. 648a; *GerberL*, 2:430

Johann Heinrich Schmelzer
(1620–1680)

NV 1790, p. 120: [no. 309] *Schmelzer, (Joh. Heinr.)* Kaiserl. Vice-Kapellmeister. Schwarze Kunst. 8. In schwarzen Rahmen, unter Glas. [PLATE 244]

Mezzotint; 16.5 x 11.5 cm

Inscription in oval frame: "JOHANNES HENRICUS SCHMELZER."

Verse:

> Qui Divum mentes qui sacras Cæsaris aures
> Tentat et Orpheâ maximus arte tentet,
> Hoc etiam, quod in are vides, tenet ore tuentum.
> Mirificeque simul pectora capta movet.
> Invidia Gallique, Italique et natio quævis
> Extera; lætitia tu bone Teuto fermis.
> f F. Gabri. Majer. Helv.

Location: A-Wn, PORT 00013418_01

References: *GerberL*, 2:434

Bernhard Schmid the elder

(1535–1592)

NV 1790, p. 120: [no. 310] *"Schmidt, (Bernh.)* Organist in Straßburg. Holzschnitt. *Fol.* In schwarzen Rahmen, unter Glas." [PLATE 245]

Woodcut; frontispiece to *Zwey Bücher einer neuen kunstlichen Tabulatur . . . allen Organisten und angehenden Instrumentisten zu nutz* (1577); 31 x 20 cm

Inscription above image: "In Effigiem Bernhardi Schmid | TETRASTICHON."

Verse:

> Non animum Sculptor, partem sed fingere doctus
> Corporis: ingenium prodit at iste liber.
> Est oris, fateor, quædam non trita venustas,
> Iudice me, partus dignior ingenij est.
> Sultzpergerus.p.

Location: D-B, Mus. P. Schmidt, Bernh. I, 1

References: Cat. Poelchau, no. 649; *GerberL*, 2:437

Melchior Schmidt

(1608–?)

NV 1790, p. 120: [no. 311] *"Schmidt, (Melchior.)* Lautenist in Nürnberg. 8. In schwarzen Rahmen, unter Glas." [PLATE 246]

Engraving by H. I. S. Schellenberger; 21 x 15 cm

Inscription below image: "MELCHIOR SCHMID, AMPHION NORICUS | *Orphea quid Thraces jactant, Amphiona Thebæ:* | *Exprimit en uno Noris utrumque Viro!* | *Auribus Hunc vidisse juvat! Pleno ore fatetur* | *Melpomene:* MEL *sit* MELCHIOR *arte* CHORI. || *Amicissima manus ac meus* | *Sigismūdi à* Birken. Com. Pal. Cæs."; at upper left: "Natus 1608."

Production details at bottom left: "H.I.S.Schollenberger fec."

Location: D-B, Mus. P. Schmid, Melchior I, 1

References: Cat. Poelchau no. 650; *GerberL*, 2:438

Johann Andreas Schmidt

(1652–1726)

NV 1790, p. 120: [no. 312] *"Schmidt, (Joh. Andr.)* Dt. Abt zu
Marienthal, Schriftsteller. Von *Uhlich.* 8." [PLATE 247]

Engraving by Gabriel Uhlich; 14 x 8.5 cm

Inscription below image: "Io: Andreas SCHMIDT | S. Theol. D. et
Prof. P. O. | ordinis Theologici Senior | et | Abbas Mariævallensis | Natus Wormatiæ,
A: 1652."

Production details at bottom left: "Uhlich sc."

Location: A-Wn, PORT 001 11317_01

References: *GerberL*, 2:437

Dirck Scholl

(1640/1–1727)

NV 1790, p. 120: [no. 313] *"Scholl, (Dirk)* Organist und Glok-
kenist in Holland. Schwarze Kunst von *van der Wiet.* Gr. 4. In
schwarzen Rahmen, unter Glas." [PLATE 248]

Mezzotint by Thomas van der Wilt, 1699; 23.5 x 17 cm

Inscription below image: "DIRK SCHOLL. | *Organist en klokkenist, voor desen tot
Arnhem, en nu, zedert den Jare 1665, tot Delft.*"

Verse:

> Dit beeld dien Phenix uijt, die Orgels, klokken, snaaren,
> Bezield met Hemel galm. Sijn vrugt'bre Geest en vlijt,
> Verbeeld zig zelf alom, door groots Musijk te baaren:
> Dies sal sijn Naam en Loff verduuren nijd en tijd.

Production details at bottom left: "Anno 1699;" at bottom right: "T. vander Wilt, pinx.
et fec."

Location: D-B, Mus. P. Scholl, Dirk

References: Cat. Poelchau no. 654; *GerberL*, 2:44–45

Johann Schop
(c. 1590–1667)

NV 1790, p. 120: [no. 314] "*Schopp, (Joh.)* Raths-Violinist in Hamburg. Quer 8. In schwarzen Rahmen, unter Glas."
[PLATE 249]

Engraving by Dirck Diricks; title page to continuo part of Schop's *Geistlicher Concerten* (Hamburg, 1644); 18 x 12.5 cm

Inscription above image: "Erster Theil | Geistlicher | CONCERTEN, | Mit 1. 2. 3. 4. und 8 Stim̃en | Sambt beÿgefügtem Basso Continuo | vor die Orgel | In die Music versetzet | durch | JOHANN SCHOPEN. | Bassus vor die Orgel, || Mit R. Keÿ: M. Freÿheit. | Hamburg | Bey Jacob Rebenlein | 1644"

Production details below: "D. Diricksen | Hamb: Fecit."

Location: D-B, Mus. P Schop, Johan I, 1

References: *GerberL*, 2:446–47

The item listed in NV 1790, in "Quer 8" format, was likely the lower part of this image. The portrait oval itself was reprinted on the title page of Schop's *Himmlischen Lieder* (1652), a copy of which CPEB owned.

Conrad Schott
(1562–1630)

NV 1790, p. 120: [no 315] "*Schottus, (Conradus)* ein blinder Orgelmacher und Mechanikus in Augsburg. Von *Kilian. Fol.*"
[PLATE 250]

Engraving by Lucas Kilian, 1625; 15 x 11 cm on sheet 31 x 19 cm

Inscription above image: "CONRADUS SCHOTTUS STUTGAR- | DIANUS."; at top of frame: "Ich Waiß daß mein Erlöser lebt. Hiob. 19."; at bottom, the same text in Latin: "SCIO, QVÒD REDEMTOR MEVS VIVIT. IOB. XIX."; in oval frame: "EFFIGIES DN̄I CONRADI SCOTI STVT-GARD: ORGANOPOEI MVSICI COECI INGENIOSISSIMI ANNO ÆTAT: LXIII. A. C. 1625."; below image: "Eidem Celeberrimo Artifici, Musico Or-ganopœo & Archi- | tecto admirando honoris & officij ergò dedicat. | Lucas Kilianus sculpsit. | Dem Ehrnvösten / Kunstreichen vnd Weitberümbten Orglen= | machern

vnd Baumaistern, H. Conrad Schotten, Burgern der Fürstl: | Hauptstadt Studtgardt
dedicirt vnd verehrt diß Contrafeyt | Dienstfreundtlich Lucas Kilian sculpsit."
Production details at lower left of image: "L. Kilian. Sculp."
Location: D-W, Portr. II 4975
References: *GerberL*, 2:448; Mortzfeld, A 19012

Tobias Heinrich Schubart
(1699–1747)

NV 1790, p. 120: [no. 316] *"Schubart, (Tob. Heinr.)* Pastor zu
Hamburg, Lyrischer Dichter. Von *Fritsch.* 4." [PLATE 251]
Engraving by Christian Fritsch, 1729; 16 x 13 cm on sheet
22.5 x 16.5 cm
Inscription below image: "Tob. Henr. Schubart | Verb. Div. Min. ad S. Michaelis
Hamburg."
Production details at bottom right: "1729. C. Fritzsch ad vivum Sculpsit"
Location: D-W, Portr. I 12181
References: Mortzfeld, A 19669

Christian Friedrich Daniel Schubart
(1739–1791)

NV 1790, p. 120: [no. 317] *"Schubart, (Chr. Fried. Dan.)* Musik-
Director und Schriftsteller. Von *Schlotterbek.* 4." [PLATE 252]
Engraving by Christian Jacob Schlotterbeck; frontispiece to
Schubart's *Gedichte*, 1 (Stuttgart, 1785); 12.5 x 10 cm on sheet
17 x 10.5 cm
Inscription below image: "Schubart."
Production details: "C. J. Schlotterbek. del. et sculp. Stuttg. 1785."
Location: D-W, Portr, I 12177b
References: *GerberL*, 2:458–60; Mortzfeld, A 19662

Heinrich Schütz

(1585–1672)

NV 1790, p. 121: [no. 318] *"Schütze, (Heinr)* Chursächsischer Ober-Kapellmeister. Von *Ramstädt.* 4. In schwarzen Rahmen, unter Glas." [PLATE 253]

Engraving by Christian Romstet after Christoph Spetner; 18.5 x 14.5 cm

Inscription in oval frame: "Herr Heinrich Schütz Churfurstl. Durchl. zu Sachsen in die LVII Jahr altester Kapellmeister. seines Alters LXXXVII Jahr."; in lower medallion: "LIBITINAM VITABIT."

Production details at bottom left: "Christian Romstet sculpsit."

Location: D-B, Mus. P. Schütz, Heinr. I, 3

References: Cat. Poelchau no. 667; *GerberL*, 2:464–66; Leaver 2007, 122

This engraving was published in 1672 with the funeral oration for Schütz by Martin Geier, a text which CPEB owned (item 367 in BA 1789).

Joseph Schuster

(1748–1812)

NV 1790, p. 121: [no. 319] *"Schuster, (Jos.)* Componist in Dresden. Von *Satzen.* 12. In schwarzen Rahmen, unter Glas."

Engraving by Satze[n] (Carl Salzer?)

References: *GerberL*, 2:476–78

NV 1790 provides too little information for this image to be conclusively identified. Gerber lists an engraving by Medard Thönert after Carl Friedrich Holtzmann as the only available portrait of this size.

Anton Schweitzer

(1735–1787)

NV 1790, p. 121: [no. 320] *"Schweizer, (Anton)* Kapellmeister in Gotha. Von *Liebe.* 12." [PLATE 254]

Engraving by Christian Gottlob August Liebe after Johann Ernst Heinsius; 8.5 x 9 cm

Inscription below image: "ANTON SCHWEIZER."

Production details at left: "Heinsius pinx."; at right: "Liebe sc. Lipsiae"

Location: D-B, Mus. P. Schweizer, Anton I, 1

References: *GerberL*, 2:484–85

Johann Heinrich von Seelen
(1688–1762)

NV 1790, p. 121: [no. 321] "Seelen, (*Joh. Heinr. a*) Lt. Lübeckischer Rector und Schriftsteller. Schwarze Kunst von *Haid. Fol.*"
[PLATE 255]

Mezzotint by Johann Jakob Haid after Jürgen Matthias von der Hude, from Jacob Brucker's *Bildersal heutiges Tages lebender und durch Gelahrtheit berühmter Schrifftsteller . . . .* 8. Zehend (Augsburg, 1750); 31 x 24 cm

Inscription below image: "IOANNES HENRICVS A SEELEN | *S. S. Theolog. Licentiatus et Gymnasii* | *Lubecensis Rector* | *nat. d. 8. Aug. A.° 1688.*"

Production details at left: "Dec. VIII. || von der Hude | pinx."; at right: "I. I. Haid exc. | A. V."

Location: D-W, Port. II 5108

References: *GerberL*, 2:493–94; Mortzfeld, A 20124

Thomas Selle
(1599–1663)

NV 1790, p. 121: [no. 322] "Selle, (*Thomas*) Hamburgischer Musik-Director. Von *Dirksen*. 4. In schwarzen Rahmen, unter Glas." [PLATE 256]

Engraving by Dirk Diricks; 18 x 13 cm

Inscription in oval frame: "THOMAS SELLIUS CERVICCÂ-SAXO. MUSICUS. CHORI MUSICI HAMBURGENSIS DIRECTOR et Ecclesiæ Cathedr. Canonicus m. NATUS AÑO 1599. 23. Martii."

Verse:

> Sellius Aonidum Decus, haud postremus eorum
> Musica qui tractant, exhibet hanc faciem.
> Si pietas, candor, Genius, si scripta probata
> Spectentur, celebrem FAMA per astra vehet.

Production details at bottom right: "DDircksen Hamb: fecit. 1653."

Location: D-B, Mus. P. Selle, Thomas I, 1

References: Cat. Poelchau no. 673; *GerberL*, 2:497–98; Hortschansky 1987, 36, 72–73

Heinrich Christoph Selmer
(1725–1787)

NV 1790, p. 121: [no. 323] *"Selmer, (Heinr-Christ.)* Mecklenb. Schwerinischer Hofrath und vorher *Virtuos* auf der Hoboe. Gezeichnet von *L. A. Abel.* Gr. 4. In schwarzen Rahmen mit goldenem Stäbchen, unter Glas."

Drawing by Leopold August Abel

Lost

References: Cat. Poelchau no. 673a; *GerberL*, 2:498–99

This portrait is listed in Cat. Poelchau no. 673a as a colored drawing (likely a pastel). What appears to be the same item is listed in the card catalogue of the portrait collection in SBB, but is now lost.

Nicolaus Selnecker
(1530–1592)

NV 1790, p. 121: [no. 324] *"Selneccerus, (Nicclaus)* anfänglich Musikus, nachher Superintendent in Leipzig. 4."

References: *GerberL*, 2:499; *GerberNL*, 4:181–82; Leaver 2007, 130

NV 1790 provides too little information for this image to be conclusively identified.

Seneca the younger
(c. 4–65 CE)

NV 1790, p. 121: [no. 325] "*Seneca*, aus Schriften. Von *Krüger*
nach einer alten *Büste*. Gr. *Fol.*" [PLATE 257]
Engraving by Andreas Ludwig Krüger, 1768; plate 11 in Krüger
1769; 25.5 x 21.5 cm
Inscription at base of bust: "LANNŒVS · SENECA:"; below: "Senèque | Marbre
di Carara; Ouvrage Romain du second rang | Dans la Collection de sa Majesté le Roy
de Prusse, à Sans Souci."
Production details at left: "Krüger delineavit et Sculpsit"; at right: "à Sans Souci 1768."
Location: A-Wn, PORT 00135269_02

Senesino (Francesco Bernardi)
(1686–1758)

NV 1790, p. 121: [no. 326] "*Senesino, (F. B.)* Sänger in Dresden.
Schwarze Kunst von *van Hæcken*. *Fol*. In schwarzen Rahmen,
unter Glas." [PLATE 258]
Mezzotint by Alexander van Haecken after Thomas Hudson,
1735; 36 x 25 cm
Inscription at top of frame: "FRANCESCO BERNARDI SENESINO."
Production details at lower left in frame: "THO: HUDSON PINXIT"; at lower
right in frame: "ALEX. VANHAECKEN FE. 1735".; on ledge below frame: a music
book with the title "Giulio Cesare—" open at the aria "Non è si vago e bello" from
Handel's *Giulio Cesare*, Act I, scene vii
Location: D-B, Mus. P. Bernardi, Fr. II, 2
References: Cat. Poelchau no. 69; *GerberL*, 1:145–46 (s.v. "Bernardi")

Franz Seydelmann
(1748–1806)

NV 1790, p. 121: [no. 327] "*Seydelmann, (F.)* Componist in
Dresden. Von *Thönert*. 4. In schwarzen Rahmen, unter Glas."
[PLATE 259]

Engraving by Medard Thönert after Johann Christoph Berkenkamp, 1782; 20 x 14 cm

Inscription below image: "F. SEYDELMANN. | *Churfürstl. Sächsisch Capellmeister.*"

Production details at bottom left: "J. C. Berkenkamp pinx"; at bottom right: "Thoenert sculps Lipsiae"; at bottom center: "zu finden in Leipzig bei A. Kühnel. | (Bureau de Musique)."

Location: D-B, Mus. P. Seydelmann, F. I, 1

References: Cat. Poelchau no. 675; *GerberL*, 2:506

José António Carlos de Seixas
(1704–1742)

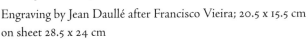

NV 1790, p. 122: [no. 328] "Seyxas, (*J. A. Carlos &*) ein Portugisischer Musikus. Von *Daucke.* 4. In schwarzen Rahmen, unter Glas." [PLATE 260]

Engraving by Jean Daullé after Francisco Vieira; 20.5 x 15.5 cm on sheet 28.5 x 24 cm

Inscription in oval frame: "JOSEPHUS ANTONIUS CARLOS & SEYXAS Vixit Annos 38. Obiit die 25. Augusti Anno 1742."; below image: "*Hanc merui citharam stellis radiantibus addi: Dissona nec vitae moribus illa fuit.*"

Production details at bottom left: "Fr. Vieira del."; at bottom right: "Daullé sculp."

Location: D-B, Mus. P. Seyxas, (Jos. Anton. Carlos de.) I, 1

References: Cat. Poelchau no. 676; *GerberL*, 2:508; *Musiker im Porträt*, 3:60–61

Baptista Siculus
(fl. late fifteenth century)

NV 1790, p. 122: [no. 329] "Siculus, (*Bapt.*) Citharædus incomp. Holzschnitt. 8. In schwarzen Rahmen, unter Glas." [PLATE 261]

Woodcut from Reusner 1589; 10 x 8 cm on sheet 15 x 9 cm

Inscription above image: "BAPTISTA SICVLVS CITHA- | ROEDVS INCOMPAR."; below image: "Da citharam, da plectra, natet Delphinus in vndis, | Da mare, da nautas, Lesbius alter ero.|| VAL. THILO L."

Location: US-I, Petrarch N7575.R44 1589

References: *GerberL*, 1:105 (s.v. "Baptista")

Justus Sieber

(1628–1695)

NV 1790, p. 122: [No. 330] *"Sieber, Von Hæckner. Gr. 8. In
schwarzen Rahmen, unter Glas."* [PLATE 262]

Engraving by Johann Caspar Höckner; 14 x 8.5 cm

Inscription above image: *"Virtute distinguimur."*; below image:
*"Hic lector, radiat per amabilis umbra SIBERT; | Gloria Phœbeis proxima fulget equis. ||
Martinus Stubritius."*

Verse:

> Dieß ist der Schaffe nur von Siebers Angesicht
> Drummuß ich wissentlich sein' hohe Kunst verschweigen.
> Dieselbe kan Unß hier die ädle Zugend [*recte:* Tugend] zeigen
> Es spiel auch wer da will, Herr Sieber ist es nicht.
>> Johann Rist.

Production details at lower left: "Joh. Caspar. Höckner. sculps."

Location: A-Wn, PORT 00085878_01

Christopher Simpson

(1602/6–1669)

NV 1790, p. 122: [no. 331] *"Simpson, (Christoph) Von Faithorne.
Gr. 4. In schwarzen Rahmen, unter Glas."* [PLATE 263]

Engraving by William Faithorne after John Carwarden, from
Simpson's *The Division-Violist* (1659); 22.5 x 16 cm on sheet
21 x 15 cm

Inscription below image: "Christophori Simpson Effigies."; motto under coat of arms:
"NEQUE LUX SINE VMBRA"

Production details at left: "J. Carwarden pinxit."; at right: "Guil: Faithorne sculp:"

Location: London, National Portrait Gallery, NPG D 22934

References: *GerberL*, 2:523

Socrates

NV 1790, p. 122: [no. 332] "*Socrates. Fol.*"

Although NV 1790 does not give detailed information for this print, the item is likely to have been published as plate 3 in Krüger 1769. NV 1790 lists eight of the twelve plates in Krüger 1769; the Socrates image would have been the ninth. The other three, which CPEB may well have owned if he had acquired the complete volume, portray figures less easy to relate to music: Marcus Aurelius, Hypocrates, and Solon (plates 12, 6, and 2, respectively, in Krüger 1769).

Anton Wilhelm Solnitz
(c. 1708–c. 1752/3)

NV 1790, p. 122: [no. 333] "*Solnitz*. Componist in Holland. Von *Tanjé*. 8. In schwarzen Rahmen, unter Glas." [PLATE 264]
Engraving by Pieter Tanjé after H. van der My, 1743; 14 x 9.5 cm on sheet 15 x 10 cm
Inscription below image: "Quem docuit nervis numeros aptare sonoros, | Arte nova et varios Musica cura modos, | SOLNIZIUM genii commendat honore tabella | Quem meritis clarum reddere fama cupit. | Sic studio gratus Batavis, licet advena, terris | Pluribus ut facies nota sit, aere nitet."
Production details at bottom left: "H. vander My pinx. 1743"; at bottom right: "P. Tanjé sculps."
Location: A-Wn, PORT 00156290_01
References: *GerberL*, 2:529

Francisco Soto de Langa
(1534–1619)

NV 1790, p. 122: [no. 334] "*Sotodalanga*, Päpstlicher Sänger. Eine italienische Zeichnung. Kl. 8. In schwarzen Rahmen, unter Glas."
Drawing
Lost

Cyriac Spangenberg
(1528–1604)

NV 1790, p. 122: [no. 335] "*Spangenberg, (Cyriacus) Theol. Histor. und Musikus, Schriftsteller. 4.*" [PLATE 265]

Engraving; 15 x 11 cm

Inscription in oval frame: "*M. CYRIÆCVS SPANGENBER-GIVS THEOLOGVS ET HISTORICVS Natus. 1528. Denatus. 1604.*"

Verse:

> So sah' im Alter aus des Spangenbergs Gesichte,
> Von seinem Erb-Sünd-Streit gibt Zeugniss die Geschichte,
> Die Substanz war ihm Ja, das Accidens ihm Nein,
> Drüm must' er bis in Todt ein Exulante seyn.

Location: A-Wn, PORT 00111497_01

References: *GerberL*, 2:537

Meinrad Spieß
(1683–1761)

NV 1790, p. 122: [no. 336] "*Spies, (Meinrad) P. und Schriftsteller. 8. In schwarzen Rahmen, unter Glas.*" [PLATE 266]

Engraving by Klauber; 15 x 9 cm

Inscription below image: "P. Meinradus Spiess Imp: Monast: | Ursin: O. S. Bened: Prior, Societ: Scien: | Mus: in Germania florentis Socius."

Production details at bottom right: "Klauber Cath. Sc. A. V."

Location: D-B, Mus. P. Spiess, Meinrad I, 2

References: Cat. Poelchau no. 685; *GerberL*, 2:544–45; *Bach-Dokumente* IV, 391, 435

Johann Staden
(1581–1634)

NV 1790, p. 122: [no. 337] "*Staden, (Joh.) Organist in Nürnberg. 8. In schwarzen Rahmen, unter Glas.*" [PLATE 267]

Engraving by Johann Pfann the younger, 1640; 12 x 10 cm on sheet 29 x 18 cm

Inscription above image: "Johannes Staden, Musicus Religiosus, Symphoïsta, | et Organista, ad d. Sebaldi Norib. Natus 1581. Obiit 1634."; in open book held by the sitter: a musical setting of the text "O mensch bedenck d: anfang vnd | wer du bist im außgang"

Verse:

> Qui nunquam vivus pingi, sculpive volebat,
> Stadius, hâc facie sistitur, ecce! tibi.
> Quanta viri at fuerit Pietas, et Musica virtus,
> Proloquitur quodvis, quod dedit ille, melos.

Production details at bottom left: "Ioh. Pfann Sculp: A.° 1640."; at bottom right: "I.V."

Location: D-W, Portr. II 5266

References: GerberL, 2:555; Musiker im Porträt, 2:42–43; Mortzfeld, A 20840

Nicolaus Stenger

(1609–1680)

NV 1790, p. 122: [no. 338] "Stenger, (Nicol.) erst Cantor, zuletzt Professor Theol. in Erfurt. Kl. Fol." [plate 268]

Engraving; 16.5 x 13 cm

Inscription in oval frame: "ADMOD. REVEREND^{US} AT$_{QUE}$ EXCELLENT^{MUS} DN^{US} M. NICOLAUS Stenger, ECCLESIÆ MERCA-TORUM PASTOR, EBR. LING. PROF. PUBLICUS etc. ANNO MDCLXI."; in upper left corner: "Nat. 1609 | 31: Aug."

Verse below:

> En tibi STENGERUM, Patriæ venerabile Lumen,
> cujus vox nectar spirat et ambrosiam.
> Dexteritate valet, seu Templum Sacra docentem,
> sive Professorem docta Lycéa vident.
> Ô benè, si tales, qualem hunc cognovimus arte,
> Consilio, atque fide, semper Hiera ferat!

Production details at lower right: "Deb. Honoris g. f. | M. Samuel Bock P. P."

Location: A-Wn, PORT 00150151_01

References: GerberL, 2:576–77; Leaver 2007, 131

Johann Christoph Stockhausen
(1725–1784)

NV 1790, p. 122: [no. 339] *"Stockhausen, (Joh. Christ.)* M. Schriftsteller. Von *Geyser.* 8." [PLATE 269]
Engraving by Christian Gottlieb Geyser; frontispiece to Georg Friedrich Götz's *Leben Heern Johann Christoph Stockhausens* (1784); 15 x 8.5 cm
Inscription below image: "M. Joh. Christoph Stockhausen | geb: 20 Oct: 1725 | gest: 4 Sept: 1784".
Location: D-B, P. Stockhausen, Joh. Christoph I, 1

This image has been closely cropped; the print originally had production details at lower right corner: "Geyser sc."

Regina Strinasacchi
(1759–1839)

NV 1790, p. 122: [no. 340] *"Strinasacchi, (Mad.)* Violinistinn. Gezeichnet von *Haack.* 4. In goldenen Rahmen, unter Glas."
Drawing by Haack
Lost
References: *GerberL*, 2:433 (s.v. "Schlick"); *GerberNL*, 4:78 (s.v. "Schlick")

Christoph Christian Sturm
(1740–1784)

NV 1790, p. 123: [no. 341] *"Sturm (Christoph Christ.)* Pastor in Hamburg, Lyrischer Dichter. Von *Fritsch.* Gr. 4." [PLATE 270]
Engraving by Johann Christian Gottfried Fritzsch after Andreas Stöttrup, 1784; 19.5 x 15 cm on sheet 23 x 18 cm
Inscription below image: "Christoph Christian Sturm, | Hauptpastor an der Haupt-kirche St. Petri und Scholarch in Hamburg. || Zum Zeichen innigster Hochachtung von Seinem Verehrer und Freunde | Johann Henrich Herold."; on page of open book:

"Betrachtungen | uber die | Werke Gottes | im Reiche der Natur | und der | Vorse-
hung | auf | alle Tage des Jahres || Erste Band . . ."; on page under wreath and quill:
"Herrn Christoph Christian Sturms, | Hauptpastors an der Hauptkirche St. Petri
und Scholarchen in Hamburg, | Geistliche Gesänge | mit | Melodien zum Singen bey
dem Claviere | vom | Herrn Kapellmeister Carl Philipp Emanuel Bach, | Musikdirek-
tor in Hamburg. | Zwyte Sammlung. || Hamburg, | bey Johann Henrich Herold,
1781."

Production details at bottom left: "gezeichnet von A. Stöttrup."; at bottom right:
"gestochen von J. C. G. Fritzsch 1784."

Location: D-W, Portr. I 13179

References: Mortzfeld, A 21461

Johann Georg Sulzer
(1720–1779)

NV 1790, p. 123: [no. 342] "*Sulzer, (Joh. George)* Professor in
Berlin, Schriftsteller. Gemahlt von *Graaf*, gestochen von *Berger*.
8." [PLATE 271]

Engraving by Daniel Berger after Anton Graff, 1779; 14 x 9 cm

Inscription below image: IOHANN GEORGE SULZER | *geb: den 16. Octobr.
1720. gest: den 25. Febr. 1779."

Production details at bottom left: "A. Graff pinxit, 1774."; at bottom right: "D. Berger
sculp. Berolini 1779."

Location: D-B, Mus. P. Sulzer, J. G. I, 1

References: Cat. Poelchau no. 705; *GerberL*, 2:610

Stephanus Kis (Szegedinus)
(1515–1572)

NV 1790, p. 123: [no. 343] "*Szegedinus, (Steph.) Theol.* und
Schriftsteller, wird von *Prætorio* bey Gelegenheit der *Missodiæ*
angeführt. Holzschnitt. 8." [PLATE 272]

Woodcut from Reusner 1589; 10 x 8 cm on sheet 15 x 9 cm

Inscription above image: "STEPHANVS SZEGEDINVS |

Vɴɢᴀʀᴠꜱ Tʜᴇᴏʟᴏɢᴠꜱ.”; below image: “Posthuma Scriptorum proles vitalibus oris |
Me retulit, volito iamque per ora virum. || N. R.”

Location: US-I, Petrarch N7575.R44 1589

References: *GerberL*, 2:613–14; Leaver 2007, 129–30

Giuseppe Tartini
(1692–1770)

NV 1790, p. 123: [no. 344] *“Tartini, (Jos.)* Violinist. Von
Calcinsta. Gr. 4. In schwarzen Rahmen, unter Glas.” [ᴘʟᴀᴛᴇ 273]
Engraving by Carlo Calcinotto, 1761; 20.5 x 13 cm
Inscription in oval frame: “JOSEPH TARTINI”; below: “Hic
fidibus, scriptis, claris hic magnus alumnis, | Cui par nemo fuit, forte nec ullus erit.”;
on sheet music: “Corelli”; on book spines: “ZARLINO | PLATO”
Production details at bottom right: “Carolus Calcinoto Sculp. in Padova.”
Location: D-B, Mus. P. Tartini I, 1
References: *GerberL*, 2:617–624; *Musiker im Porträt*, 3:46–47

Georg Philipp Telemann
(1681–1767)

NV 1790, p. 123: [no. 345] *“Telemann, (George Phil.)* Kapellmeister und Musik-Direc-
tor in Hamburg. Auf *Schiefer* in Gips. In gipsernen Rahmen, unter Glas.”
Plaster relief on slate in plaster frame
Lost
References: *GerberL*, 2:628–35

Carlo Tessarini
(1690–after 1766)

NV 1790, p. 123: [no. 346] *“Tessarini, (Carlo)* Professor, Musikus
und Violinist. Schwarze Kunst von *Pether. Fol.* In schwarzen
Rahmen, unter Glas.” [ᴘʟᴀᴛᴇ 274]

Mezzotint by William Pether after Jan Palthe; 37.5 x 27 cm

Inscription below image: "Carlo Tessarini da Rimini | Professeur de Fiolon en la Metropolitaine d'Urbino."

Production details at left: "J. Palthe pinxit."; at right: "Wm Pether fecit."

Location: D-B, Mus. P. Tessarini, Carlo II, 1

References: Cat. Poelchau no. 717; *GerberL*, 2:640

Zaccaria Tevo
(1651–c. 1709/12)

NV 1790, p. 123: [no. 347] "*Tevo, (F. Z.) Theol. Baccal.* und *Mag. Mus.* in Venedig, Schriftsteller. 4. In schwarzen Rahmen, unter Glas." [PLATE 275]

Engraving; 21 x 14 cm

Inscription in oval frame: "F. ZACHARIAS TEVO SACCENSIS. ADOP. TAR. SAC. THEO. BAC. ET MVSI. MAGIS. AN. IL"; on book held by the sitter: "Musico | Testore"; below: "Quidquid melliflui exoptas ex arte canendi | Cuncta tibi Textor Musicus ecce dabit."

Location: D-B, Mus. P. Tevo, Zach. I, 1

References: Cat. Poelchau no. 718; *GerberL*, 2:642

Gabriel-Vincent Thévenard
(1669–1741)

NV 1790, p. 123: [no. 348] "*Thevenard, (G. V.) Pens. du Roi de France*, ein *Baritonist*. Von *G. F. Schmidt* in Berlin. 8. In schwarzen Rahmen, unter Glas" [PLATE 276]

Engraving by Georg Friedrich Schmidt after Charles Etienne Geuslain; 24 x 16 cm

Inscription below image: "GABRIEL VINCENT THEVENARD | Pension.^re du Roi pour la Musique | Né à Paris, le 10. Août 1669."

Production details at left: "Geuslain Pinx."; at right: "G. F. Schmidt Sculp."; at bottom: "A Paris chez Odieuvre, M.^d d'Estampes, quay del'Ecole vis-à-vis la Samaritaine, à la belle Image. C.P.R."

Location: D-B, Mus. P. Thevenard, Gab. Vinc. I, 1
References: Cat. Poelchau no. 720; *GerberL*, 2:664–65

Salomon van Til
(1643–1713)

NV 1790, p. 123: [no. 349] *"Til, (Salomon van) Dt.* und *Prof.*
Theol. in Leyden. Schriftsteller. 8. In schwarzen Rahmen, unter
Glas." [PLATE 277]

Engraving from *Acta Eruditorum*; 15 x 9.5 cm

Inscription below image: "Salomon van Til. | S. S. Theol. Doct. et Professor in |
Academia Lugduno Batava."

Location: A-Wn, PORT 00111651_01

References: *GerberL*, 1:652

Maria Giustina Turcotti
(c. 1700–after 1763)

NV 1790, p. 123: [no. 350] *"Turcotti, (M. Just.)* Sängerinn im Bayreithschen. Von
Tiepolo in *Carricatur* gezeichnet. *Fol.* In schwarzen Rahmen, unter Glas."

Caricature drawing by Tiepolo

Lost

References: *GerberL*, 2:691; *GerberNL*, 4:739–40

Johann August Unzer
(1727–1799)

NV 1790, p. 124: [no. 351] *"Unzer, (Joh. Aug) Dt.* Schriftsteller,
im Arzt, im 141 Stück von der Musik. Von *Fritsch.* 8."
[PLATE 278]

Engraving by Johann Christian Gottfried Fritzsch, 1768; 13 x
10 cm on sheet 20 x 12 cm

Inscription below image: "D. JOANNES AUGUSTUS | UNZER, Medicus. | Ann: ætat. XXXXII."

Production details at bottom right: "J. C. G. Fritzsch del. et sc: 1768"

Location: D-W, Portr. I 13790.1

References: *GerberL*, 2:700; Mortzfeld, A 22524

Nicolas Vallet

(1583–after 1642)

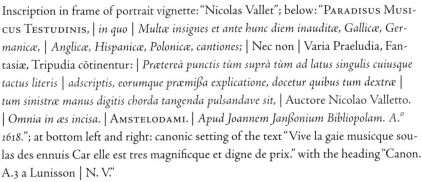

NV 1790, p. 124: [no. 352] *"Valet, (Nicol.) Lautenist. Fol. oblongo. In schwarzen Rahmen, unter Glas."* [PLATE 279]

Engraving by Joannes Berwinckel after David Vinckeboons; title page from Vallet's *Paradisus Musicus Testudinis* (1618); 13 x 20.5 cm

Inscription in frame of portrait vignette: "Nicolas Vallet"; below: "PARADISUS MUSI-CUS TESTUDINIS, | in quo | *Multæ insignes et ante hunc diem inauditæ, Gallicæ, Germanicæ,* | *Anglicæ, Hispanicæ, Polonicæ, cantiones;* | Nec non | *Varia Praeludia, Fantasiæ, Tripudia côtinentur:* | *Prætereà punctis tùm suprà tùm ad latus singulis cuiusque tactus literis* | *adscriptis, eorumque præmißa explicatione, docetur quibus tum dextræ* | *tum sinistræ manus digitis chorda tangenda pulsandave sit,* | Auctore Nicolao Valletto. | *Omnia in æs incisa.* | AMSTELODAMI. | *Apud Joannem Janßonium Bibliopolam. A.*° *1618.*"; at bottom left and right: canonic setting of the text "Vive la gaie musicque sou-las des ennuis Car elle est tres magnificque et digne de prix." with the heading "Canon. A.3 a Lunisson | N. V."

Production details at left: "Davit Vinckebons inuentor"; at right: "Ioan. Berwinckel sculpsit"

Location: A-Wn, PORT 00015480_01

References: *GerberL*, 2:706–7

Georg Venzky

(1704–1757)

NV 1790, p. 124: [no. 353] *"Venzky, (George) Dt. und Rector in Prenzlau, Schriftsteller. 8."* [PLATE 280]

Engraving from L. C. Mizler's *Neu eröffnete musikalische Bibliothek*, 2 (1743); 14 x 18.5 cm

Inscription below image: "GE. VENZKY. | S. S. Th. Doct. Gymnas. Primisi. Rect. | *Membrum Societ. regiar. Regiomonti | honorarium et Gryphisio Lips. et musicalium | veritatum ordinarium.*"

Production details at bottom left: "v. P pinxit."

Location: D-B, Mus. P. Venzky, Ge. I, 1

References: *GerberL*, 2:718

Daniel Vetter
(1657/8–1721)

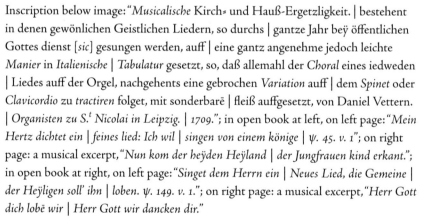

NV 1790, p. 124: [no. 354] "*Vetter, (Daniel)* Organist in Leipzig. Von *M. Ph. Fol. oblongo.* In schwarzen Rahmen, unter Glas." [PLATE 281]

Engraving; title page to *Musicalische Kirch= und HaußErgetzligkeit* (1709); 29 x 15 cm

Inscription below image: "*Musicalische* Kirch= und Hauß-Ergetzligkeit. | bestehent in denen gewönlichen Geistlichen Liedern, so durchs | gantze Jahr beÿ öffentlichen Gottes dienst [*sic*] gesungen werden, auff | eine gantz angenehme jedoch leichte *Manier* in Italienische | *Tabulatur* gesetzt, so, daß allemahl der *Choral* eines iedweden | Liedes auff der Orgel, nachgehents eine gebrochen *Variation* auff | dem *Spinet* oder *Clavicordio* zu *tractiren* folgt, mit sonderbarē | fleiß auffgesetzt, von Daniel Vettern. | *Organisten zu S.ᵗ Nicolai in Leipzig.* | 1709."; in open book at left, on left page: "*Mein Hertz dichtet ein | feines lied: Ich wil | singen von einem könige | ψ. 45. v. 1*"; on right page: a musical excerpt, "*Nun kom der heÿden Heÿland | der Jungfrauen kind erkant.*"; in open book at right, on left page: "*Singet dem Herrn ein | Neues Lied, die Gemeine | der Heÿligen soll' ihn | loben. ψ. 149. v. 1.*"; on right page: a musical excerpt, "*Herr Gott dich lobē wir | Herr Gott wir dancken dir.*"

Production details at bottom left: "Zu finden beÿ dem Autore,"; at bottom right: "M.B. sc."

Location: D-B, Mus. P. Vetter, I, 1

References: Cat. Poelchau no. 731; *GerberL*, 2:722; Leaver 2007, 124

Leonardo da Vinci

(1452–1519)

NV 1790, p. 124: [no. 355] *"Vintius, (Leonhardus)* Mayländischer Violinist und Mahler. Holzschnitt. 8." [PLATE 282]

Woodcut from Reusner 1589; 10 x 8 cm on sheet 15 cm x 9 cm

Inscription above image: LEONARDVS VINTIVS |
FLORENT. PICTOR."; below image: "Laudis Apellææ metuit sua sidera fulgor | Sospite me vinci, me moriente mori. | VAL. THILO L. || ANDREAS."

Location: US-I, Petrarch N7575.R44 1589

References: *GerberL*, 2:730–31; *GerberNL*, 4:451

A German Violinist [possibly Gottlob Harrer] and an Italian Secretary

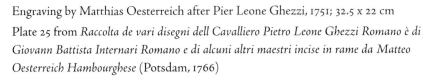

NV 1790, p. 124: [no. 356] *"Violinist,* ein Deutscher und ein italienischer Secretär. Von *Oesterreich* in *Carricatur. Fol."* [PLATE 283]

Engraving by Matthias Oesterreich after Pier Leone Ghezzi, 1751; 32.5 x 22 cm

Plate 25 from *Raccolta de vari disegni dell Cavalliero Pietro Leone Ghezzi Romano è di Giovann Battista Internari Romano e di alcuni altri maestri incise in rame da Matteo Oesterreich Hambourghese* (Potsdam, 1766)

Inscription:

> Vomini sono di Cervello fresco,
> Nella Profession di gusto vario,
> L'uno in Musica esperto, ed è Tedesco,
> L'altro Italiano dotto Segretario.

Below verse: "Il Disegno Originale si conserva nel Gabinetto di Sua Ecc.za | Monsignore Conte de Brühl Primo Ministro di Sua Maestà | IL RÈ DI POLONIA ELETTORE DI SASSONIA."

Production details at left: "Cavalliere Pietro Leone Ghezzi disegnò"; at right: "Matteo Oesterreich jncise Roma. 1751."; within frame at lower right, in reverse: "Oesterreich Sculpsit Roma 1751"

Location: US-CAh, Typ 720.66.423 F

References: Rostirolla, 181–82, 379–80; Heartz 2003, 331

The index to Oesterreich's 1766 publication identifies the two figures portrayed here as "Il Signor, Consigliere de' Rossi, è il Musico, Haar." Ghezzi's annotation to the drawing on which the engraving is based, dated 18 June 1739, gives more detailed information about the musician: "Composer of music and player of the violin of German nationality, who was in the service of the Prince Elector of Poland and was very fine, and who favored me by coming to my musical academy." (Compositor di musica e sonator di violino di natione tedesco il quale stava al servitio del signor principe elettorale di Polonia et era bravo assai, il quale mi favoriva di venire alla mia accademia di musica.) The violinist and composer "Haar" is likely Gottlob Harrer (1703–1755), who served the Saxon prime minister Count von Brühl from 1731 to 1750 and would have been with him in Rome in 1739. Harrer was J.S. Bach's successor in Leipzig in 1750. Further corroboration for this identification is given by Ernst Florens Friedrich Chladni in his "Beyträge zu dem Gerberschen Tonkünstler-Lexicon," *Journal der Tonkunst*, 2. Stück (Erfurt and Braunschweig, 1795), 201.

Virgil
(70–19 BCE)

NV 1790, p. 124: [no. 357] *"Virgilius, (Maro) aus Schriften. Von Krüger nach einer alten Büste. Gr. Fol."*
Engraving by Andreas Ludwig Krüger, 1769; plate 9 in Krüger 1769
Location: D-B, 2° Ns 4811

Tomaso Antonio Vitali
(1663–1745)

NV 1790, p. 124: [no. 358] *"Vitali, (Thomaso)* Violinist, Lehrmeister des *Pat. Martini* auf der Geige. Italienische Zeichnung. 8. In schwarzen Rahmen, unter Glas." [PLATE 284]
Drawing in black chalk on white paper; 12.5 x 9 cm

Annotation in CPEB's hand, in dark ink: "Tomaso Vitali, | gran Sonator | di Violino | e famoso Com | positore."

Location: D-B, Mus. P. Vitali, Tommaso I, 1

Provenance: CPEB's estate—Georg Poelchau—SBB (1841)

References: Cat. Poelchau no. 738; *GerberL*, 2:733

Antonio Vivaldi
(1678–1741)

NV 1790, p. 124: [no. 359] *"Vivaldi, (Anton)* Violinist und Kapellmeister in Venedig am Hospital *della Pietà.* Von *la Cave.* 4. In schwarzen Rahmen, unter Glas." [PLATE 285]

Engraving by Francois Morellon de la Cave, 1725; 26 x 20 cm

Inscription below image: "EFFIGIES ANTONII VIVALDI."

Production details at bottom right: "F. M. la Cave Sculpsit 1725"

Location: D-B, Mus. P. Vivaldi, Ant. I, 2

References: Cat. Poelchau no. 739; *GerberL*, 2:736–39; *Bach-Dokumente* IV, 388, 432; *Musiker im Porträt,* 3:22–23

Georg Joseph Vogler
(1749–1814)

NV 1790, p. 124: [no. 360] *"Vogler, (George Jos.)* Churpfalz-bayerscher Kapellmeister. In einer sehr gut getroffenen *Büste,* in Lebensgröße, von Gips."

Life-sized plaster bust

Lost

References: *GerberL*, 2:73–76

Gerhard Johann Voss
(1577–1649)

NV 1790, p. 124: [no. 361] *"Vossius, (Gerh. Joh.)* Professor zu Amsterdamm, Schriftsteller. 16." [PLATE 286]

Woodcut from Paulus Freher's *Theatrum virorum eruditione clarorum* (Nuremberg, 1688)

Inscription below image: "GERHARDUS IOH. VOSSIUS | *Eloquent. Prof. Ludg. Batav.*"

Location: A-Wn, PORT 00150079_03

References: *GerberL*, 2:750–51

Christoph Thomas Walliser
(1568–1648)

NV 1790, p. 125: [no. 362] "*Walliser, (Christ. Thom.) Mag.* und Componist in Strasburg. Von *Heyden.* 8. In schwarzen Rahmen, unter Glas." [PLATE 287]

Engraving by Jacob van der Heyden, 1625; 18.5 x 12 cm

Inscription above image: "EFFIGIES VIRI CLARISSIMI, DN. M. CHRI⸗ | STOPHORI THOMÆ WALLISERI, ARGENTORATENSIS, | PRÆCEP-TORIS IN GYMNASIO PATRIO FIDELISSIMI, | ET MUSICI ORDI-NARII. CELEBERRIMI."; at upper left corner: "Anno Christi | M. D. C. XXV."; at upper right corner: "Ætatis suæ | LVII."; below: "*Orphea miraris? Miraris Ariona? Thracum | qvòd resonâ traherent saxa ferásque, lyrâ? | WALLISER hic potiùs mirandus; Nam trahit ad se | Europam totam, totam Asiam; et Libyam. || M. Casp. Brülovius P. C. | Poët. Prof. et Gymnas.*"

Production details at bottom left: "Iacob, ab Heydē sculpsit ad vivum."

Location: D-B, Mus. P. Walliser, Chr. Tom. I, 1

References: Cat. Poelchau no. 746; *GerberL*, 2:760–61

Thomas Christian Walther
(1749–1788)

NV 1790, p. 125: [no. 363] "*Walther,* Secretär, Componist und Director des Königl. Theaters in Kopenhagen. Eine Zeichnung von *Hardrich.* 4. In goldenen Rahmen, unter Glas." [PLATE 288]

Drawing by Hardrich in black and colored chalk on vellum; 19 x 15 cm

On verso, in Poelchau's hand, in upper right corner: "G. Poelchau"; along bottom edge: "Walther, Komponist u. ehemaliger Director des kopenhageners Theater. Gezeichnet von Hardrich. Aus der Bachschen Sammlung."

Location: D-B, Mus. P. Walther, I, 1

Provenance: CPEB's estate—Georg Poelchau—SBB (1841)

References: Cat. Poelchau no. 748; GerberL, 2:762

Other drawings by Hardrich in CPEB's collection are Mme Benda (no. 47) and Antonio Lolli (no. 210). The latter is similar in format and medium to this portrait, and was likely made at about the same time, probably in Hamburg.

Silvius Leopold Weiss
(c. 1687–1750)

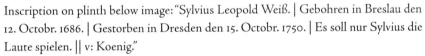

NV 1790, p. 125: [no. 364] "Weiss. (Sylvius Leopold) Königl. Polnischer und Churfürstl. Sächsischer Lautenist in Dresden. Von *Folick*. 8. In schwarzen Rahmen, unter Glas." [PLATE 289]

Engraving by Bartolomeo Folin after Balthasar Denner; 19 x 13 cm

Inscription on plinth below image: "Sylvius Leopold Weiß. | Gebohren in Breslau den 12. Octobr. 1686. | Gestorben in Dresden den 15. Octobr. 1750. | Es soll nur Sylvius die Laute spielen. || v: Koenig."

Production details at left: "B: Denner pinx:"; at right: "B: Folin sc:"

Location: D-B, Mus. P. Weiß I, 1

References: Cat. Poelchau no. 759; GerberL, 2:790; *Bach-Dokumente* IV, 388, 431; *Musiker im Porträt*, 3:42–43; Leaver 2007, 126

Johann Wellter
(1614–1666)

NV 1790, p. 125: [no. 365] "Wellter, (Joh.) Stadtmusikus und Lautenist in Nürnberg. Von *Leonart*. 4." [PLATE 290]

Engraving by Johann Friedrich Leonart, 1668; 12.5 x 10 cm on sheet 30 x 12.5 cm

Inscription below image: "Johann Wellter Stadt *Musicus* in Nürnberg, | ward ge-
bohren A.° 1614 starb A.° 1666"

Verse:

> Zuvor war ich ein Holtz, und hörte Orfeus Lieder;
> Jetzt bin ich eine Laut', und Orfeus hört mich wieder:
> So sprach diß Seitenspiel, in unsers Wellters Hand.
> Sein Nam ihn Orfeus nennt, dem Wellter zugerañt.

At upper left on scroll of paper: "Dießes wenige | machte zu freundl. | angedencken. |
J. F. Leonart Anno 1668."; at lower right of scroll: "28"

Location: D-W, Port. II 5887

References: *GerberL*, 2:793; *GerberNL*, 4:542–43; Mortzfeld, A 23710

Carl August Friedrich Westenholz
(1736–1789)

NV 1790, p. 124: [no. 366] "*Westenholz, (Carl Aug.)* Kapellmeister in Ludwigslust.
Kniestück in *Miniatur* gemahlt. In goldenen Rahmen, unter Glas."

Miniature; likely a pendant to no. 367

Lost

References: *GerberL*, 2:801–2

Barbara Lucietta Fricemelica Westenholz (née Affabili)
(1725–1776)

NV 1790, p. 125: [no. 367] "*Westenholz, (Mad. Affabali)* des vorigen erste Gattinn,
Sängerinn. Kniestück in *Miniatur* gemahlt. In goldenen Rahmen, unter Glas."

Miniature; likely a pendant to no. 366

Lost

References: *GerberL*, 1:14 (s.v. "Affabali")

Christian Friedrich Wilisch

(1684–1759)

NV 1790, p. 125: [no. 368] *"Wilisch, (Christ. Fried) Dt. und Pastor in Freyberg. Schriftsteller. 8."* [PLATE 291]

Engraving by Martin Bernigeroth; frontispiece to *Acta Eruditorum* (Leipzig, 1731); 14.5 x 9 cm on sheet 16.5 x 9.5 cm

Inscription below image: "Christianus Fridericus Wilisch, | S. S. Theol. Doctor, Pastor Primar: | Ecclesiar. Freibergensium vicinarumque | Superintendens."

Location: D-W, Portr. I 14571

References: *GerberL*, 2:814; Mortzfeld, A 24019

Ernst Wilhelm Wolf

(1735–1792)

NV 1790, p. 125: [no. 369] *"Wolf, (Ernst Wilh.) Kapellmeister in Waimar. Gr. 4. In schwarzen Rahmen, unter Glas."* [PLATE 292]

Engraving, with additions in ink and watercolor, from Johann Caspar Lavater's *Physiognomische Fragmente zur Beförderung der Menschenkenntnis und Menschenliebe*, 4 (Leipzig and Winterthur, 1778); 25.5 x 20 cm

Inscription below image: engraved "W."; in ink, in Lavater's hand: "olf."; at bottom: "Musikalisch Talent—Reichhaltig, leicht, und lebendig."

Location: D-B, Mus. P. Wolf, Ernst Wilh. I, 1

References: Cat. Poelchau no. 773; Lavater, *Physiognomische Fragmente*, 4:373–74; *GerberL*, 2:824–27; Schmid 1988, 518

Wilhelm Xylander

(1532–1576)

NV 1790, p. 125: [no. 370] *"Xylander, (Gvieliel) Musikus und Schriftsteller. Holzschnitt. 8."* [PLATE 293]

Woodcut from Reusner 1587; 10 x 8 cm on sheet 15 x 9 cm

Inscription above image: "GVILIELMVS XYLANDER. |

Philologus."; below image: "Quàm benè Plutarchi Græcè sonat antè: Latinè | Per me nunc loquitur tam benè Musa mei. | M. D. LXXV."

References: *GerberL*, 2:834–35; Lemmer 1973, 484

Friedrich Wilhelm Zachariä
(1726–1777)

NV 1790, p. 125: [no. 371] *"Zachariæ, (Fried. Wilh.)* Professor in Braunschweig, Componist. 8. In schwarzen Rahmen, unter Glas." [PLATE 294]

Engraving by Christian Gottlieb Geyser; 17 x 13 cm

Inscription below image: "F.W. ZACHARIAE."

Location: D-B, Mus. P. Zachariae, Fr. W. I, 1

References: Cat. Poelchau no. 776; *GerberL*, 2:837–38; *CPEB-Briefe*, 2:1042, 1049; *CPEB-Letters*, 215, 218

Maximilian Zeidler
(1680–1745)

NV 1790, p. 126: [no. 372] *"Zeidler, (Maxim.)* Kapellmeister in Nürnberg. Von *Heumann. Fol.* In schwarzen Rahmen, unter Glas." [PLATE 295]

Engraving by Georg Daniel Heumann; 34.5 x 24.5 cm

Inscription below image: "MAXIMILIAN ZEIDLER | CAPELL DIERECTOR | IN NÜRNBERG."

Production details at bottom: "Monument d'une Veritable affection, par George Danieli, Heümann sc:"

Location: D-B, Mus. P. Zeidler, Maximilian II, 1

References: Cat. Poelchau no. 779; *GerberL*, 2:844–45

Georg Bernhard Leopold Zeller
(1728–1803)

NV 1790, p. 126: [no. 373] *"Zeller,* Concertmeister in Strelitz. In Oel von *Cogho.* 1 Fuß, 9 Zoll hoch, 15 Zoll breit. In goldenen Rahmen."
Oil painting by Johann Samuel Cogho; c. 53 x 38 cm
Lost
References: *GerberL,* 2:847

Johann Samuel Cogho was a cellist and a painter at the court of Mecklenburg-Strelitz; he was also the owner of a fine collection of engravings. CPEB owned another painting by him, a portrait in oils of Cogho's wife, the soprano Therese Petrini (see no. 81).

Johann Gotthilf Ziegler
(1688–1747)

NV 1790, p. 126: [no. 374] *"Ziegler, (Joh. Gotthilf)* Musik-Director in Halle. Gezeichnet von *Joh. Seb. Bach.* Gr. Fol. In schwarzen Rahmen, unter Glas."
Drawing by Johann Sebastian Bach the younger, possibly a copy of no. 375
Lost

✳ ✳ ✳

NV 1790, p. 126: [no. 375] "Derselbe in Oel. 2 Fuß, 9 Zoll hoch, 2 Fuß, 3 Zoll breit. In goldenen Rahmen."
Oil painting; c. 84 x 68.5 cm
Lost
References: *GerberL,* 2:850–51; *GerberNL,* 4:643–44

Theodor Zwinger the elder
(1533–1588)

NV 1790, p. 126: [no. 376] *"Zvingerus, (Theodor) Medic. & Mus. peritus.* Holzschnitt. 8" [PLATE 296]

Woodcut from Reusner 1589; 10 x 8 cm on sheet 15 x 9 cm

Inscription above image: "THEODORVS ZVINGERVS | Basil. Medicvs.";
below image: "Quæ mihi Zuingeri mentem, quæ pectoris artes | Pinget, & ô terras
pinget & astra manus. | V. T. L. || Trinv-"

Location: US-I, Petrarch N7575.R44 1589

References: *GerberL*, 2:358–59

Nicolaus Zygmuntowski
(c. 1771–c. 1782/86)

NV 1790, p. 126: [no. 377] *"Zygmantowsky, (Nicol.)* Virtuos auf
dem Violoncell; ein Kind von 6¾ Jahren. Von *Satzen.* Gr. 4."
[PLATE 297]

Engraving by Satze[n] (Carl Salzer?); 21 x 16 cm

Inscription below image: "Nicolaus Zygmuntowski | Ein Kind von 6¾ Jahren Virtuos
in Violino≈Zello."

Production details at lower right: "Nach dem Leben gezeichnet u: gestochē von C:
Satzen"

Location: D-B, Mus. P. Zygmuntowski, Nicolaus I, 1

References: *GerberL*, 2:860; *GerberNL*, 4:658

APPENDIX A

This appendix lists the "little collection of musical silhouettes" (eine kleine Sammlung Musikalischer Silhouetten) in NV 1790 (pp. 126–28). What is immediately distinctive and striking about this collection, in comparison to C. P. E. Bach's portrait gallery, is the number of younger composers and musicians included. This probably reflects the vogue for silhouette portraits in the last quarter of the eighteenth century, when Bach and his family also had their silhouettes done (see appendix B). Unfortunately, it is not possible to identify all of the musicians listed, and only half of the silhouettes can be identified. Twelve were published in a volume by Heinrich Philipp Bossler in 1784 as *Schattenrisse berühmter Tonsetzer* (see Schneider 1985, 260). Bach probably owned a copy of this book, perhaps as a gift from Bossler himself, who had published some of Bach's music in *Blumenlese* and other anthologies. But we cannot be absolutely sure that these silhouettes were the ones Bach owned. For example, silhouettes of Neefe and Hiller were also published in the *Taschenbuch für die Schaubühne auf das Jahr 1778*, edited by H. A. O. Reichard (Gotha, 1785), and a silhouette of Mozart was engraved by Hieronymus Löschenkohl for his *Musik- und Theater-Almanach* (Vienna, 1785). Bossler's *Schattenrisse* was originally published in black and white; the hand-colored frames presented here are not necessarily representative of the exemplars owned by Bach. Some of the other silhouettes were probably given to Bach by his students, friends, and admirers—including the Dušeks and Mašeks from Prague. A number of them are musicians from Copenhagen, who might have met Bach in Hamburg or come to his attention through his former student, Niels Schiørring.

EINE KLEINE SAMMLUNG MUSIKALISCHER SILHOUETTEN.

Charlotte Wilhelmine Franzisca (Minna) Brandes
(1765–1788)

NV 1790, p. 126: [no. 1] "*Demoiselle Minna Brandes*, Sängerinn und Schauspielerinn."
References: *GerberL*, 1:197–98

Carlo Concialini
(1744–1812)

NV 1790, p. 126: [no. 2] "Herr *Concialini*, Sänger in Königl. Preußischen Diensten."
See main catalogue, no. 82 (plate 61)
References: *GerberL*, 1:294–95

Marianne Crux
(1774–after 1807)
NV 1790, p. 126: [no. 3] "*Demoiselle Crux*, Violinistinn."
References: *GerberL*, 1:315; *GerberNL*, 1:829

Herr Daemen

NV 1790, p. 127: [no. 4] "Herr *Daemen*, Musikus in Copenhagen."

Johann Philipp Degen
(1728–1789)

NV 1790, p. 127: [no. 5] "Herr *Joh. Phil. Degen*."
References: *GerberL*, 1:329–30

František Xaver Dušek (Duschek)
(1731–1799)

NV 1790, p. 127: [no. 6] "Herr *Duscheck*, Musikus in Prag."
References: *GerberL*, 1:365–66; *GerberNL*, 1:965–66

Josefa Dušková (Duschek)
(1754–1824)

NV 1790, p. 127: [no. 7] "*Madame Duscheck, dessen Gattin, Sängerinn.*"
See main catalogue, no. 98
References: *GerberL*, 1:366; *GerberNL*, 1:966

Hans Adolf Friedrich von Eschstruth
(1756–1792)

NV 1790, p. 127: [no. 8] "Herr Freyherr *von Eschstruth*, Componist in Kassel."
See main catalogue, nos. 105–6 (plate 79)
References: *GerberL*, 1:386–88; *GerberNL*, 2:51

Carl Friedrich Christian Fasch
(1736–1800)

NV 1790, p. 127: [no. 9] "Herr *Carl Fasch*, Königl. Preußischer Kammermusikus."
See main catalogue, no. 113 (plate 86)
References: *GerberL*, 1:399; *GerberNL*, 2:77–89

Wilhelm Hans Rudolph Rosenkrantz Giedde
(1756–1816)

NV 1790, p. 127: [no. 10] "Herr. *W.H.R.R. von Giedde* in Kopenhagen."
References: *GerberNL*, 2:325; Inge Bittman, *Catalogue of Giedde's Music Collection in the Royal Library of Copenhagen* ([Copenhagen]: Edition Egtved, 1976)

Franz Kreibich
(1728–1797)

NV 1790, p. 127: [no. 11] "Herr *Greibich*, Componist." [PLATE 1]
References: *GerberL*, 1:757; *GerberNL*, 3:111; Schneider 1985, 114

[Johann] Hartmann
(fl. 1768–1791)

NV 1790, p. 127: [no. 12] "Herr *Hartmand*."
References: *GerberL*, 2:511

Johann Adam Hiller
(1728–1804)

NV 1790, p. 127: [no. 13] "Herr *Hiller*, Kapellmeister und Componist." [PLATE 2]
See main catalogue, no. 166 (plate 127)
References: *GerberL*, 1:636–48; *GerberNL*, 2:674–78; Schneider 1985, 115

Joseph Kämpfer

NV 1790, p. 127: [no. 14] "Herr *Joseph Kempfer*, Contrabaßist."
References: *GerberL*, 2:703–4; *GerberNL*, 3:36

Leopold Kozeluch
(1747–1818)

NV 1790, p. 127: [no. 15] "Herr *Kozeluch*, Componist." [PLATE 3]
References: *GerberL*, 1:749–51; *GerberNL*, 3:99–100; Schneider 1985, 116

Johann Georg Lang
(c. 1722–1798)

NV 1790, p. 127: [no. 16] "Herr *J. G. Lang*, Componist."
[PLATE 4]
References: *GerberL*, 1:784; Schneider 1985, 117

[Peter] Lem
(1753–?)

NV 1790, p. 127: [no. 17] "Herr *Lem*."
References: *GerberL*, 3:211

Vincenc Mašek
(1755–1831)

NV 1790, p. 127: [no. 18] "Herr *Mascheck* aus Prag,"

Johanna Mašek

NV 1790, p. 127: [no. 19] "*Madame Mascheck*, dessen Gattinn, (spielen beyde die Harmonica.)"
References: *CPEB-Briefe*, 2:1224, 1226; *CPEB-Letters*, 268; *GerberL*, 1:896; *GerberNL*, 3:349–50

Wolfgang Amadeus Mozart
(1756–1791)

NV 1790, p. 127: [no. 20] "Herr *Mozard*. Componist." [PLATE 5]
References: *GerberL*, 1:977–79; *GerberNL*, 3:475–98; *Mozart and His World in Contemporary Pictures*, ed. Otto Erich Deutsch (Kassel: Bärenreiter, 1961), 18, plate 14; Schneider 1985, 113

Christian Friedrich Müller
(1752–1827)

NV 1790, p. 127: [no. 21] "Herr *Müller*, Violinist in Königl. Schwedischen Diensten."
References: *GerberL*, 1981–82

Carolina Fredrika Müller
(1755–1826)

NV 1790, p. 127: [no. 22] "*Madame Müller*, dessen Gattinn, Sängerinn und Schaus-pielerinn in Königl. schwedischen Diensten."
See main catalogue, no. 245 (plate 192)
References: *GerberL*, 1:980–81

Johann Gottlieb Naumann
(1741–1801)

NV 1790, p. 128: [no. 23] "Herr *Naumann*."
References: *GerberL*, 2:6–12; *GerberNL*, 3:548–59

Christian Gottlob Neefe
(1748–1798)

NV 1790, p. 128: [no. 24] "Herr *Neefe*, Componist." [PLATE 6]
See main catalogue, no. 248 (plate 195)
References: *GerberL*, 2:13–16; *GerberNL*, 3:563–65; Schneider 1985, 118

Peter Paulsen

NV 1790, p. 128: [no. 25] "Herr *Paulsen*, Organist in Flensburg."
References: *GerberL*, 2:85

Ignace Joseph Pleyel
(1757–1831)

NV 1790, p. 128: [no. 26] "Herr *Ign. Pleyel*, Componist."
[PLATE 7]
References: *GerberL*, 2:160–64; *GerberNL*, 3:733–39; Schneider
1985, 119

Christian Wilhelm Pobielsky

NV 1790, p. 128: [no. 27] "Herr *Podbielsky*."
References: *GerberL*, 2:164–65

Antonio Rosetti
(1750–1792)

NV 1790, p. 128: [no. 28] "Herr *Rosetti*, Componist." [PLATE 8]
References: *GerberL*, 2:324–25; Schneider 1985, 120

[Christian Gottlieb] Sauppe

NV 1790, p. 128: [no. 29] "Herr *Sauppe*. Cantor in Hadersleben."
References: *GerberL*, 2:395

Joseph Aloys Schmittbaur
(1718–1809)

NV 1790, p. 128: [no. 30] "Herr *Schmittbaur*, Componist."
[PLATE 9]
References: *GerberL*, 2:439–41; Schneider 1985, 121

Christian Friedrich Daniel Schubart
(1739–1791)

NV 1790, p. 128: [no. 31] "Herr *Schubart*, Componist." [PLATE 10]
See main catalogue, no. 317 (plate 252)
References: *GerberL*, 2:458–60; Schneider 1985, 122

Maddalena Laura Sirmen
(1745–1818)

NV 1790, p. 128: [no. 32] "*Madame Syrmen*, Violinistinn und Sängerinn. Ganze Figur auf gelben Altlas."
References: *GerberL*, 2:524

Joseph Anton Steffan
(1726–1797)

NV 1790, p. 128: [no. 33] "Herr *Steffan*. Componist." [PLATE 11]
References: *GerberL*, 2:577–78 (s.v. "Stephan"); *GerberNL*, 4:254–57; Schneider 1985, 123

Johann Baptist Vanhal
(1739–1813)

NV 1790, p. 128: [no. 34] "Herr *Johann Wanhal*. Componist." [PLATE 12]
References: *GerberL*, 2:767–68; Schneider 1985, 124

Johann Georg Witthauer
(1751–1802)

NV 1790, p. 128: [no. 35] "Herr *Witthauer*, Musikus in Berlin."
References: *GerberL*, 2:821–22; *GerberNL*, 4:596

Herr Zeyer

NV 1790, p. 128: [no. 36] "Herr *Zeyer*."

Hans Heinrich Zielche
(1741–1802)

NV 1790, p. 128: [no. 37] "Herr *H. H. Zielche*."
References: *GerberL*, 2:852

Acknowledgments

I want to thank Hans Schneider for allowing us to reproduce the silhouettes from Heinrich Philipp Bossler's *Schattenrisse berühmter Tonsetzer,* and Matthias Röder for helping to identify some of the obscure musicians.

Paul Corneilson

APPENDIX B

This appendix contains the surviving portraits of Carl Philipp Emanuel Bach and his family, none of which are listed in NV 1790.[1] The only portrait of C. P. E. Bach that is listed in NV 1790 (no. 31), a plaster bust ("in Gips") by Schubart, is lost or missing. Bach's daughter, Anna Carolina Philippina, sent this to J. J. H. Westphal on 15 June 1798.[2] Obviously, his widow and daughter wanted to keep some of the portraits of him (see below), but it is unlikely that the family owned all the paintings and engravings included here.

We are fortunate that portraits survive of Bach from each stage of his life. Only one is lost.[3] The number of surviving portraits—all but the last two presented here were done during his lifetime—bear witness to the fame of the composer. Charles Burney left us one of the few verbal descriptions of Bach, after meeting him in Hamburg in 1772: "He is now fifty nine, rather short in stature, with black hair and eyes, and brown complexion, has a very animated countenance, and is of a chearful and lively disposition."[4] We may also have a musical self-portrait in the form of a character piece, Wq 117/27, which he had originally titled "La Bach" and later changed to the more fanciful "L'Aly Rupalich."[5] Were it not for his early death in 1778 in Rome, Bach's artist son might well have done his father's portrait.[6]

---

1. Wotquenne includes six of the portraits in his catalogue as items 273–78.

2. "Von den verzeichneten Bildnissen [NV 1790] bitte ich das von meinem lieben seel. Vater / in Gips / zu seinem Andenken anzunehmen; . . ." Schmid 1988, 518.

3. According to *GerberNL*, 4:735 (Anhang II): "Bach (Carl Phil. Em.) in Oel vom Kanzleyrath Brünnich 1772 sehr ähnlich gemalt. Er sitzt, mit einem Notenblatte, worauf das von Reichardt (s. Th. II. S. 22. seiner Briefe die Mus. betr.) eingerückte B.A.C.H. steht. Es befand sich in des verstorbenen Schiörrings Sammlung, auf dessen Bitte Bach auch seinen Namen so in Musik gesetzt hatte."

4. Burney 1775, 2:271.

5. See the introduction to CPEB:CW, I/8.2, xiv–xvii, on the identity of other musical portraits Bach created in his "petites pièces pour le clavecin."

6. Although J. S. Bach the younger was primarily a landscape artist, he did make copies of two portraits (Buffardin and Mingotti) for his father's collection, as well as an oil painting of C. F. Abel, and drawings of Padre Martini and J. G. Ziegler (all lost).

The earliest extant portrait of Bach is a pastel by one of his Meiningen cousins, Gottlieb Friedrich Bach (plate 1), depicting the teenaged musician who was still living with his family in Leipzig. (A similar portrait of the young Wilhelm Friedemann, probably by the same artist, also survives from around the same time.) The next portrait, probably by Johann Friedrich Reiffenstein (plate 2), dates from mid-career, around Bach's fortieth birthday. He refers to this painting several years later, in a letter to Forkel of 20 April 1774:

> Who then, painted the portrait of me that you own? Perhaps it is a copy by Herr Reiffenstein, who painted me in Kassel in 1754 with dry colors. Perhaps I will be fortunate enough to present to you soon a clean engraving of my portrait, if it would be of value to you. The one you have does not have wrinkles, but the one I hope to send you will have all the more.[7]

The later portrait Bach mentions is probably the one from 1773 by Johann Philipp Bach, which C.P.E. Bach refers to in the family genealogy he sent to Forkel:

> The son [Gottlieb Friedrich Bach] of the Capellmeister of Meinungen [Johann Ludwig Bach, 1677–1731] is still living there, as Court Organist and Court Painter; his son [Johann Philipp] is engaged as his assistant in both capacities. Both father and son are excellent portrait painters. (The latter visited me last summer, and painted my portrait, catching the likeness excellently.)[8]

Schwickert wanted to include an engraving of Bach in the revised edition of the *Versuch*, but in a letter of 27 January 1786, Bach wrote:

> Drop the expensive plans with the portrait. My only appropriate portrait is with dry colours, framed, under glass and may not be sent [to Berlin]. My family will not permit it. Someone will make a good copy here in oil for 4 ducats. Since I have been engraved badly often enough, who is looking particularly for something new?[9]

---

7. See introduction for German text. *CPEB-Briefe*, 1:392; *CPEB-Letters*, 54. One of the former owners confidently attributed this portrait to "A.E. Oeser," the painting teacher to C.P.E. Bach's son, Johann Sebastian the younger.

8. "Des Meinungschen Capellmeisters Sohn lebt noch da, als Hoforganist u. Hofmahler; deßen H. Sohn ist ihm adjungirt in beÿden Stationen. Vater und Sohn sind vortrefliche Portraitmahler. (Lezterer hat mich vorigen Sommer besucht u. gemahlt, u. vortreflich getroffen.)" *NBR*, 286. See also C.S. Terry, *The Origin of the Family of Bach Musicians* (London, 1929), 10n. The exemplar in D-B is reproduced in Ernst Bücken, *Die Musik des Rokokos und der Klassik* (Wildpark-Potsdam: Akademische Verlagsgesellschaft Athenaion, 1927).

9. See introduction for German text. *CPEB-Briefe*, 2:1139–40; *CPEB-Letters*, 245.

This portrait by Johann Philipp Bach survives in two copies: one in D-B (plate 3), one in D-LEb (plate 4). Another copy, formerly owned by Paul Bach in Weimar, is now lost.[10] Of these three copies Bach himself probably owned the one in Berlin.

Another pastel portrait exists from around the same time, signed "J.C. Löhr" (plate 5), which is a nearly identical pose to the portrait by Johann Philipp Bach. This was presumably the model for the engraving by Johann Heinrich Lips (plate 6), published in Johann Caspar Lavater's *Physiognomische Fragmente*.[11] Lavater's commentary, with its quirky anatomical analysis, is worth quoting at length:

> Yet the painter has politely disguised the defect of the left eye … thereby inevitably losing some of the unique forcefulness of Bach's expression. None the less, spirit remains in the eyes and eyebrows. The nose, rather too rounded, still manages to convey an impression of refinement and creative power. The mouth, for all its simplicity, such a fine expression of delicacy, richness, dryness, assurance, and security; the lower lip somewhat artful and weak—with only a faint hint of awkwardness!
>
> Firmness, cheerfulness, courage, and conviction can be seen on the forehead. I do not know whether it is simply an illusion, but it seems to me at least that in most portraits of virtuosi the lower part of the face is not entirely successful; here, though, the outline of the chin is masterly.[12]

---

10. This lost pastel is reproduced in Gustav Kanth, ed., *Bilder-Atlas zur Musikgeschichte von Bach bis Strauss* (Berlin: Schuster & Loeffler, 1912).

11. Lavater had written to Bach on 13 May 1775 to ask him to send a portrait for his book; Lavater confirmed he had received the portrait on 1 September, and Bach asked about it in his letter dated 6 September. *CPEB-Briefe*, 1:499–500, 514–15; *CPEB-Letters*, 82–83.

12. "Doch den Fehler am linken Auge in der Natur hat der Mahler aus Höflichkeit vermuthlich und schonender Güte weggepinselt … und ganz unfehlbar damit zugleich—ein beträchtliches von Ausdruck. Seele genug bleibt übrigens noch in Aug und Augenbrauen übrig. Die Nase, zu sehr abgerundet, läßt indeß immer noch genug von Feinheit und würkender Kraft durchscheinen. Der Mund—welch ein einfach gewordener Ausdruck von Feingefühl, Sattheit, Trockenheit, Selbstbewußtheit und Sicherheit; die Unterlippe etwas listig und schwach—aber nur leiser Hauch der Lästigkeit drüber! Die nah an die Lippe gränzende Einkerbung—kräftigt wieder sehr.

"Feste, Heiterkeit, Muth und Drang ist in der Stirne. Ich weiß nicht, ob's Trug ist—wenigstens scheint's mir, daß der untere Theil des Gesichtes bey den mehresten Virtuosen, die ich im Urbilde oder Nachbilde sah, nicht ganz vortheilhaft ist. Der Umriß vom Oberkinn ist indeß hier nicht gemein." Quoted in Ottenberg, 1.

After publication of volume 3 of the *Physiognomische Fragmente* in which Bach's portrait appears, Bach confided in Breitkopf on 9 August 1777:

> And have you seen my Lavater portrait, which, it is generally agreed, is anything but a good likeness and more resembling someone sleeping than someone awake? The good Lavater reasons so conclusively and certainly, although from what I know and have seen only 2 pieces are characterized fairly well, namely Friedrich and Rameau.[13]

Other engravings, by Heinrich Pfenninger (plate 7) and Johann Conrad Krüger (plate 8), also seem to derive from Johann Philipp Bach's pastel portraits, and the latter engraving was published by Forkel as the frontispiece to his *Allgemeine Deutsche Bibliothek*, volume 34 (Berlin, 1778).

There are two silhouettes of C. P. E. Bach, one by Jacob von Döhren (plate 9), and the other what seems to be its reverse image (plate 10). The first (Wq 275) was published in Hamburg in 1778 by "C. Herolds Wittwe." The second silhouette (Wq 276) was published in *Musikalische Bibliothek*, volume 1 (Marburg, 1784), edited by Hans Adolph Friedrich von Eschstruth.[14] The former was part of a series of silhouettes of Bach's entire family (plates 17–20), which he refers to in a letter to Breitkopf dated 19 December 1778.

> You will receive through Herr Professor Oeser a silhouette of my dear late son. I know you loved him too. The likeness is very good. A young artist here used this style to great advantage. Darker and better than those of Lavater. Inexpensive. Keep this portrait in memory of me.[15]

---

13. "Und mein Lavatorisch Portrait, welches nach allgemeiner Beurtheilung, nichts weniger, als getroffen ist u. mehr einem schlafenden als wachenden gleicht, haben Sie gesehen? Der gute Lavater raisonirt so bündig und gewiß, ohngeacht, was ich kenne u. gesehen habe, blos 2 Stück ziemlich getroffen sind, nehmlich Friedrich und Rameau." *CPEB-Briefe*, 1:647; *CPEB-Letters*, 113. In addition to Bach and Rameau, Jommelli's portrait is discussed immediately preceding Bach's in Lavater's *Physiognomische Fragmente*. See Gerda Mraz, "Musikerportraits in der Sammlung Lavater," in *Studies in Music History Presented to H. C. Robbins Landon*, ed. Otto Biba and David Wyn Jones (London: Thames & Hudson, 1996), 165–76. For a modern-day analysis of C. P. E. Bach's physiognomy, see Peter Rummenhöller, "Er ist der Vater, wir sind die Buben: Zur Physiognomik Carl Philipp Emanuel Bachs," in *Carl Philipp Emanuel Bach: Beiträge zu Leben und Werk*, ed. Heinrich Poos (Mainz: Schott, 1993), 15–20.

14. This journal included a musical supplement, in which appeared Bach's *Passionslied*, Wq 197/6.

15. "Sie werden durch den Herrn Profeßor Oeser einen Schattenriß von meinem lieben seeligen Sohn erhalten. Ich weiß, Sie haben ihn auch geliebt. Er ist sehr gut getroffen. Ein junger

A posthumous drawing of J. S. Bach the younger was done by Oeser (plate 21), apparently as a gift for C. P. E. Bach in 1778 and thus must have been in his collection. This drawing was eventually used for an engraving by Carl Wilhelm Grießmann, published in 1791 (plate 22). Another portrait of J. S. Bach the younger, now in the Goethe-Museum in Düsseldorf, does not seem to have a connection with C. P. E. Bach.[16]

The last formal portrait of C. P. E. Bach was done by Andreas Stöttrup in Hamburg, c. 1780 (plate 11).[17] At around the same time, Bach and Pastor Christoph Christian Sturm were depicted together on the title page of Bach's "Sturm Lieder" (Hamburg: Johann Henrich Herold, 1780; plate 12), with a cityscape of Hamburg designed by Oeser and engraved by Christian Gottlieb Geyser. But the publisher must have been dissatisfied with the likenesses of the composer and poet, because he commissioned Stöttrup to prepare a new portrait of Bach and Sturm for the revised, second edition (1781; plate 13).[18] While it is difficult to distinguish Bach and Sturm in the first edition, they have been more clearly delineated in the new profiles of the second edition. Here Pastor Sturm is on the inside and to the right of Bach; it is easy to see the resemblance in the engraving of Sturm (cf. plate 270 in the main text). Stöttrup also depicted himself drawing the two men (plate 14), with a few portraits hanging on the walls in the background.

Stöttrup's engraving (plate 11) also served as a model for his posthumous engraving of C. P. E. Bach: a memorial bust (Wq 277, plate 15), published as a frontispiece to the piano-vocal score of Bach's *Passions-Cantate*, Wq 233. Bach's

---

Künstler hier hat diese Art sehr hoch gebracht. Schwärzer und beßer, wie die Lavaterschen. Wohlfeil. Verwahren Sie dies Bild mir zum Andenken." *CPEB-Briefe*, 1:719; *CPEB-Letters*, 131.

16. See Maria Hübner, "Ein Brief von Carl Philipp Emanuel Bach an Adam Friedrich Oeser," *BJ* (2007): 243–54, esp. 248. A third portrait by Friedrich Rehberg was published in 1926 but is now apparently lost; see *ibid.*, 249. The function of the Oeser portrait as a posthumous monument was discovered by Helmut Börsch-Supan in his review of Fröhlich, in *BJ* (2008): 356.

17. The works directly above CPEB's head seem to be similar in style to the portrait of Mercury (plate 181), though the one on the left might depict Orpheus. The original drawing in pencil for this portrait survives in the Kunsthalle, Hamburg, Inv. Nr. 49473, signed and dated "gezeichnet von A. Stöttrup. 1784." A second drawing by Stöttrup, a variant of this one, is in the Klassik Stiftung Weimar und Kunstsammlungen, Graphische Sammlung Inv. Nr. KK 3004. See Peter Prange, *Deutsche Zeichnungen 1450–1800* (Cologne: Böhlau, 2007), items 981–82.

18. The complete title pages are reproduced in CPEB:CW, VI/2, plates 9–10.

widow, Johanna Maria, refers to this in a letter to J.J.H. Westphal dated 24 September 1790:

> I have enclosed a copper engraving that was made here, and which, like all of the other engravings of him, does not really resemble him; because I believe that it will be pleasing to a friend, even though a connoisseur would be very reproachful about the mixing together of Roman and German costume.[19]

Indeed, the bewigged Bach is dressed in a toga as a winged cherub crowns him with a laurel wreath while another sobs at the base of the monument.

The medallion by Johann Friedrich Schröter (Wq 278, plate 16), published on the title page of the *Allgemeine musikalische Zeitung,* volume 3 (Leipzig: Breitkopf & Härtel, 1800) also appears to be based on Stöttrup's engraving (plate 11). The lithograph by Heinrich E. von Wintter, dated 1816, is clearly posthumous and part of a series of portraits of famous composers, including J.S. Bach.[20]

Finally, there is also an engraving by Peter Haas of a "Concert by Frederick the Great" (c. 1786), which was done as part of a series on Frederick's court. If it dates from the end of his reign, that would mean the keyboard player depicted could not have been C.P.E. Bach.[21] This engraving appears to be one of the sources for the famous painting by Adolph Menzel depicting a musical entertainment at Sanssouci Palace.[22]

---

19. "Ich habe ein Kupfer, was hier verfertigt ist, und welches ihn freylich nicht recht ähnlich vorstellt, wie keines Kupferstiche, die von ihm vorhanden sind, mit beygelegt, weil ich glaube, daß es einem Freunde angenehm seyn kann, wenn ein Kenner die Mischung von römischer und deutscher Tracht gleich sehr tadeln wird." Schmid 1988, 488.

20. For the J.S. Bach portrait, see *Bach-Bildnisse als Widerspiegelung des Bach-Bildes. Katalog zur Sonderausstellung im Bachhaus Eisenach März – Oktober 1994,* ed. Gisela Vogt (Munich: Musikverlag Emil Katzbichler, 1994), 27 and plate 13.

21. This engraving is reproduced, among other places, in Bücken, 75, figure 43; Karl Michael Komma, *Musikgeschichte in Bildern* (Stuttgart: Kröner, 1961); and in Neal Zaslaw, ed., *The Classical Era* (London: Macmillan, 1989), 243, figure 53.

22. For further discussion of this mid-nineteenth-century tribute to Prussia's past, see Gabriele Busch-Salmen, "Adolph Menzels 'Flötenkonzert,'" *Music in Art* 28/1–2 (2003): 127–46, and Jost Hermand, *Adolph Menzel: Das Flötenkonzert in Sanssouci* (Frankfurt: Fischer, 1985).

PORTRAITS OF C.P.E. BACH
AND HIS FAMILY

1. C. P. E. Bach

Pastel by Gottlieb Friedrich Bach, c. 1730; 20 x 15 cm

Location: D-EIb, 5.1.0.22

References: Conrad Freyse, "Unbekannte Jugendbildnisse Friede-
mann und Emanuel Bachs," in *Bericht über die wissenschaftliche
Bachtagung der Gesellschaft für Musikforschung Leipzig 23. bis 26.
Juli 1950*, ed. Walther Vetter and Ernst Hermann Meyer (Leipzig: C.F. Peters, 1951),
349–54; *Bach-
Dokumente* IV, 237 (plate 403)

2. C. P. E. Bach

Pastel attributed to Adam Friedrich Oeser, but probably by
Johann Friedrich Reiffenstein, c. 1754; 27 x 30 cm

Location: Sir Ralph Kohn F.R.S., London

References: Walter Haacke, *Die Söhne Bachs* (1962); Sotheby's
Catalogue (17 May 2002), 12–13

3. C. P. E. Bach

Pastel by Johann Philipp Bach, 1773; 15 x 11.5 cm

Location: D-B, Mus. P. Bach, K.Ph.E. I,1

References: Cat. Poelchau no. 30; Dragan Plamenac, "New Light
on the Last Years of Carl Philipp Emanuel Bach," *Musical Quar-
terly* 35 (1949): 565–87, esp. 571–72; Biehahn 1961, 10 and plate 4

4. C. P. E. Bach

Pastel after Johann Philipp Bach, c. 1773; 16 x 12 cm
Location: D-LEb, BS 1
References: *CPEB-Briefe*, 2:1139–40; *CPEB-Letters*, 245

5. C. P. E. Bach

Pastel by Franz Conrad Löhr after J. P. Bach, c. 1775; 16 x 13 cm
Signature: "*F. C. Lo[hr] | pinxit*" [F. C. Löhr painted this image]
Location: Gemäldegalerie, Staatliche Museen zu Berlin, M.589

6. C. P. E. Bach

Engraving by Johann Heinrich Lips after J. P. Bach, c. 1777; 20 x
16 cm on a plate 31 x 22 cm
Inscription: "*Emanuel Bach*"
Location: Lavater's *Physiognomische Fragmente zur Beförderung
der Menschenkenntnis und Menschenliebe*, 3 vols. (Leipzig and
Winterthur, 1777), 3:200–201 (exemplars in D-LEb, Graph. Slg. 7145 and D-B, Mus.
P. Bach, K.Ph.E. I,2)
References: *CPEB-Briefe*, 1:499–500, 514–15, 647; *CPEB-Letters*, 82–83, 113; "*Er ist
Original!*", 110–11

7. C. P. E. Bach

Engraving by Heinrich Pfenninger after J. H. Lips, c. 1777/8;
22.5 x 15 cm on sheet 37.5 x 30.5 cm
Inscription: "*Emanuel Bach*"
Production details at bottom left: "*Joh. H. Lips*"
Location: D-LEb, Graph. Slg. 12/1 (also D-B, Mus. P. Bach,
K.Ph.E. I,4)
References: *Bach-Dokumente* IV, 257 (plate 440)

8. C. P. E. Bach

Engraving by Johann Conrad Krüger after J. H. Lips, c. 1778,
17 x 10.5 cm
Inscription: "KARL PHILIPP EMANUEL | BACH."
Production details at bottom right: "J.C. Krüger Sc."
Location: frontispiece to *Allgemeine Deutsche Bibliothek*, 34
(Berlin, 1778) (exemplars in D-LEb, Graph. Slg. 4/2 and D-B, Mus. P. Bach, K.Ph.E.
I,1a–1b)
References: Wq 274; *Bach-Dokumente* IV, 324 (plate 573); *"Er ist Original!"*, 109, 111;
CPEB-Musik und Literatur, 84 and plate 39; Mortzfeld, A 742

9. C. P. E. Bach

Silhouette by Jacob von Döhren, c. 1776, 15 x 19 cm
Inscription: "C. P. E. BACH."
Location: US-NYp, Muller Collection (digital ID 1100908)
References: Wq 275; Lavater's *Physiognomische Fragmente*, 3:201

10. C. P. E. Bach

Silhouette after Jacob von Döhren, c. 1784
Inscription: "CARL PHILIPP EMANUEL BACH."
Location: frontispiece to *Musikalische Bibliothek*, 1 (Marburg,
1784), ed. Hans Adolph Friedrich von Eschstruth (exemplar in
D-Mbs, Mus. th. 980–1/2)
References: Wq 276; Haacke, *Die Söhne Bachs*, 19

11. C. P. E. Bach

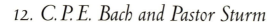

Engraving by Andreas Stöttrup, c. 1780; 21.5 x 16.5 cm on sheet
26.5 x 21 cm

Inscription: "Carl Philipp Emanuel Bach, | Kapellmeister und
Musikdirektor in Hamburg. | Aus Hochachtung gezeichnet und
gestochen von A. Stöttrup."

Location: D-LEb, Graph. Slg. 12/14 (also D-B, Mus. P. Bach, K.Ph.E. I,6)

References: Wq 273; *"Er ist Original!"* 109, 111; *CPEB-Musik und Literatur*, 17 and
plate 1

12. C. P. E. Bach and Pastor Sturm

Engraving by Christian Gottlieb Geyser; cityscape designed by
Adam Friedrich Oeser, c. 1780, 14 x 19 cm

Production details at bottom left: "Oeser inv."; at bottom right:
"Geyser sc."

Location: title page to *Sturms geistliche Gesänge*, 1st ed. (Hamburg, 1780) (exemplar in D-B, Mus. P. Bach, K.Ph.E. I,3)

References: CPEB:CW, VI/2

13. C. P. E. Bach and Pastor Sturm

Engraving by Johann Christian Gottfried Fritzsch; cityscape
designed by Adam Friedrich Oeser, and a new medallion by
Andreas Stöttrup, 1781; 27 x 31.5 cm

Production details at bottom left: "Oeser inv."; center: "A.
Stöttrup imagines p."; at bottom right: "F. C. G. Fritzsch sc. 1781."

Location: title page to *Sturms geistliche Gesänge*, 2nd ed. (Hamburg, 1781) (exemplar in
US-AAu, M2112.B12 G36)

References: *CPEB-Musik und Literatur*, 94 and plate 32; CPEB:CW, VI/2

14. C. P. E. Bach with Pastor Sturm and Stöttrup

Drawing by Andreas Stöttrup, in pen and ink, c. 1784; 25.5 x 20.5 cm

Production details in brown pen: "Nach dem Leben gezeichnet und zusammengesetzt von And. Stöttrup. Hamburg 1784."

Location: Hamburger Kunsthalle, Kupferstichkabinett, Inv. Nr. 23790

References: *"Er ist Original!"* 111; *CPEB-Musik und Literatur*, 93 and plate 35; *Musiker im Porträt*, 3:80–81; Peter Rummenhöller, "Zur zeitgenössischen Portraitierung Carl Philipp Emanuel Bachs," *Musica* (Germany) 48 (1994): 215–18; Peter Prange, *Deutsche Zeichnungen 1450–1800* (Cologne: Böhlau, 2007), 342

15. C. P. E. Bach

Memorial bust by Andreas Stöttrup, c. 1789; 9 x 14 cm; published as frontispiece to *Passions-Cantate*, Wq 233

Inscription: "BACH"

Production details at lower right: "A. Stöttrup inven. et sculps Hamburg"

Location: D-B, Mus. P. Bach, K.Ph.E. 1,5

References: Wq 277

16. C. P. E. Bach (posthumous)

Engraving by Johann Friedrich Schröter, c. 1800; 11 x 9 cm on sheet 25 x 21 cm

Inscription below image: *"Carl Phil: Em: Bach."*

Production details: "J.F. Schröter. scul. Lipsia"

Location: title page to *Allgemeine musikalische Zeitung*, 3 (Leipzig: Breitkopf & Härtel, 1800) (exemplar in D-LEb, Graph. Slg. 12/6)

References: *"Er ist Original!"* 111

17. Johanna Maria Bach
(1724–1795)

Silhouette by Jacob von Döhren, c. 1776, 8.8 cm high

Location: Museum für Hamburgische Geschichte

References: *CPEB-Briefe*, 1:719; *CPEB-Letters*, 131; *CPEB-Musik und Literatur*, 65 and plate 18

18. Johann August Bach
(1745–1789)

Silhouette by Jacob von Döhren, c. 1776, 8 cm high

Location: Museum für Hamburgische Geschichte

References: *CPEB-Briefe*, 1:719; *CPEB-Letters*, 131; *CPEB-Musik und Literatur*, 65 and plate 18

19. Anna Carolina Philippina Bach
(1747–1804)

Silhouette by Jacob von Döhren, c. 1776, 9.8 cm high

Location: Museum für Hamburgische Geschichte

References: *CPEB-Briefe*, 1:719; *CPEB-Letters*, 131; *CPEB-Musik und Literatur*, 65 and plate 18

20. Johann Sebastian Bach the younger
(1748–1778)

Silhouette by Jacob von Döhren, c. 1776, 6.6 cm high

Location: Museum für Hamburgische Geschichte

References: *CPEB-Briefe*, 1:719; *CPEB-Letters*, 131; *CPEB-Musik und Literatur*, 65 and plate 18; Fröhlich, 23

21. J. S. Bach the younger

Drawing by Adam Friedrich Oeser, 1778
Inscription: "I.S. BACH."
Location: Klassik Stiftung Weimar, Goethe-Nationalmuseum
References: Fröhlich, 32

22. J. S. Bach the younger

Engraving by Carl Wilhelm Grießmann after Adam Friedrich
Oeser, 1791
Inscription: "I.S. BACH."
Location: D-LEb, Graph. Slg. 4–3
References: *CPEB-Musik und Literatur*, 65 and plate 19;
Fröhlich, frontispiece

Acknowledgments

I am grateful to the following individuals for their assistance in providing portraits of C. P. E. Bach: Gisela Vogt at the Sammlung Bachhaus Eisenach / Neue Bachgesellschaft e.V.; Kristina Funk-Kunath at the Bach-Archiv Leipzig; Martina Rebmann at the Staatsbibliothek zu Berlin; and Stephen Roe at Sotheby's. I also want to thank Annette Richards, Peter Wollny, and Christoph Wolff for providing information about some of the portraits, and my colleagues at the editorial office, especially Lisa DeSiro, Ruth Libbey, and Jason B. Grant, for their suggestions for improvement.

Finally, we could not have completed this volume without the expertise and good humor of our designer, Dean Bornstein.

Paul Corneilson

CLASSIFIED INDEX

The classified index groups the portraits, including the silhouettes in appendix A, into four categories:

A. Items known to have been owned by CPEB;

B. Engraved portraits concordant with items listed in NV 1790 and perhaps originally in the possession of CPEB;

C. Portraits for which NV 1790 gives only partial information, but for which a likely match is available, based on provenance, on the inscription, on the rarity of portraits of a particular sitter, on the absence of artists' names, and on availability to CPEB;

D. Portraits for which NV 1790 provides enough information but which are known to be lost or otherwise have not been identified; in a few cases NV 1790 provides too little information for conclusive identification.

Items in appendix B are listed in category E, portraits of CPEB and his family not included in NV 1790.

The subject names are listed in alphabetical order within each section. References to the introduction and catalogue in part I are given in roman type; references to plates in part II are given in italic. (Plates in the appendices are preceded by the letter A or B.)

Category A
Abel, Leopold August, 27; *1*
Abel, Carl Friedrich, 11, 27–28; *2*
Bach, Johann Ambrosius, 7, 38; *20*
Bach, Johann Sebastian, 7, 8, 20, 38; *21*
Bach, Johann Ludwig, 9n, 42; *24*
Bedeschi, Paolo, 19, 45–46; *31*
Benda, Maria Felicitas, 47–48; *36*
Buffardin, Pierre-Gabriel, 11, 20, 54; *46*
Cecilia, Saint, 20, 32, 55; *47*
Concialini, Carlo, 63; *61*
Eberlin, Daniel, 71; *74*
Fasch, Carl Friedrich Christian, 77; *86*
Jürgensen, Johann Christian, 107; *138*
Lolli, Antonio, 13, 121; *164*
Mara, Gertrud Elisabeth (née Schmeling), 13, 19, 124; *169*
Mingotti, Caterina Regina, 11, 19, 20, 133; *185*

Pisendel, Johann Georg, 150–51; *213*
Quantz, Johann Joachim, 151, 155–56; *221*
Reichardt, Johann Friedrich, 20, 158–59; *226*
Schiørring, Niels, 12, 168; *243*
Vitali, Tomaso Antonio, 190; *284*
Walther, Thomas Christian, 192–93; *288*

Category B
Accorso, Mariangelo, 28; *3*
Agrell, Johan Joachim, 28–29; *4*
Alardus Amstelredamus, 30; *6*
Alberti, Leon Battista, 31; *8*
Albertus Magnus, 30; *7*
Alciati, Andrea, 31; *9*
d'Alembert, Jean le Rond, 32; *10*
Alexander the Great, 32; *11*
Allegranti, Maddalena, 33; *12*
André, Johann, 34; *14*

d'Anglebert, Jean-Henry, 34; *15*

Annibali, Domenico, 35–36; *17*

Apollo, 36; *18*

Aristotle, 37; *19*

Bach, Hans, 41; *23*

Bagge, Charles Ernest, Baron de, 43; *26*

Baron, Ernst Gottlieb, 43–44; *27*

Bartholin, Caspar, 44; *28*

Beard, John, 45; *30*

Beer, Johann, 43; *25*

Bembo, Pietro, 46; *32*

Benda, Franz, 46–47; *33, 34*

Benda, Georg, 47; *35*

Besard, Jean-Baptiste, 48–49; *37*

Bianchini, Francesco, 49–50; *39*

Biber, Heinrich Ignaz Franz von, 49; *38*

Blankenburg, Quirinus Gerbrandszoon van, 50; *40*

Briegel, Wolfgang Carl, 52; *42*

Brockes, Barthold Heinrich, 52; *43*

Bümler, Georg Heinrich, 53; *45*

Callimachus (Filippo Buonaccorsi), 55–56; *48*

Calvisius, Sethus, 56; *49*

Calvör, Caspar, 56; *50*

Camerarius, Philippus, 57; *51*

Capricornus, Samuel Friedrich, 57; *52*

Carestini, Giovanni, 58; *53*

Chéron, Elisabeth Sophie, 60; *55*

Christophorus (Cristoforo Marcello), 60; *56*

Cicero, Marcus Tullius, 61; *57*

Cisner, Nicolaus, 20, 61; *58*

Cochlaeus, Johannes, 62; *60*

Colas, Domenico and his brother, 51–52; *41*

Conring, Hermann, 63; *62*

Corelli, Arcangelo, 64; *63*

Cosimi, Nicola, 64–65; *64*

Crüger, Johannes, 65–66; *66*

Curti, 66; *67*

Daquin, Louis-Claude, 67; *68*

De Fesch, Willem, 68; *69*

Denis, Michael, 68; *70*

Descartes, René, 59; *54*

Dieterich, Johann Conrad, 68–69; *71*

Dionysius, Aelius, 24n, 69

Dolet, Étienne, 69–70; *72*

Ebeling, Christoph Daniel, 10, 71; *73*

Eccard, Johannes, 72; *75*

Engel, Johann Jakob, 15, 72; *76*

Epicurus, 73; *77*

Erasmus, Desiderius, 73; *78*

Eschstruth, Hans Adolf Friedrich von, 12, 74; *79*

Ettmüller, Michael Ernst, 74; *80*

Euler, Leonhard, 75; *82*

Fabricius, Johann Albertus, 76; *84*

Fabricius, Werner, 75–76; *83*

Farinelli (Carlo Broschi), 76–77; *85*

Ficino, Marsilio, 78–79; *89*

Fiorillo, Ignazio, 79; *90*

Fordyce, Margaret, 81; *92*

Fracastoro, Girolamo, 81; *93*

Franciscello (Francesco Alborea), 81–82; *94*

Franck, Michael, 82; *95*

Franckenau, Georg Frank von, 82; *96*

Franklin, Benjamin, 83; *97*

Frescobaldi, Girolamo, 83; *98*

Fritz, Barthold, 84; *99*

Gaultier, Jacques, 88; *108*

Gellert, Christian Fürchtegott, 85; *100*

Geminiani, Francesco, 85; *101*

Gerbert, Martin, 86; *102*

German Violinist and Italian Secretary, 189–90; *283*

Gerstenberg, Heinrich Wilhelm von, 86; *103*

Gesner, Conrad, 87; *104*

Gluck, Christoph Willibald, 87; *106*

Góis, Damião de, 19n, 88; *107*

Graphaeus (Cornelis Schryver), 90; *109*

Graun, Carl Heinrich, 91; *110*

Guignon, Jean Pierre, 92; *112*

Gumpelzhaimer, Adam, 92–93; *113*

Hagedorn, Friedrich von, 94; *115*

Hainlein, Paul, 99; *124*

Hammerschmidt, Andreas, 94; *116*

Handel, George Frideric, 95; *117*

Handl, Jacobus, 95; *118*

Hardt, Johann Daniel, 96; *119*

I Iasse, Faustina (née Bordoni), 97; *121*

Hasse, Johann Adolph, 97; *120*

Hässler, Johann Wilhelm, 93; *114*

Haydn, Joseph, 98; *122*

Hebden, John, 98; *123*

Herbst, Johann Andreas, 100; *126*
Hessus, Helius Eobanus, 99; *125*
Hiller, Johann Adam, 10, 11, 100; *127*
Hintze, Jacob, 101; *128*
Höffler, Konrad, 101; *129*
Hölty, Ludwig Christoph Heinrich, 102; *130*
Homer, 24n, 102
Horace, 24n, 102
Hunt, Arabella, 103; *132*
James I, 104; *133*
Jeep, Johannes, 104; *134*
Jommelli, Niccolò, 105–6; *135*
Journet, Françoise, 106; *136*
Kayser, Philipp Christoph, 108; *139*
Kellner, Johann Christoph, 15, 109; *140*
Kepler, Johannes, 109–10; *141*
Kindermann, Johann Erasmus, 110; *142*
Kis, Stephanus (Szegedinus), 183; *272*
Koch, Franziska, 112; *146*
Kremberg, Jakob, 112–13; *147*
Krieger, Adam, 113; *148*
Kuhnau, Johann, 114; *149*
Kupecký, Christoph Johann Frideric, 114; *150*
Lalande, Michel-Richard de, 115; *151*
Lallouette, Jean François, 116; *152*
Lampe, Friedrich Adolph, 116; *153*
Lampe, John Frederick, 116–17; *154*
Lange, Aloysia (née Weber), 117; *155*
Lanier, Nicholas, 35; *16*
Lasso, Orlando di, 117–18; *156*
Leclair, Jean-Marie, 61; *59*
Legros, Joseph, 92; *111*
Leibniz, Gottfried Wilhelm, 118; *157*
Leonardo da Vinci, 189; *282*
Leopold I (emperor), 118–19; *158*
Lessing, Gotthold Ephraim, 119; *159*
Leveridge, Richard, 119; *160*
Liberti, Hendrik, 120; *161*
Lingke, Georg Friedrich, 120; *162*
Löwe, Johann Jakob, 121; *163*
Lully, Jean-Baptiste, 122–23; *166*
Luther, Martin, 123; *167*
Lutter, Johann Balthasar, 124; *168*
Marchand, Louis, 125; *170*
Marot, Clement, 126; *172*
Marpurg, Friedrich Wilhelm, 126; *173*

Mattheson, Johann, 128; *175*
Mayer, Johann Friedrich, 129; *176*
Medici, Lorenzo di, 129; *177*
Meiland, Jacob, 129–30; *178*
Melanchthon, Philipp, 130; *179*
Mendelssohn, Moses, 131; *180*
Mercury, 131, 213n; *181*
Merulo, Claudio, 132; *182*
Metastasio, Pietro, 132; *183*
Milton, John, 134; *186*
Mondonville, Jean-Joseph Cassanéa de, 134; *187*
Monte, Philippe de, 135; *188*
Montesson, Charlotte-Jeane Béraud de la Haye de Riou, Marquise de, 127; *174*
Monticelli, Angelo Maria, 135–36; *189*
Morhof, Daniel Georg, 136; *190*
Mozart, Leopold, 137; *191*
Müller, Carolina Fredrika, 137–38; *192*
Musculus, Wolfgang, 138; *193*
Nardini, Pietro, 138; *194*
Neefe, Christian Gottlob, 139; *195*
Neumeister, Erdmann, 139; *196*
Niklas, Marie Sophie, 140; *197*
Noordt, Sybrandus van, 141; *198*
Nozemann, Jacob, 141; *199*
Ochsenkuhn, Sebastian, 142; *200*
Paix, Jakob, 143; *202*
Paminger, Leonhard, 144; *203*
Passeri, Giovanni Battista, 146; *206*
Pécour, Louis Guillaume, 147; *208*
Pepusch, Johann Christoph, 147; *207*
Philidor, François-André Danican, 149; *210*
Piccinni, Niccolò, 149–50; *211*
Pico della Mirandola, Giovanni, 150; *212*
Plato, 151; *214*
Poliziano, Angelo, 151–52; *215*
Pontano, Giovanni, 106–7; *137*
Postel, Guillaume, 152; *216*
Praetorius, Michael, 153; *217*
Ptolemy, 153–54; *218*
Punto, Giovanni (Johann Wenzel Stich), 154; *219*
Quantz, Johann Joachim, 155–56; *222*
Rameau, Jean-Philippe, 157; *223*
Ramler, Karl Wilhelm, 157; *224*

Rebel, Jean-Fery, 158; *225*

Reiche, Gottfried, 159; *227*

Reincken, Johann Adam, 159–60; *228*

Reusner, Nikolaus, 160; *229*

Reyher, Andreas, 160; *230*

Rhenanus, Beatus, 161; *231*

Richey, Michael, 161; *232*

Rist, Johann, 10n, 162; *233*

Rolle, Johann Heinrich, 162–63; *234*

Rousseau, Jean-Jacques, 163; *235*

Sachs, Hans, 164; *236*

Saint-Huberty, Anne-Antoinette Clavel de, 15, 103; *131*

Salimbeni, Felice, 164; *237*

Scalichius, Paul, 165; *238*

Scheidemann, Heinrich, 165–66; *239*

Scheidt, Samuel, 166; *240*

Schelwig, Samuel, 167; *241*

Schenck, Johannes, 167; *242*

Schmelzer, Johann Heinrich, 168; *244*

Schmid, Bernhard, the elder, 169; *245*

Schmidt, Johann Andreas, 170; *247*

Schmidt, Melchior, 169; *246*

Scholl, Dirck, 170; *248*

Schop, Johann, 171; *249*

Schott, Conrad, 171–72; *250*

Schubart, Christian Friedrich Daniel, 172; *252*

Schubart, Tobias Heinrich, 172; *251*

Schütz, Heinrich, 173; *253*

Schweitzer, Anton, 173–74; *254*

Seelen, Johann Heinrich von, 174; *255*

Seixas, José Antonio Carlos de, 177; *260*

Selle, Thomas, 174–75; *256*

Seneca the younger, 176; *257*

Senesino (Francesco Bernardi), 176; *258*

Seydelmann, Franz, 176–77; *259*

Siculus, Baptista, 177; *261*

Sieber, Justus, 178; *262*

Simpson, Christopher, 178; *263*

Solnitz, Anton Wilhelm, 179; *264*

Spieß, Meinrad, 180; *266*

Staden, Johann, 180–81; *267*

Stenger, Nicolaus, 181; *268*

Stockhausen, Johann Christoph, 182; *269*

Sturm, Christoph Christian, 182–83; *270,* *B 12–B 13*

Sulzer, Johann Georg, 183; *271*

Tartini, Giuseppe, 184; *273*

Tessarini, Carlo, 184–85; *274*

Tevo, Zaccaria, 185; *275*

Thévenard, Gabriel-Vincent, 185; *276*

Til, Salomon van, 186; *277*

Unzer, Johann August, 186; *278*

Vallet, Nicholas, 187; *279*

Venzky, Georg, 187–88; *280*

Vetter, Daniel, 188; *281*

Virgil, 24n, 190

Vivaldi, Antonio, 191; *285*

Walliser, Christoph Thomas, 192; *287*

Walpurgis, Maria Antonia, 125; *171*

Weiss, Silvius Leopold, 193; *289*

Wellter, Johann, 193–94; *290*

Wilisch, Christian Friedrich, 195; *291*

Wolf, Ernst Wilhelm, 18, 195; *292*

Xylander, Wilhelm, 195; *293*

Zachariä, Friedrich Wilhelm, 12, 196; *294*

Zeidler, Maximilian, 196; *295*

Zwinger, Theodor, the elder, 197–98; *296*

Zygmuntowski, Nicolaus, 198; *297*

Category C

Agrippa, Heinrich Cornelius, 29–30; *5*

Alsted, Johann Heinrich, 33; *13*

Bach, Johann Christoph Friedrich, 40; *22*

Bastard, Ann [mistaken for La Bastardella], 44–45; *29*

Browne, Sir Thomas, 53; *44*

Critopulus, Metrophanes, 65; *65*

Euclid of Megara, 75; *81*

Ferdinand I (emperor), 77–78; *87*

Ferdinand III (emperor), 78; *88*

Fludd, Robert, 80; *91*

Giovannini (Count of St. Germain), 87; *105*

Hiller, Johann Adam, 199, 202; *A 2*

Kircher, Athanasius, 111; *143*

Kirnberger, Johann Philipp, 9n, 111; *144*

Klopstock, Friedrich Gottlieb, 112; *145*

Kozeluch, Leopold, 202; *A 3*

Kreibich, Franz, 202; *A 1*

Lang, Johann Georg, 203; *A 4*

Le Jeune, Claude, 62

Ludecus, Matthäus, 122; *165*

Meursius, Johannes, 133; *184*
Mozart, Wolfgang Amadeus, 199, 203; *A 5*
Neefe, Christian Gottlob, 199, 204; *A6*
Olearius, Johannes, 142; *201*
Pan, 144; *204*
Panciroli, Guido, 145; *205*
Penna, Lorenzo, 148; *209*
Pleyel, Ignace Joseph, 205; *A 7*
Puteanus, Erycius, 155; *220*
Rosetti, Antonio, 205; *A 8*
Schmittbaur, Joseph Aloys, 205; *A 9*
Schubart, Christian Friedrich Daniel, 206;
　A 10
Socrates, 24n, 179
Spangenberg, Cyriac, 180; *265*
Steffan, Joseph Anton, 206; *A 11*
Vanhal, Johann Baptist, 206; *A 12*
Voss, Gerhard Johann, 191–92; *286*

Category D
Abel, Carl Friedrich, 27
Agricola, Rudolf, 11, 29
Alcaeus, 31
Ambrose, Saint, 34
Augustine of Hippo, Saint, 37
Bacchus, 38
Bach, Anna Magdalena, 7, 39
Bach, Carl Philipp Emanuel, 40, 209
Bach, Johann Christian, 40, 41
Bach, Wilhelm Friedemann, 9, 39
Bernacchi, Antonio Maria, 48
Bona, Giovanni Cardinal, 50
Bononcini, Giovanni, 17, 51
Brandes, Charlotte Wilhelmine Franzisca
　(Minna), 200
Cardinal, [Jeanne Cecile], 58
Cecilia, Saint, 55
Charlemagne, 58
Charles V (emperor), 59
Charles VI (emperor), 59
Cogho, (Marie) Therese, 62
Concialini, Carlo, 200
Crux, Marianne, 200
Cuzzoni, Francesca, 67
Daemen, 200
David, 67

Degen, Johann Philipp, 200
Dülon, Friedrich Ludwig, 13, 70
Dušek, František Xaver (Duschek), 199, 201
Dušková, Josefa (Duschek), 13, 70, 199, 201
Eschstruth, Hans Adolf Friedrich von, 74, 201
Fasch, Carl Friedrich Christian, 201
Faun, 77
Fischer, John Abraham, 17, 80
Folega, Abbate, 18, 80
Frederick II (king of Prussia), 84
Galileo Galilei, 84
Giedde, Wilhelm Hans Rudolph Rosen-
　krantz, 201
Graf, Christian Ernst, 89
Graf, Friedrich Hartmann, 89
Gräfe, Johann Friedrich, 89
Graul, Markus Heinrich, 90
Graun, Johann Gottlieb, 90
Gregory, Saint, 91
Guido of Arezzo (Aretino), 37
Hartmann, [Johann], 202
Hermann of Reichenau, 100
Johann Georg II, 105
Junius, Hadrian, 108
Juno, 108
Jupiter, 108
Kämpfer, Joseph, 202
Latilla, Gaetano, 115
Lem, [Peter], 203
Lotti, Santa Stella, 17, 122
Martini, Giovanni Battista, 10n, 11, 127–28
Mašek, Johanna, 199, 203
Mašek, Vincenc, 199, 203
Mena, Maria Anna de, 130
Minerva, 134
Montanari, Francesco, 135
More, Sir Thomas, 136
Müller, Christian, 137
Müller, Carolina Fredrika, 204
Müller, Christian Friedrich, 204
Naumann, Johann Gottlieb, 204
Noëlli, Georg, 18, 140
Orting, Benjamin, 143
Palestrina, Giovanni Pierluigi da, 11, 18, 143
Paradis, Maria Theresia, 13, 17, 145–46
Paulsen, Peter, 204

Perez, David, 148–49
Pobielsky, Christian Wilhelm, 205
Porphyry, 152
Pugnani, Gaetano, 18, 154
Pythagoras, 155
Quiersfeld, Johann, 156–57
Reginelli, Nicolò, 158
Sauppe, [Christian Gottlieb], 205
Scaliger, Joesph Justus, 165
Scaliger, Julius Caesar, 164
Schuster, Joseph, 173
Selmer, Heinrich Christoph, 175
Selnecker, Nicolaus, 175
Sirmen, Maddalena Laura, 206
Soto de Langa, Francisco, 179
Strinasacchi, Regina, 13, 182
Telemann, Georg Philipp, 18, 184
Turcotti, Maria Giustina, 186
Vogler, Georg Joseph, 191

Westenholz, Barbara Lucietta Fricemelica
    (née Affabili), 194
Westenholz, Carl August Friedrich, 194
Witthauer, Johann Georg, 207
Zeller, Georg Bernhard Leopold, 197
Zeyer, 207
Ziegler, Johann Gotthilf, 11, 197

Category E
Bach, Anna Carolina Philippina, 209, 220;
    B 19
Bach, Carl Philipp Emanuel, 209–19;
    B 1–B 16
Bach, Johann August, 220; B 18
Bach, Johann Sebastian, the younger, 5n, 11,
    17n, 20, 27, 29, 54, 127, 133, 197, 209n, 213,
    220–221; B 20–B 22
Bach, Johanna Maria, 220; B 17

INDEX OF SUBJECTS

This index includes only the names of subjects in C. P. E. Bach's portrait collection. The names are listed in alphabetical order (not the order in NV 1790). References to the introduction and catalogue in part I are given in roman type; references to plates in part II are given in italic. (Plates in the appendices are preceded by the letter A or B.)

Abel, Leopold August, 27; 1
Abel, Carl Friedrich, 11, 27–28; 2
Accorso, Mariangelo, 28; 3
Agrell, Johan Joachim, 28–29; 4
Agricola, Rudolf, 11, 29
Agrippa, Heinrich Cornelius, 29–30; 5
Alardus Amstelredamus, 30; 6
Alberti, Leon Battista, 31; 8
Albertus Magnus, 30; 7
Alcaeus, 31
Alciati, Andrea, 31; 9
d'Alembert, Jean le Rond, 32; 10
Alexander the Great, 32; 11
Allegranti, Maddalena, 33; 12
Alsted, Johann Heinrich, 33; 13
Ambrose, Saint, 34
André, Johann, 34; 14
d'Anglebert, Jean-Henry, 34; 15
Annibali, Domenico, 35–36; 17
Apollo, 36; 18
Aristotle, 37; 19
Augustine of Hippo, Saint, 37
Bacchus, 38
Bach, Anna Carolina Philippina, 209, 220; B 19
Bach, Anna Magdalena, 7, 39
Bach, Carl Philipp Emanuel, 9, 18, 40, 209–19; B 1–B 16
Bach, Hans, 41; 23
Bach, Johann Ambrosius, 7, 38; 20
Bach, Johann August, 220; B 18
Bach, Johann Christian, 40, 41
Bach, Johann Christoph Friedrich, 9n, 40; 22

Bach, Johann Ludwig, 9n, 42; 24
Bach, Johann Sebastian, 7, 8, 20, 38; 21
Bach, Johann Sebastian, the younger, 5n, 11, 17n, 20, 27, 29, 54, 127, 133, 197, 209n, 213, 220–221; B 20–B 22
Bach, Johanna Maria, 214, 220; B 17
Bach, Wilhelm Friedemann, 9, 39
Bagge, Charles Ernest, Baron de, 43; 26
Baron, Ernst Gottlieb, 43–44; 27
Bartholin, Caspar, 44; 28
Bastard, Ann [mistaken for La Bastardella], 44–45; 29
Beard, John, 45; 30
Beer, Johann, 43; 25
Bedeschi, Paolo, 19, 45–46; 31
Bembo, Pietro, 46; 32
Benda, Franz, 46–47; 33, 34
Benda, Georg, 47; 35
Benda, Maria Felicitas, 47–48; 36
Bernacchi, Antonio Maria, 48
Bernardi, Francesco. See Senesino
Besard, Jean-Baptiste, 48–49; 37
Bianchini, Francesco, 49–50; 39
Biber, Heinrich Ignaz Franz von, 49; 38
Blankenburg, Quirinus Gerbrandszoon van, 50; 40
Bona, Giovanni, 50
Bononcini, Giovanni, 17, 51
Brandes, Charlotte Wilhelmine Franzisca (Minna), 200
Bresciani. See Colas, Domenico
Briegel, Wolfgang Carl, 52; 42
Brockes, Barthold Heinrich, 52; 43

Broschi, Carlo. *See* Farinelli

Browne, Sir Thomas, 53; *44*

Buffardin, Pierre-Gabriel, 11, 20, 54; *46*

Bümler, Georg Heinrich, 53; *45*

Callimachus (Filippo Buonaccorsi), 55–56; *48*

Calvisius, Sethus, 56; *49*

Calvör, Caspar, 56; *50*

Camerarius, Philippus, 57; *51*

Capricornus, Samuel Friedrich, 57; *52*

Cardinal, Jeanne Cecile, 58

Carestini, Giovanni, 58; *53*

Cecilia, Saint, 20, 32, 55; *47*

Charlemagne, 58

Charles V (emperor), 59

Charles VI (emperor), 59

Chéron, Elisabeth Sophie, 60; *55*

Christophorus (Cristoforo Marcello), 60; *56*

Cicero, Marcus Tullius, 61; *57*

Cisner, Nicolaus, 20, 61; *58*

Cochlaeus, Johannes, 62; *60*

Cogho, Marie Therese, 62

Colas, Domenico and his brother, 51–52; *41*

Concialini, Carlo, 63, 200; *61*

Conring, Hermann, 63; *62*

Corelli, Arcangelo, 64; *63*

Cosimi, Nicola, 64–65; *64*

Critopulus, Metrophanes, 65; *65*

Crüger, Johannes, 65–66; *66*

Crux, Marianne, 200

Curti, 66; *67*

Cuzzoni, Francesca, 67

Daemen, 200

Daquin, Louis-Claude, 67; *68*

David, 67

De Fesch, Willem, 68; *69*

Degen, Johann Philipp, 200

Denis, Michael, 68; *70*

Descartes, René, 59; *54*

Dieterich, Johann Conrad, 68–69; *71*

Dionysius, Aelius, 24n, 69

Dolet, Étienne, 69–70; *72*

Dülon, Friedrich Ludwig, 13, 70

Dušek, František Xaver (Duschek), 199, 201

Dušková, Josefa (Duschek), 13, 70, 199, 201

Ebeling, Christoph Daniel, 10, 71; *73*

Eberlin, Daniel, 71; *74*

Eccard, Johannes, 72; *75*

Engel, Johann Jakob, 15, 72; *76*

Epicurus, 73; *77*

Erasmus, Desiderius, 73; *78*

Eschstruth, Hans Adolf Friedrich von, 12, 74, 201; *79*

Ettmüller, Michael Ernst, 74; *80*

Euclid of Megara, 75; *81*

Euler, Leonhard, 75; *82*

Fabricius, Johann Albert, 76; *84*

Fabricius, Werner, 75–76; *83*

Farinelli (Carlo Broschi), 76–77; *85*

Fasch, Carl Friedrich Christian, 77, 201; *86*

Faun, 77

Ferdinand I (emperor), 77–78; *87*

Ferdinand III (emperor), 78; *88*

Ficino, Marsilio, 78–79; *89*

Fiorillo, Ignazio, 79; *90*

Fischer, John Abraham, 17, 80

Fludd, Robert, 80; *91*

Folega, Abbate, 18, 80

Fordyce, Margaret, 81; *92*

Fracastoro, Girolamo, 81; *93*

Franciscello (Francesco Alborea), 81–82; *94*

Franck, Michael, 82; *95*

Franckenau, Georg Frank von, 82; *96*

Franklin, Benjamin, 83; *97*

Frederick II (king of Prussia), 84

Frescobaldi, Girolamo, 83; *98*

Fritz, Barthold, 84; *99*

Galileo Galilei, 84

Gaultier, Jacques, 88; *108*

Gellert, Christian Fürchtegott, 85; *100*

Geminiani, Francesco, 85; *101*

Gerbert, Martin, 86; *102*

German Violinist and Italian Secretary, 189–90; *283*

Gerstenberg, Heinrich Wilhelm von, 86; *103*

Gesner, Conrad, 87; *104*

Giedde, Wilhelm Hans Rudolph Rosenkrantz, 201

Giovannini (Count of St. Germain), 87; *105*

Gluck, Christoph Willibald, 87; *106*

Góis, Damião de, 19n, 88; *107*

Graf, Christian Ernst, 89

Graf, Friedrich Hartmann, 89

Gräfe, Johann Friedrich, 89
Graphaeus (Cornelis Schryver), 90; 109
Graul, Marcus Heinrich, 90
Graun, Carl Heinrich, 91; 110
Graun, Johann Gottlieb, 90
Gregory, Saint, 91
Guido of Arezzo (Aretino), 37
Guignon, Jean Pierre, 92; 112
Gumpelzhaimer, Adam, 92–93; 113
Hagedorn, Friedrich von, 94; 115
Hainlein, Paul, 99; 124
Hammerschmidt, Andreas, 94; 116
Handel, George Frideric, 95; 117
Handl, Jacobus, 95; 118
Hardt, Johann Daniel, 96; 119
Harrer, Gottlob. See German Violinist
Hartmann, [Johann], 202
Hasse, Faustina (née Bordoni), 97; 121
Hasse, Johann Adolf, 97; 120
Hässler, Johann Wilhelm, 93; 114
Haydn, Joseph, 98; 122
Hebden, John, 98; 123
Herbst, Johann Andreas, 100; 126
Hermann of Reichenau, 100
Hessus, Helius Eobanus, 99; 125
Hiller, Johann Adam, 10, 11, 100, 199, 202;
    127, A 2
Hintze, Jacob, 101; 128
Höffler, Konrad, 101; 129
Hölty, Ludwig Christoph Heinrich, 102; 130
Homer, 24n, 102
Horace, 24n, 102
Hunt, Arabella, 103; 132
James I, 104; 133
Jeep, Johannes, 104; 134
Johann Georg II, 105
Jommelli, Niccolò, 105–6; 135
Journet, Françoise, 106; 136
Junius, Hadrian, 108
Juno, 108
Jupiter, 108
Jürgensen, Johann Christian, 107; 138
Kämpfer, Joseph, 202
Kayser, Philipp Christoph, 108; 139
Kellner, Johann Christoph, 15, 109; 140
Kepler, Johannes, 109–10; 141

Kindermann, Johann Erasmus, 110; 142
Kircher, Athanasius, 111; 143
Kirnberger, Johann Philipp, 9n, 111; 144
Kis, Stephanus (Szegedinus), 183; 272
Klopstock, Friedrich Gottlieb, 112; 145
Koch, Franziska, 112; 146
Kozeluch, Leopold, 202; A 3
Kreibich, Franz, 202; A 1
Kremberg, Jakob, 112–13; 147
Krieger, Adam, 113; 148
Kuhnau, Johann, 114; 149
Kupecký, Christoph Johann Frideric, 114; 150
Lalande, Michel-Richard de, 115; 151
Lallouette, Jean François, 116; 152
Lampe, Friedrich Adolph, 116; 153
Lampe, John Frederick, 116–17; 154
Lang, Johann Georg, 203; A 4
Lange, Aloysia (née Weber), 117; 155
Lanier, Nicholas, 35; 16
Lasso, Orlando di, 117–18; 156
Latilla, Gaetano, 115
Leclair, Jean-Marie, 61; 59
Legros, Joseph, 92; 111
Leibniz, Gottfried Wilhelm, 118; 157
Le Jeune, Claude, 62
Lem, [Peter], 203
Leonardo da Vinci, 189; 282
Leopold I (emperor), 118–19; 158
Lessing, Gotthold Ephraim, 119; 159
Leveridge, Richard, 119; 160
Liberti, Hendrik, 120; 161
Lingke, Georg Friedrich, 120; 162
Lolli, Antonio, 13, 121; 164
Lotti, Santa Stella, 17, 122
Löwe, Johann Jakob, 121; 163
Ludecus, Matthäus, 122; 165
Lully, Jean-Baptiste, 122–23; 166
Luther, Martin, 123; 167
Lutter, Johann Balthasar, 124; 168
Mara, Gertrud Elisabeth (née Schmeling), 13,
    19, 124; 169
Marchand, Louis, 125; 170
Marot, Clement, 126; 172
Marpurg, Friedrich Wilhelm, 126; 173
Martini, Giovanni Battista, 10n, 11, 127–28
Mašek, Johanna, 199, 203

Mašek, Vincenc, 199, 203
Mattheson, Johann, 128; *175*
Mayer, Johann Friedrich, 129; *176*
Medici, Lorenzo di, 129; *177*
Meiland, Jacob, 129–30; *178*
Melanchthon, Philipp, 130; *179*
Mena, Maria Anna de, 130
Mendelssohn, Moses, 131; *180*
Mercury, 131, 213n; *181*
Merulo, Claudio, 132; *182*
Metastasio, Pietro, 132; *183*
Meursius, Johannes, 133; *184*
Milton, John, 134; *186*
Minerva, 134
Mingotti, Caterina Regina, 11, 19, 20, 133; *185*
Mondonville, Jean-Joseph Cassanéa de, 134; *187*
Montanari, Francesco, 135
Monte, Philippe de, 135; *188*
Montesson, Charlotte-Jeanne Béraud de la Haye de Riou, Marquise de, 127; *174*
Monticelli, Angelo Maria, 135–36; *189*
More, Sir Thomas, 136
Morhof, Daniel Georg, 136; *190*
Mozart, Leopold, 137; *191*
Mozart, Wolfgang Amadeus, 199, 203; *A 5*
Müller, Carolina Fredrika, 137–38, 204; *192*
Müller, Christian, 137
Müller, Christian Friedrich, 204
Musculus, Wolfgang, 138; *193*
Nardini, Pietro, 138; *194*
Naumann, Johann Gottlieb, 204
Neefe, Christian Gottlob, 139, 199, 204; *195*, *A 6*
Neumeister, Erdmann, 139; *196*
Niklas, Marie Sophie, 140; *197*
Noëlli, Georg, 18, 140
Noordt, Sybrandus van, 141; *198*
Nozemann, Jacob, 141; *199*
Ochsenkuhn, Sebastian, 142; *200*
Olearius, Johannes, 142; *201*
Orting, Benjamin, 143
Paix, Jakob, 143; *202*
Palestrina, Giovanni Pierluigi da, 11, 18, 143
Paminger, Leonhard, 144; *203*
Pan, 144; *204*

Panciroli, Guido, 145; *205*
Paradis, Maria Theresia, 13, 17, 145–46
Passeri, Giovanni Battista, 146; *206*
Paulsen, Peter, 204
Pécour, Louis Guillaume, 147; *208*
Penna, Lorenzo, 148; *209*
Pepusch, Johann Christoph, 147; *207*
Perez, David, 148–49
Philidor, François-André Danican, 149; *210*
Piccinni, Niccolò, 149–50; *211*
Pico della Mirandola, Giovanni, 150; *212*
Pisendel, Johann Georg, 150–51; *213*
Plato, 151; *214*
Pleyel, Ignace Joseph, 205; *A 7*
Pobielsky, Christian Wilhelm, 205
Poliziano, Angelo, 151–52; *215*
Pontano, Giovanni, 106–7; *137*
Porphyry, 152
Postel, Guillaume, 152; *216*
Praetorius, Michael, 153; *217*
Ptolemy, 153–54; *218*
Pugnani, Gaetano, 18, 154
Punto, Giovanni (Johann Wenzel Stich), 154; *219*
Puteanus, Erycius, 155; *220*
Pythagoras, 155
Quantz, Johann Joachim, 151, 155–56; *221*, *222*
Quiersfeld, Johann, 156–57
Rameau, Jean-Philippe, 157; *223*
Ramler, Karl Wilhelm, 157; *224*
Rebel, Jean-Fery, 158; *225*
Reginelli, Nicolò, 158
Reichardt, Johann Friedrich, 20, 158–59; *226*
Reiche, Gottfried, 159; *227*
Reincken, Johann Adam, 159–60; *228*
Reusner, Nikolaus, 160; *229*
Reyher, Andreas, 160; *230*
Rhenanus, Beatus, 161; *231*
Richey, Michael, 161; *232*
Rist, Johann, 10n, 162; *233*
Rolle, Johann Heinrich, 162–63; *234*
Rosetti, Antonio, 205; *A 8*
Rousseau, Jean-Jacques, 163; *235*
Sachs, Hans, 164; *236*
Saint-Huberty, Anne-Antoinette Clavel de, 15, 103; *131*

Salimbeni, Felice, 164; *237*
Sauppe, [Christian Gottlieb], 205
Scalichius, Paul, 165; *238*
Scaliger, Joseph Justus, 165
Scaliger, Julius Caesar, 164
Scheidemann, Heinrich, 165–66; *239*
Scheidt, Samuel, 166; *240*
Schelwig, Samuel, 167; *241*
Schenck, Johannes, 167; *242*
Schiørring, Niels, 12, 168; *243*
Schmelzer, Johann Heinrich, 168; *244*
Schmid, Bernhard the elder, 169; *245*
Schmidt, Johann Andreas, 170; *247*
Schmidt, Melchior, 169; *246*
Schmittbaur, Joseph Aloys, 205; *A 9*
Scholl, Dirck, 170; *248*
Schop, Johann, 171; *249*
Schott, Conrad, 171–72; *250*
Schubart, Christian Friedrich Daniel, 172, 206; *252, A 10*
Schubart, Tobias Heinrich, 172; *251*
Schuster, Joseph, 173
Schütz, Heinrich, 173; *253*
Schweitzer, Anton, 173–74; *254*
Seelen, Johann Heinrich von, 174; *255*
Seixas, José Antonio Carlos de, 177; *260*
Selle, Thomas, 174–75; *256*
Selmer, Heinrich Christoph, 175
Selnecker, Nicolaus, 175
Seneca the younger, 176; *257*
Senesino (Francesco Bernardi), 176; *258*
Seydelmann, Franz, 176–77; *259*
Siculus, Baptista, 177; *261*
Sieber, Justus, 178; *262*
Simpson, Christopher, 178; *263*
Sirmen, Maddalena Laura, 206
Socrates, 24n, 179
Solnitz, Anton Wilhelm, 179; *264*
Soto de Langa, Francisco, 179
Spangenberg, Cyriac, 180; *265*
Spieß, Meinrad, 180; *266*
Staden, Johann, 180–81; *267*
Steffan, Joseph Anton, 206; *A 11*
Stenger, Nicolaus, 181; *268*
Stich, Johann Wenzel. *See* Punto, Giovanni

Stockhausen, Johann Christoph, 182; *269*
Strinasacchi, Regina, 13, 182
Sturm, Christoph Christian, 182–83, 213, 218; *270, B 12–B 13*
Sulzer, Johann Georg, 183; *271*
Szegedinus. *See* Kis, Stephanus
Tartini, Giuseppe, 184; *273*
Telemann, Georg Philipp, 18, 184
Tessarini, Carlo, 184–85; *274*
Tevo, Zaccaria, 185; *275*
Thévenard, Gabriel-Vincent, 185; *276*
Til, Salomon van, 186; *277*
Turcotti, Maria Giustina, 186
Unzer, Johann August, 186; *278*
Vallet, Nicholas, 187; *279*
Vanhal, Johann Baptist, 206; *A 12*
Venzky, Georg, 187–88; *280*
Vetter, Daniel, 188; *281*
Virgil, 24n, 190
Vitali, Tomaso Antonio, 190; *284*
Vivaldi, Antonio, 191; *285*
Vogler, Georg Joseph, 191
Voss, Gerhard Johann, 191–92; *286*
Walliser, Christoph Thomas, 192; *287*
Walpurgis, Maria Antonia, 125; *171*
Walther, Thomas Christian, 192–93; *288*
Weiss, Silvius Leopold, 193; *289*
Wellter, Johann, 193–94; *290*
Westenholz, Barbara Lucietta Fricemelica (née Affabili), 194
Westenholz, Carl August Friedrich, 194
Wilisch, Christian Friedrich, 195; *291*
Witthauer, Johann Georg, 207
Wolf, Ernst Wilhelm, 18, 195; *292*
Xylander, Wilhelm, 195; *293*
Zachariä, Friedrich Wilhelm, 12, 196; *294*
Zeidler, Maximilian, 196; *295*
Zeller, Georg Bernhard Leopold, 197
Zeyer, 207
Ziegler, Johann Gotthilf, 11, 197
Zielche, Hans Heinrich, 207
Zwinger, Theodor, the elder, 197–98; *296*
Zygmuntowski, Nicolaus, 198; *297*

INDEX OF ARTISTS

This index lists the artists who created the portraits in C.P.E. Bach's collection. Names are based on the *Allgemeines Lexikon der bildenden Künstler von der Antike bis zur Gegenwart*, edited by Ulrich Thieme, Felix Becker, and Hans Vollmer (Leipzig, 1908–50), commonly known as Thieme-Becker. The artists are listed in alphabetical order with their birth and death dates (if known); where no artists' names are given in NV 1790, the entries (plates only) are listed here as "Anonymous." The woodcuts from Reusner 1587, 1589, and 1590 are all listed under Reusner, though at least some of the woodcuts were the work of Tobias Stimmer (1539–1584). References to the introduction and catalogue in part I are given in roman type; references to plates in part II are given in italic. (Plates in the appendices are preceded by the letter A or B.)

Abel, Ernst Heinrich (1737–after 1783), 27, 41, 70; *2*

Abel, Leopold August (1718–1794), 27, 124, 175; *1, 169*

Adam, Jakob (1748–1811), 68; *70*

Andrea, S., 117; *154*

Anonymous, *13, 19, 20, 23, 28, 55, 65, 88, 91, 107, 109, 118, 124, 145, 149, 165, 178, 182, 200, 202, 203, 205, 207, 209, 217, 220, 226, 228, 240, 244, 245, 265, 268, 275, 277, 280, 281, 284, 286, 292*

Argentina, 109; *141*

Aubert, Michel (1704–1757), 144; *204*

Bach, Gottlieb Friedrich (1714–1785), 42, 210, 215; *24, B 1*

Bach, Johann Philipp (1752–1846), 10n, 210–12, 215, 216; *B 3–B 6*

Bach, Johann Sebastian, the younger (1749–1778), 5n, 11, 17n, 20, 27, 29, 54, 127, 133, 197, 209n, 213, 220–221; *46, 185, B 20–B 22*

Battoni, Pompeo (1708–1787), 61; *57*

Berger, Daniel (1744–1824), 34, 112, 117, 140, 183; *14, 146, 155, 197, 271*

Berkenkamp, Johann Christoph (1739–1824), 177; *259*

Berndt, J.O., 108; *139*

Bernigeroth, Martin (1660–1733), 74, 118, 195; *80, 158, 291*

Berwinckel, Joannes (fl. first half seventeenth century), 187; *279*

Beyel, Daniel (1760–1828), 71; *73*

Bloemaert, Cornelis (c. 1603–after 1684), 111; *143*

Blond, Jean le (1590/4–1666), 131; *181*

Bock, Christoph Wilhelm (1755–1835), 86; *102*

Böcklin, Johann Christoph (1657–c. 1709), 63, 167; *62, 241*

Bodenehr, Moritz (1665–1748), 101, 112; *128, 147*

Boetius, Christian Friedrich (1706–1782), 118; *157*

Boissard, Robert (1570?–c. 1603), 29, 135; *5, 188*

Bottschild, Samuel (1641–1706), 76, 112; *83, 147*

Bruhn, T., 168; *243*

Brühl, Johann Benjamin (1691–1763), 82; *95*

Bry, Theodor de, 133, 135, 136; *184, 188*

Bürglin, Christoph Leonhard (1727–1772), 34, 37, 67, 91

Busch, Georg Paul (d. 1756), 65; *66*

Calcinotto, Carlo (fl. 1760s), 184; *273*

Carlone, Giovanni Battista (1592–1677), 126; *172*

Carmontelle, Louis (1717–1806), 137; *191*

Carracci, Annibale (1560–1609), 66, 131, 144–45; *67, 181, 204*

Carstens, Asmus Jakob (1754–1798), 14, *70*

Carwarden, John (fl. 1636–1660), 178; *263*

Casali, Andrea (1705–1784), 135; *189*

Casse, D., 33; *12*

Cassieri, J. J., 157; *223*

Cathelin, Louis-Jacques (1739–1804), 149; *211*

Cave, Francois Morellon de la (fl. 1700–1755), 68, 191; *69, 285*

Cecchi, Giovanni Battista (1748/9 –1807), 138; *194*

Chéreau, François (1680–1729), 147; *208*

Chodowiecki, Daniel (1726–1801), 72, 102; *76, 130*

Clerc, [Pierre Thomas] le (1740–after 1796), 92; *111*

Cochin, Charles Nicolas, the younger (1715–1790), 32, 43, 83, 134, 149, 154; *10, 26, 97, 187, 210, 219*

Cogho, Johann Samuel (fl. second half eighteenth century), 63, 197

Colomba, N. N., 79; *90*

Corbutt, Charles/Philip. *See* Purcell, Richard

Cranach, Lucas (1515–1586), 130; *179*

Creite, Ernst Ludwig (fl. first half eighteenth century), 50; *40*

Cristofori, Antonio (1701–1737), 39

Daullé, Jean (1703–1763), 177; *260*

Darbes, Joseph Friedrich August (1747–1810), 75; *82*

Delafosse, Jean Baptiste (1721–1806), 137; *191*

Delâtre, Jean Marie (c. 1745–1840), 134; *187*

Denner, Balthasar (1685–1749), 52, 67, 193; *43, 289*

Descombes, Charles (fl. mid-eighteenth century), 67; *68*

Desrochers, Étienne (1668–1741), 67, 106, 115, 123; *68, 136, 151, 166*

Diricks, Dirck (1613–1653), 171, 174; *249, 256*

Döhren, Jacob von (1746–1800), 212, 217, 220; *B 9–B 10, B 17–B 20*

Donner, Ignaz (1752–1803), 68; *70*

Duflos, Claude Augustin (1700–1786), 126; *172*

Duplessis, Joseph Siffred (1725–1802), 87; *106*

Dupuis, Charles (1685–1742), 125; *170*

Dürr, Johann (fl. c. 1640–1680), 121; *163*

Eberling, J.C., 84; *99*

Eichler, Joseph (1724–after 1783), 39

Endner, Gustav Georg, 103; *131*

Faber, John, the younger (c. 1695–1756), 45, 58, 95, 98, 135; *30, 53, 117, 123, 189*

Faithorne, William (1616–1691), 178; *263*

Falbe, Joachim Martin (1709–1782), 46; *33*

Ferdinand, 116; *152*

Fialetti, Odoardo (1573–1636/37), 66; *67*

Fischer, Jacob Adolph (1755–after 1799), 163; *234*

Fleischberger, Johann Friedrich (fl. second half seventeenth century), 110, 165; *142, 239*

Folin, Bartolomeo (1730–after 1808), 193; *289*

Franke, Johann Heinrich Christian (1738–1792), 45, 150, 156; *31, 213, 221, 222*

François, Jean Charles (1717–1769), 58, 61; *59*

Frisch, Johann Christoph (1738–1815), 34, 131; *14, 180*

Fritsch, Christian (1695–1769), 134, 139, 161, 172; *186, 196, 232, 251*

Fritsch, Christian Friedrich (1719–before 1774), 141; *199*

Fritzsch, Johann Christian Gottfried (1720–1802/3), 58, 85, 94, 119, 182, 186, 218; *100, 115, 159, 270, 278, B 13*

Frye, Thomas (1710–1762), 119; *160*

Füger, Heinrich (1751–1818), 100; *127*

Furck, Sebastian (c. 1600–1655), 77, 100; *87, 126*

Geuslain, Charles Étienne (1685–1765), 185; *276*

Geyser, Christian Gottlieb (1742–1803), 47, 74, 100, 163, 182, 196, 213, 218; *35, 79, 127, 234, 269, 294, B 12*

Ghezzi, Pier Leone (1674–1755), 35–36, 51, 105, 115, 148–49, 154, 189–90; *17, 41, 135, 283*

Graf, Christian Ernst (1723–1804), 89

Graff, Anton (1736–1813), 119, 183; *159, 271*

Gregory F. (fl. second half eighteenth century), 132; *183*

Grießmann, Carl Wilhelm, 213, 221; *B 22*

Gründler, Gottfried August (1710–1775), 152; *216*

Haack, 182

Haas, Jonas (1720–1775), 116; *153*

Haecken, Alexander van (1701–1758), 77, 176; *85, 258*

Haffner, Melchior (fl. early seventeenth century), 56; *49*

Haid, Johann Elias (1739–1809), 72; *76*

Haid, Johann Jakob (1704–1767), 55, 82, 128, 146, 174; *94, 175, 206, 255*

Hals, Frans (c. 1580–1666), 59; *54*

Hardrich, 48, 121, 192–93; *36, 164, 288*

Haußmann, Elias Gottlob (1695–1774), 38–39, 159; *21, 227*

Heinsius, Johann Ernst (1740–1812), 32, 174; *11, 254*

Herman, Johann (fl. 1641–58), 72; *75*

Herz, Johann Daniel (1693–1754), 77

Heumann, Georg Daniel (1691–1759), 196; *295*

Heyden, Jacob van der (1573–1645), 192; *287*

Höckner, Johann Caspar (1629–c. 1670), 113, 178; *148, 262*

Holtzmann, Carl Friedrich (1740–1811 or 1818), 173

Howard, Hugh (1675/6–1738), 64; *63*

Høyer, Cornelius (1741–1804), 138; *192*

Hude, Jürgen Matthias von der (1690–1751), 174; *255*

Hudson, Thomas (1701–1779), 95, 176; *117, 258*

Jenkins, Thomas (d. 1798), 85; *101*

Jode, Pieter de, II (1601–1674?), 120, 155; *161*

Kauke, Johann Friedrich (fl. 1755–77), 126, 157; *173, 224*

Kilian, Lucas (1579–1637), 48, 57, 93, 171; *37, 51, 113, 250*

Kilian, Philip (1628–1693), 57, 76; *52, 83*

Kilian, Wolfgang (1566–1625), 104; *133*

Klauber, 180; *266*

Kleve, Johan T. (1743–1797), 138; *192*

Knapton, George (1698–1778), 58; *53*

Kneller, Sir Godfrey (1646–1723), 64, 103; *64, 132*

Kniep, Christoph Heinrich (1755–1825), 20, 55, 71, 107; *47, 73, 138*

Knorr, Georg Wolfgang (1705–1761), 164; *236*

Krüger, Andreas Ludwig (1743–c. 1805), 24n, 61, 69, 73, 102, 151, 176, 179, 190; *57, 77, 214, 257*

Krüger, Johann Conrad (fl. late eighteenth century), 212, 217; *B 8*

Kupezky, Jan (1667–1740), 114; *150*

Kütner, Samuel Gottlob (1747–1828), 75; *82*

Lange, Joseph (1751–1831), 117; *155*

Lemkus, Diederich (fl. early eighteenth century), 136; *190*

Leonart, Johann Friedrich (1633–1687), 193; *290*

Leuchter, Johann Heinrich (fl. seventeenth century), 52; *42*

Leygeben, Gottfried (1630–1683), 118; *157*

Liebe, Christian Gottlob August (1746–1819), 139, 174; *195, 254*

Lievens, Jan (1607–1674), 35, 88; *16, 108*

Lips, Johann Heinrich (1758–1817), 211, 216, 217; *B 6–B 8*

Lisiewski, Christian Friedrich Reinhold (1725–1794), 111; *144*

Löhr, Franz Conrad (1735–1812), 211, 216; *B 5*

Loir, Alexis (1712–85), 61; *59*

Lucy, Charles (1692–after 1736), 77; *85*

Macret, Charles François (1751–1789), 92; *111*

Mansfeld, Johann Ernst (1739–1796), 98; *122*

Martin, David (1737–1797), 163; *235*

Mathieu, Georg David (1737–1778), 40; *22*

McArdell, James (1729–1765), 85, 117; *101, 154*

Mechau, Jacob Wilhelm (1745–1808), 47; *35*

Mellan, Claude (1598–1688), 83; *98*

Mengs, Anton Raphael (1728–1779), 133; *185*

Mentzel, Johann Georg (1677–1743), 56, 82, 129; *50, 96, 176*

Menzel, 157

Mercier, Philippe (1689–1760), 98; *123*

Meurs, Jacob van (1619/20–before 1680), 59; *54*

Meytens, Martin van (1695/98–1770), 82; *94*

Miger, Simon Charles (1736–1820), 43, 87, 154; *26, 106, 219*

Mignard, Paul (1639–1691), 34, 123; *15, 166*

Moine, Jacques Antoine Marie le, 103; *131*

Möller, Andreas (1684–1762), 91; *110*

Moyreau, Jean (1691–1762), 158; *225*

Müller, Christian (1766–1824), 93; *114*

Müller, Johann Gotthard (1747–1830), 131; *180*

My, H. van der, 179; *264*

Nachenius, Jacob Jan (1712–after 1746), 50; *40*

Nessenthaler, Elias (c.1664–1714), 52; *42*

Oeser, Adam Friedrich (1717–1799), 11, 12, 210n, 213, 215, 218, 221; *B 2, B 12–B 13, B 21–B 22*

Oesterreich, Matthias (1716–1778), 35–36, 48, 51, 105, 115, 148–49, 189–90; *17, 41, 135, 283*

Palthe, Jan (1719–1769), 185; *274*

Pechwell, August Joseph (c. 1757–1811), 123; *167*

Pether, William (1731–1821), 119, 185; *160, 274*

Pfann, Johann, the younger (fl. mid-seventeenth century), 180; *267*

Pfenninger, Heinrich (1749–1815), 212, 216; *B 7*

Pinssio, Sébastien (1721–after 1777), 92; *112*

Preisler, Daniel (1627–1665), 110; *142*

Preisler, Johann Justin (1698–1771), 29; *4*

Preisler, Johann Martin (1714–1794), 36; *18*

Preisler, Valentin Daniel (1717–1765), 29, 79, 91, 96, 124; *4, 90, 110, 119, 168*

Purcell, Richard (fl. 1744–1766), 44, 81; *29, 92*

Ramsay, Allan (1713–1784), 163; *235*

Reiffenstein, Johann Friedrich (1719–1793), 9, 210, 215; *B 2*

Reusner, Nikolaus (1545–1602), 22, 28, 30, 31, 46, 55, 60, 61, 62, 70, 73, 79, 81, 87, 99, 106, 129, 138, 150, 152, 154, 160, 161, 165, 177, 183, 189, 195, 198; *3, 6, 7, 8, 9, 32, 48, 56, 58, 60, 72, 78, 89, 93, 104, 125, 137, 177, 193, 212, 215, 218, 229, 231, 238, 261, 272, 282, 293, 296*

Reynolds, Sir Joshua (1723–1792), 44, 81; *29, 92*

Robert, Nicolas (1614–1685), 125; *170*

Robineau, Charles Jean (1745–1799), 149; *211*

Romstet, Christian (1640–1721), 101, 113, 142, 173; *129, 148, 201, 253*

Rosbach, Johann Friedrich (fl. 1720–28), 159; *227*

Rosenberg, Johann Georg (1739–1808), 139; *195*

Rotari, Pietro (1707–1762), 97; *120*

Sadeler, Johann (1550–1600), 117; *156*

Saint-Aubin, Augustin de (1736–1807), 127, 149, 157; *174, 210, 223*

Satze[n] (Carl Salzer?), 173, 198; *297*

Schäffer, Christian (fl. second half seventeenth century), 121; *163*

Schaup, 111; *144*

Schellenberger, H. I. S., 169; *246*

Schenck, Pieter (1660–1718/19), 43, 141, 167; *25, 198, 242*

Schleuen, Johann David (fl. second half eighteenth century), 156; *222*

Schlotterbeck, Christian Jacob (1757–1811), 172; *252*

Schmidt, Georg Friedrich (1712–1775), 164, 185; *237, 276*

Schönemann, Friedrich (fl. 1745–60), 49; *39*

Schreyer, Johann Friedrich Moritz (1768–1795), 86; *103*

Schröter, Johann Friedrich (d. 1811), 214, 219; *B 16*

Schubart, 17, 18, 40, 145–46, 209

Schuster, Johann Matthias (1715–1758), 46; *33*

Schwenterley, Christian Heinrich (1749–1815), 109; *140*

Seel, Paulus (fl. second half seventeenth century), 49; *38*

Skerl, Friedrich Wilhelm (1752–1810), 17, 47, 54; *34*

Smith, John (1652–1743), 64, 103; *63, 64, 132*

Soldi, Andrea (c. 1703–after 1771), 68; *69*

Specht, 74; *79*

Sperling, [Johann Christian] (1690/91–1746), 53; *45*

Spetner, Christoph (1617–99), 173; *253*

Steiner, Johann Nepomuk (1725–1793), 132; *183*

Steürhelt, Franz (fl. mid-seventeenth century), 162; *233*

Stölzel, Christian Friedrich (1751–1816), 33; *12*

Stör, Johann Wilhelm (fl. 1727–1755), 43, 59; 27

Stöttrup, Andreas (1754–1811), 182, 213, 214, 218–19; *270, B 11, B 13–B 15*

Stranz, Emanuel Gottlieb (fl. 1780s), 63; *61*

Strauch, Georg (1613–1675), 71; *74*

Sysang, Johann Christoph (1703–1757), 53, 120; *45, 162*

Tanjé, Pieter (1706–1761), 179; *264*

Tardieu, Jacques Nicolas (1716–1791), 116; *152*

Thelott, Johann Philipp, the elder (d. 1671), 69; *71*

Thevet, André (1516–1590), 75; *81*

Thomas, Nicolas, 87; *105*

Thönert, Medard (1754–1814), 87, 173, 177; *105, 259*

Tiepolo, 18, 80, 158, 186

Torelli, Stefano (1712–1784), 97, 125; *121, 171*

Tournières, Robert Le Vrac (1668–1752), 147; *208*

Uhlich, Gabriel (1682–c. 1741), 170; *247*

Ullrich, Heinrich (d. 1621), 104; *134*

Vaillant, Jacques (c. 1625–1691), 135

Van Dyck, Anthony (1599–1641), 35, 120, 155; *161*

Vanloo, 92; *112*

Vermeulen, Cornelis (c. 1644–1708/9), 34; *15*

Vestri, Marco (fl. eighteenth century), 138; *194*

Vieira, Francisco (1765–1806), 177; *260*

Vinckeboons, David (1576–1629), 187; *279*

Vogel, Bernhard (1683–1737), 114; *150*

Vorstermann, Lucas (1595–1675), 35; *16*

Wagener, Friedrich Erhard (1759–1813), 77; *86*

Wahl, Johann Salomon (1689–1765), 128, 139; *175, 196*

Walch, Georg (fl. 1632–54), 160; *230*

Watelet, Claude Henri (1718–1786), 32; *10*

Watteau, Antoine (1684–1721), 158; *225*

Weisch, Samuel (fl. mid-seventeenth century), 94; *116*

White, Robert (1645–1703), 53; *44*

Wilt, Thomas van der (1659–1733), 170; *248*

Williams, John Michael (1710–c. 1780), 45; *30*

Wolfgang, Johann Georg (1662–1744), 52; *43*

Wolffgang, Gustav Andreas (1692–1775), 76; *84*

Zucchi, Lorenzo (1704–1779), 97, 125; *120, 121, 171*